Praise for this edition:

'Sally Marks has the historical debates at her fingertips, and she writes with clarity, verve and wit. This revised edition of *The Illusion of Peace* draws on the research of the last quarter-century, and deserves the widest possible readership.' – **P. M. H. Bell**, *University of Liverpool*

'Extensive knowledge, sound historical judgment, felicitous prose, and the courage to debunk myths make Sally Marks one of the best historians of international relations of this generation. With wide vision and a keen focus on power, this second edition of *The Illusion of Peace* peers behind the illusions of interwar diplomacy to analyze the erosion of European strength in the world and of French predominance over Germany on the European continent.' – **Joel Blatt**, *University of Connecticut*

'I am delighted to see a second edition of *The Illusion of Peace*. It is an especially valuable book for teaching, since it provides a succinct and lucid overview of international relations before the rise of Hitler. It is informed by the latest scholarship and written in a style that is both accessible and witty. Sally Marks' controversial thesis that the Germans were the only ones who knew what they wanted and were determined to get it continues to stimulate historical discussion.' – **Peter Kent**, *University of New Brunswick*

'This is a most welcome second edition. Sally Marks has skilfully incorporated the findings of new research into her original authoritative text, offering students clear and well-judged historical explanations and a comprehensively updated bibliography. This remains the best overview of the 1920s, the years that became, but need not have been, "The Years of Illusion".' – **Alan Sharp**, *University of Ulster*

The Making of the 20th Century

This series of specially commissioned titles focuses attention on significant and often controversial events and themes of world history in the twentieth century. Each book provides sufficient narrative and explanation for the newcomer to the subject while offering, for more advanced study, detailed source-references and bibliographies, together with interpretation and reassessment in the light of recent scholarship.

The Illusion of Peace

International Relations in Europe, 1918–1933

Second Edition

Sally Marks

First published 2003 by
PALGRAVE MACMILLAN
Houndmills, Basingstoke, Hampshire RG21 6XS and
175 Fifth Avenue, New York, N.Y. 10010
Companies and representatives throughout the world

PALGRAVE MACMILLAN is the global academic imprint of the
Palgrave Macmillan division of St. Martin's Press, LLC and of
Palgrave Macmillan Ltd. Macmillan® is a registered trademark in
the United States, United Kingdom and other countries. Palgrave
is a registered trademark in the European Union and other countries.

ISBN 1–4039–0419–7 hardcover
ISBN 0–333–98589–3 paperback

This book is printed on paper suitable for recycling and
made from fully managed and sustained forest sources.

A catalogue record for this book is available from the British
Library.

A catalogue record for this book is available from the Library of
Congress.

10   9   8   7   6   5   4   3   2   1
12   11   10   09   08   07   06   05   04   03

Printed in China

Contents

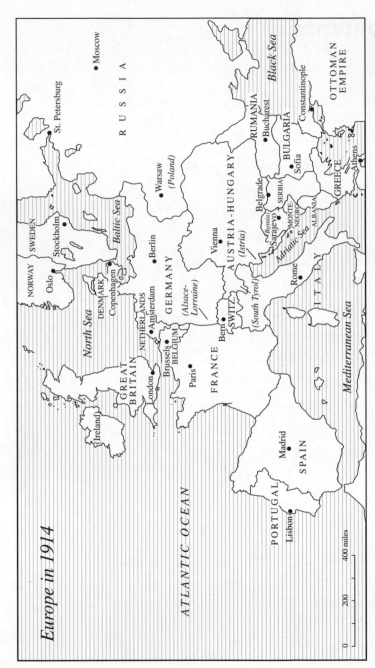

Map 1   Europe in 1914, adapted from Richard Goff et al., *The Twentieth Century: A Brief Global History*, 5th edn (Boston, MA, 1998), p. 33.

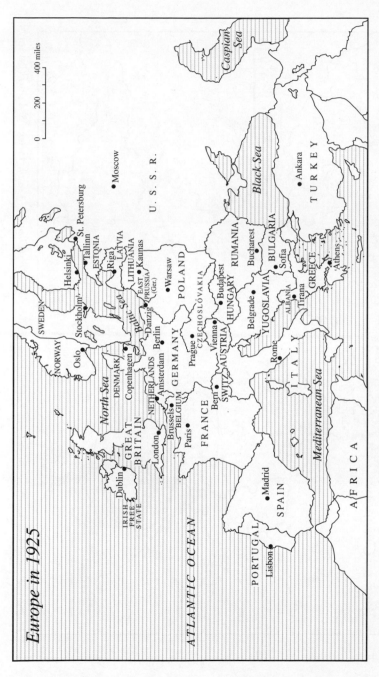

Map 2   Europe in 1925, adapted from Richard Goff et al., *The Twentieth Century: A Brief Global History*, 5th edn (Boston, MA., 1998), p. 144.

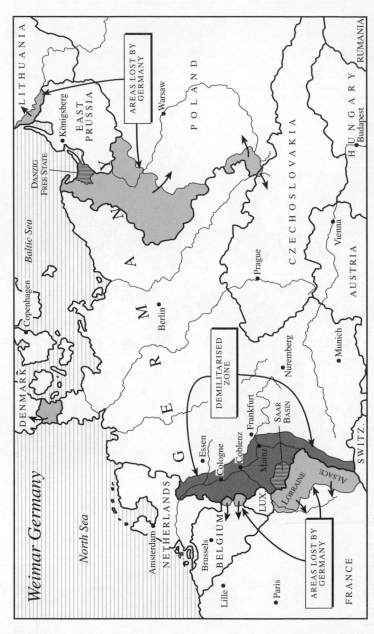

Map 3   Weimar Germany, adapted from Robert Ergang, *Europe in Our Time: 1914 to the Present*, 3rd edn (Boston, MA, 1958), p. 122.

Map 4   Eastern Europe in 1925, adapted from Eugene N. Anderson,
Modern Europe in World Perspective: 1914 to the Present (New York,
1941), p. 243.

1 The Pursuit of Peace

Major wars often provide the punctuation marks of history, primarily because they force drastic realignments in the relationships among states. To this rule the First World War was no exception. Long before the fighting ceased in November 1918, it was evident that the map of Europe must be redrawn and that reallocation of colonies, creation of a new international organisation, and changes in the economic balance must considerably affect the rest of the world as well. The First World War heralded the end of European dominance as the true victors in this predominantly European war were the United States and Japan: two non-European powers. The European victors were bled white and suffered a Pyrrhic victory from which none of them ever really recovered. While this fact was not evident at the war's end, it was clear that the forthcoming settlement must far exceed in geographic scope and complexity those other periodic realignments of the power balance, the 1648 Treaty of Westphalia and the 1815 Final Act of Vienna, to which it is often compared. Nobody doubted the magnitude of the task ahead, but nobody was properly prepared to undertake it.

As often happens, the sudden collapse of the enemy took the victors by surprise. Germany had been expected to hold out until mid-1919 and, in the autumn of 1918, Allied energy was more concentrated upon winning the war than upon planning the peace. True, some planning was in progress, but not always in the most effectual quarters. In the final year of the war, the smaller Allied states pursued their limited, specific aims with energy, but achieved only cautious and qualified commitments. Exile organisations representing ethnic groups within the Central Powers did the same with similar results. They recognised that the ultimate court of appeal would consist of Britain, France and the United States, but these three, who had the task of planning for much of the world, were also responsible for winning the war. Not surprisingly, that came first.

Of the major Allies, the French were perhaps the best organised in planning ahead, mainly because they knew precisely what mattered to them and because their interests were not really global. In London the Foreign Office was industriously preparing position papers on every conceivable topic, but, since its views often did not coincide with those of the Cabinet, and even less with those of Prime Minister David Lloyd George, much of the work proved futile. In the United States the situation was more obscure. A special organisation called the Inquiry had been established late in 1917 under the supervision of the President's confidant, Edward M. House, to research the problems of the peace and to prepare a programme designed to pre-empt those of European leaders. The Inquiry, composed largely of academicians and functioning independently of the State Department, was hard at work, but its influence was still uncertain and House himself was in Paris during the closing weeks of the war.[1] Secretary of State Robert Lansing was preparing his views, which did not coincide with those of the Inquiry and which could be expected to clash with those of the President. As for Woodrow Wilson himself, so far as could be ascertained, the American President had no views beyond the hazy slogans of his Fourteen Points, enumerated as a peace programme in an address to Congress on 8 January 1918.[2] While these provided a splendid propaganda platform of high moral tone, they were too ambiguous to serve as the basis for a settlement.

* * *

When the Germans, recognising the advantages of ambiguity, suddenly on 4 October 1918 requested an armistice on the basis of the Fourteen Points, they addressed themselves to Wilson alone in hopes of easier terms, and he negotiated unilaterally for nearly a month while the Allies watched nervously. In deference to the American tradition of isolationism and fear of 'entangling alliances', Wilson had insisted that the United States was not an Ally but rather an 'Associated Power', and Allied statesmen recognised that the distinction was apt. Despite some similarity in Wilson's and Lloyd George's public pronouncements, Allied leaders knew that American war aims had little in common with theirs. France's chief concern was security *vis-à-vis* Germany. Italy and Japan wanted as much territory as possible at the expense of their neighbours, and the smaller states tended to be territorially ambitious as well.

Britain cared mainly about restoration of the traditional balance of power and economic patterns on the continent, preservation of British naval supremacy, and enlargement of the Empire. These were time-honoured objectives, understood and acknowledged by European leaders. Yet the United States, to whom most states directly or indirectly owed enormous sums of money, had no territorial or economic claims and no financial demands beyond the substantial one of debt repayment, a burden to be levied on the victors, not on the foe. Furthermore, Allied leaders feared that Wilson was a genuine idealist and suspected he really believed his own rhetoric about 'permanent peace' and 'the world must be made safe for democracy'. They suspected as well that Wilson viewed himself as the Angel of the Lord, coming to deliver Europe from decadence and corruption, and they worried that the Fourteen Points, which no Allied leader had endorsed, might have become Holy Writ in his eyes. Above all, as October 1918 progressed, they feared that he might still be imbued with the 'peace without victory' sentiments he had uttered before America's entry into the war, and fretted that he might give too much away to Germany as he negotiated alone.

While Allied assessments of Wilson were accurate in some respects, the fears about Germany were groundless. He had given nothing away before the Allies were brought into the negotiations late in October. Allied leaders in Paris, together with House, hastily settled the terms. Britain wanted to end the war before the United States became even more dominant. France wished to ensure that the Armistice was a surrender and that Germany could not resume hostilities. This was achieved by draconian military terms requiring rapid German withdrawal behind the Rhine, which had the unanticipated effect of tightening the German Army's grip on the nascent Weimar Republic.[3] The chief American concern was to ensure the inclusion of Wilson's Fourteen Points and his subsequent pronouncements, some of which were contradictory,[4] to serve as the basis for the peace. Despite much reinterpretation and one British reservation on freedom of the seas, this also was achieved.[5] On 9 November, a revolt in Berlin ended the monarchy and brought to power for the first time moderate but politically inexperienced Social Democrats. On 11 November they accepted the Allied terms, thereby incurring responsibility for what their predecessors had wrought and the cessation of hostilities the monarchic regime had sought as well as for the peace which followed. Germany's most democratic forces were soon labelled 'November criminals', which contributed to dislike of the new Weimar Republic, named for the town where its constitution was approved in 1919.

At this juncture, the German people entered upon what one German called 'the dreamland of the Armistice period'.[6] Jolted by the shock of the abrupt shift from their anticipation of victory to the humiliation of defeat, they soon convinced themselves that the war had been fought to a draw and that they had not lost. The misleading term Armistice, implying a truce but not a surrender, contributed to this belief, as did Allied inattention during the next six months; so did the fact that German Armies were still in France and Belgium, along with the lack of damage in Germany and absence of occupation even briefly of any area other than the westernmost Rhineland. Had the Allies known how incapable Germany was of resuming fighting, they might have paraded troops through major German cities to make their victory plain, but they did not. Thinking the matter of who won and who lost was perfectly clear, they did little to bring defeat home to the German people and set about planning and holding a peace conference to write a peace treaty based upon Allied victory. A few German leaders and diplomats knew from the outset roughly what the terms would be, but the German people interpreted Wilson's utterances in the most favourable way possible for Germany, ignoring his qualifying phrases, and came to expect a treaty with rewards rather than penalties.[7]

* * *

After Germany accepted the Armistice on 11 November 1918 and the guns fell silent on the Western Front, the victors set about planning for an Allied peace conference to be followed, they assumed, by a peace congress with Germany and the other defeated Central Powers, but administrative chaos set in. France insisted upon Paris as the site of the conference, but it was a poor choice. Not only did wartime passions run higher there than in any other likely location but, after four years of the strains of war, the French capital was in no condition to provide hotel rooms, offices, limousines, printing presses, and the myriad other facilities required by the thousands of delegates, experts, clerks and newsmen pouring into Paris – all of them male except secretaries. Wilson, delayed by the opening of Congress and by the Atlantic crossing, arrived in mid-December to find nothing prepared. Britain and France had not even named their delegates. Statesmen who needed to contemplate the problems ahead were instead coping with a ceaseless flow of querulous complaints about room allocations, despatch boxes, and all the administrative trivia essential to the functioning of so large a conference. The confusion in Paris before and during the deliberations was almost indescribable and contributed considerably to the erratic course of events.

The problems facing the peacemakers were staggering in their magnitude and compounded by a bewildering array of wartime promises, pronouncements and treaty commitments. The range of agreement among the Allied and Associated Powers was narrow. It was established that all Allied territories occupied by the enemy should be evacuated and restored, but there was no real agreement on what 'restoration' meant. It was understood that France would receive Alsace-Lorraine without a plebiscite, that Belgium's territorial and legal status would be improved, and that Poland would be re-created, although its location and size remained uncertain. Until the Armistice, there was also an agreed ambiguity about the future of the Habsburg Empire. Despite constant *émigré* pressure, particularly from the Czechs,[8] Allied and American statements had been vague because, almost to the end, Allied leaders hoped for a separate peace with Austria-Hungary and were prepared to subordinate national self-determination to that aim.

Beyond this there was little agreement. Much of the difficulty derived from several secret treaties entered into by Britain and France during the war.[9] Sweeping concessions to Russia and Romania had been nullified, since both states had signed separate peace treaties with the enemy. As to Russia, however, the situation had not simplified. The publication by the Bolsheviks of the secret treaties they discovered upon their accession to power late in 1917 had the effect of portraying the Allies as cynically carving up subject peoples among themselves and also heightened popular Italian territorial expectations. In Russia itself, a multi-faceted collection of civil and international wars wheezed indeterminately on. The Bolshevik government was under attack in both European Russia and Siberia by Russian forces of nearly every possible political persuasion, backed at times by various Allied powers. The situation was further complicated by anti-Soviet attacks, often with British or French blessing, by Polish, Finnish and Ukrainian forces, and by the presence in several areas of military detachments and commissions from Britain, France, Japan and the United States. Beyond that, the sizeable Czech Legion was determinedly trying to fight its way out of Russia via Vladivostok, while assorted Allied powers and Russian groups tried equally determinedly to use it to their own varying ends. No Allied state had a clear-cut, consistent policy in the fluid Russian situation; much less was there any agreed Allied policy. Despite, or perhaps because of, the abrogation of the secret treaties, the entire Russian area, including its important European borderlands, remained a large question mark.[10]

The other secret treaties remained in effect. They concerned the Middle East, the Balkans and the Pacific area. These commitments had been made under the urgent wartime necessity of aid from Italy, Japan, the Arabs and the Zionist movement. Some British radicals, liberals and junior officials found these allocations of the spoils distasteful and, noting Wilson's view that he was not bound by these arrangements, hoped that he would somehow force Britain and France to abandon their treaty commitments.[11] This was expecting more than Wilson could accomplish. Spurred by Chinese pleas and domestic political considerations, he strenuously opposed Japanese administrative and economic control of Shantung (Shandong) province in China, but, faced by united opposition from Britain and France, tied to their treaty commitments, and with Japan in occupation, he had to give way.[12] Similarly, once Lloyd George had gained the German Pacific islands south of the Equator for Australia and New Zealand, he had no choice but to support Japan's undoubted treaty right to the German islands north of the Equator and defeat Wilson on that issue, too.

Wilson's efforts to modify the other secret treaties were more limited and no more successful. While he apparently had not been informed of the promises to Japan, he had been told of the Middle Eastern and Italian arrangements upon American entry into the war, and perhaps this fact, coupled with his ignorance of the areas concerned and the absence of domestic pressure for revision, accounts for the half-heartedness of his efforts to upset the secret wartime arrangements. The chief beneficiary of these arrangements was Italy, who in 1915 had been bribed by the secret Treaty of London into a declaration of war against the Central Powers by promise of massive amounts of Habsburg and Ottoman territory. Italy was to gain the Trentino, the South Tyrol (Alto Adige), the Istrian peninsula, Trieste, portions of Dalmatia and Albania, and the Dodecanese Islands, plus some undefined rights to German colonies and to a share in the Ottoman Empire, particularly in Adalia in Anatolia. The entire Turkish situation was especially confused. With the collapse of the Russian commitments, there were no arrangements for European Turkey, but there was in 1917 a further concession of the Smyrna (Izmir) area in Anatolia to Italy and a series of conflicting commitments concerning the Arabic portions of the Ottoman Empire. The British had promised in 1915 that this territory, except perhaps Lebanon (a French interest), would become an Arab national state; had entered in 1916 into an Anglo-French division of the area between themselves; and in 1917 had endorsed the creation of a Jewish 'national home' in Palestine, which now was the subject of three conflicting arrangements. When in 1918 Wilson endorsed 'secure sovereignty' for the Turkish portions of the Ottoman Empire and 'autonomous development' for the remainder, the situation was in no way clarified.[13]

Allied oratory, while less binding than treaties, also muddied the situation and led to inflated expectations. In the hiatus before the peace conference, politicians in the victor states raised in their battered, war-weary constituents unrealisable expectations of territorial aggrandisement, immediate prosperity, and a golden era of peace and happiness, as in Britain's 'land fit for heroes'. By war's end, the political leaders had committed themselves also to the growing movement for an international organisation to ensure lasting peace. From 1915 on, a variety of groups such as Britain's Fabian Society, Union of Democratic Control, and League of Nations Society, the American World Peace Foundation and League to Enforce Peace, and smaller movements on the continent earnestly planned for a new world order. Early in 1915 one of the Americans involved exulted: 'We have societies galore advocating a parliament of man and an equally large number of organizations and people advocating a supreme court of the world, all of them making innumerable suggestions and proposals at different times.'[14] By war's end the concept of an international organisation was widely accepted in Britain and the United States and to a lesser degree on the continent, leading Wilson, Lloyd George and some continental politicians to endorse the idea of a League of Nations, charged with the impossible task of preserving peace in perpetuity. Equally unrealisable were the implied promises by the politicians that the vanquished would assume the war costs of the victors, leaving them free to return to a prosperous prewar life.

Except with the Arabs, the victors were more cautious about commitments to subject nationalities, but repeated statements endorsing 'autonomy' came in time to be viewed by such peoples as support for independence. With the sudden collapse of the Central Powers, the untiring efforts of the *émigré* groups had their reward. The Allies never really sanctioned the break-up of the Habsburg Empire.[15] It simply happened. In central Europe and on the Russian borderlands, as also briefly in the Middle East, new states seemed to emerge almost daily. Commitments or not, they were factors to be dealt with.

In the confused period before the peace conference opened, this complicated state of affairs was further compounded by an imperative need for haste. Winter was settling in, millions were starving (though not in Germany),* and influenza was sweeping Europe. It appeared that Russian communism, new and equally feared as a fatal disease, might sweep westward as well. East of the Rhine, there existed a dangerous power vacuum as the four great eastern empires were in disarray. Despite much uncertainty, Germany retained some coherence, as did Turkey, but the vast Habsburg and Romanov domains were in complete collapse.[16] In this vacuum, the new states were emerging. Often they had no governments, and generally they had no boundaries, but they did

---

* The persistent myth of deliberate Allied starvation of Germany is demonstrably untrue. Germans were undernourished and hungry, but not afflicted with the starvation conditions prevalent in many areas of victor states. *FRUS PPC*, II, 139–42, XII, 115; PRO, FO 371/2776, *passim*. The related tale of the Allied blockade is equally mythical. True, under the Armistice terms Allied warships remained in place to prevent a resumption of hostilities, but the Allies, who were short of merchant shipping and who had all Europe to feed, told the Germans to send out their ships to be filled with Allied food. This the Germans refused to do. In the end, Allied food was provided in Allied ships, the first deliveries arriving at the end of March 1919, well before German supplies were exhausted. Erich Eyck, *A History of the Weimar Republic* (Cambridge, MA, 1962) I, pp. 88–9; Admiralty to FO, 19 Apr 1919, m. 10630, FO 371/3776. See also the treatments by Elisabeth Glaser, 'The Making of the Economic Peace', in Boemeke et al., pp. 388–92; and Klaus Schwabe, *Woodrow Wilson, Revolutionary Germany, and Peacemaking, 1918–1919*, tr. Robert and Rita Kimber (Chapel Hill, NC, 1985), pp. 191–208.

seem to exist. Poland and Czechoslovakia were developing of their own accord. Bavaria was trying to detach itself from Germany; the Ukraine was resisting Russian control; and a short-lived republic of Kuban announced its existence. What eventually became the Baltic states were clamouring for independence, but nobody wanted to make decisions about that area until the outcome of the Russian civil wars became clear. In central and eastern Europe, even the elementary problem of feeding people was rendered excruciatingly difficult by the fact that all administrative structure had been swept away by war and civil war, and none had yet been devised to replace it. There were, of course, less pressing problems affecting other parts of the globe, but parcelling out colonies and dividing up the German merchant fleet could wait. Europe could not. There the task was urgent.

* * *

Yet in the end Europe had to wait. When the plenipotentiaries finally convened at the French Foreign Ministry on the Quai d'Orsay – and thus so called – in mid-January 1919, they did not deal with first things first. After the opening ceremonies, the urgent European tasks were avoided for some weeks. There were several reasons for this. Understandably, the Allied leaders wished to take each other's measure before they clashed head-on in the major battles, most of which were clearly going to come over European issues. The difficult question of Russian representation in the absence of any single Russian government, combined with deep-seated reluctance to recognise that of the Bolshevik V. I. Lenin while there remained any lingering hope of its defeat, led to postponement of east European issues. As the great powers busied themselves with less pressing non-European problems, Lloyd George, with dazzling diplomatic skill, secured most of Britain's desiderata and then hopped up to join Wilson on the pedestal where together they posed as the impartial arbiters of the world's destinies. Since he wished to turn away from Europe and hoped not to have to enforce the treaty, Lloyd George soon held that one should ask only what Germany would accept, so enforcement would be unnecessary, a view unacceptable to France. In addition, the five great states of Britain, France, America, Italy and Japan had arrogated all power of decision to themselves, leaving the 22 other countries officially present with little to do; as House remarked, they 'might as well be in Patagonia.'[17] To obscure this truth, these smaller states had to be given the appearance of some activity to placate their domestic opinion and prevent the fall of their governments. Accordingly, the two senior plenipotentiaries of each of the five great powers constituted themselves the Council of Ten, before which the smaller states could plead and thus receive their day in the limelight. The smaller states made the most of this, reciting at interminable length documents already submitted and consuming weeks of valuable time. Another factor often considered to have increased the delay was Wilson's insistence on writing the Covenant of the League of Nations at the outset. He was probably correct in believing that it must be written first or not at all, and it is true that his League Commission met at night, not delaying the droning daytime sessions; but much of his energy and that of other senior officials was diverted for several weeks from the European issues which were becoming more urgent with each passing day.[18]

When the conference finally got down to business, it functioned haphazardly. Much work was done by committees. The various frontiers of Germany were assigned to several committees which functioned independently of each other. Most of these, in the belief that they were preparing bargaining documents for a subsequent peace congress with Germany, arrived at more stringent boundaries than might otherwise have been chosen. When the heads of the major delegations, minus Japan, tired of the Council of Ten, and constituted themselves the Big Four to meet at Wilson's home and settle matters, they proceeded in slipshod fashion without agenda, minutes or any record of decisions until the British delegation's secretary, the supremely efficient Colonel Sir Maurice Hankey, insinuated himself into their midst and rescued them from disaster.[19] Even then, the agenda darted from topic to topic, and the Big Four were startlingly erratic in either accepting, ignoring or rejecting expert reports, and in reserving a variety of questions, both major and minor, exclusively to themselves. For no ascertainable reason, the tangled but relatively trivial problem of Luxemburg was handled entirely by the Big Four without benefit of expert advice. In addition, while there was general agreement that the German treaty should be written first, the Italians, who were 'moral absentees'[20] on German issues and uninterested therein, demanded time for their concerns, thus forcing disastrous and heated forays by an ill-prepared Big Four into the morass of Balkan politics.

Influence and idiosyncracy, personality and prejudice all played a role in the haphazardness of decisions. The legalistic Lansing was officially the second American delegate, but the entire conference recognised that only House had Wilson's ear and beat a path to his door. Similarly, in the French delegation André Tardieu, charged with guarding France's vital interests in Western Europe, was the confidant of Premier Georges Clemenceau, and the others counted for nothing. In the British delegation, Lloyd George and the Foreign Secretary, Arthur James Balfour, mattered and perhaps Sir Eyre Crowe of the Foreign Office, but nobody else. The Italian Foreign Minister, Sidney Sonnino, was probably more influential than the Prime Minister, Vittorio Orlando, for he spoke English as well as French and the British trusted him since his mother was Scottish. Wilson's inexperience in debate and penchant for involvement in trivia were factors, as were Lloyd George's refusal to read memoranda and reluctance to instruct his delegation. His secretary shielded him too well, and able British experts often worked at cross-purposes from lack of information. Much has been written about the charm of Eleutherios Venizelos of Greece and the prickly personality of Paul Hymans of Belgium, and these, too, played a part.

The role of prejudice is perhaps best illustrated by the Polish question. For strategic reasons, France wanted a powerful Poland. The Italians also supported Polish claims to set a precedent for their own territorial demands elsewhere. Lloyd George, who was intensely anti-Polish, thought Poland was going to be a dangerously unstable nuisance, so he fought to keep it as small as possible. On the other hand, the influential American expert on Poland, Robert Lord, a historian recently converted to Roman Catholicism, viewed Poland as a vital Christian outpost against the barbarian hordes to the east. When such prejudices were added to the inherent geographic, ethnic and political difficulties, it is a wonder that any decisions were reached about Poland at all.

Yet somehow the decisions were made. They took so long that a certain realism intruded, and the idea of a subsequent congress with Germany was tacitly abandoned. Time pressures became so acute that the Versailles Treaty was, in the end, thrown together in a tremendous flurry and, despite the work of a territorial committee, never properly co-ordinated. When it was rushed to the printers while a German delegation patiently waited behind protective fencing at Versailles,[21] nobody had read it in full and nobody was very sure of its contents. None the less, this lengthy document of 440 clauses and over 200 pages was presented to the Germans in a tense ceremony at Versailles on 7 May 1919, essentially in the form of an ultimatum.

* * *

The Versailles Treaty,[22] which German representatives eventually had to sign on 28 June 1919 with little modification, was severe, but it is amazing that it was not more so. The interminable Allied battles throughout the spring over specific clauses amounted to a struggle between Anglo-American complacency, reinforced by the seas separating them from Germany, and French fear, based on a long frontier with Germany.[23] In Wilson's mind there lingered some residue of the 'peace without victory' sentiment[24] and he was determined to see what he considered a just peace. The British wanted German ships and colonies but, in Europe, they still distrusted France,[25] the ancient rival, and were already instinctively reverting to their traditional balance of power stance, designed to ensure that no state, especially including France, dominated the continent. Clemenceau, on the other hand, had seen two German invasions of France in his lifetime and knew well that France had not won this war but had been rescued. Like most Frenchmen, he craved security against what he saw as a continuing menace.

In the end it was two against one, and Clemenceau, appeased by the promise of an Anglo-American defensive guarantee which never materialised, gave way on many particulars. Thanks to Wilson's insistence that there be no dismemberment, Germany lost remarkably little territory, considering how thoroughly it had lost the war. True, the colonies were gone, but the European losses were relatively modest. In the south Germany lost nothing, and in the north only a small strip of Schleswig to neutral Denmark. In the West Germany was obliged to transfer two small districts, Eupen and Malmédy, to Belgium; to return Alsace-Lorraine to France, to the displeasure of many of its inhabitants; and, after a great battle among the Big Four, to cede the Saar coal-mines to France and the Saarland to the League of Nations for 15 years, after which a plebiscite would decide its future. The Rhineland was to be permanently demilitarised and temporarily occupied, but, despite its centrality to France's military security, it remained German. To the east, the losses were greater. Memel (Klaipeda) went eventually to Lithuania, Danzig (Gdansk) to the League of Nations as a Free City, and 122 square miles (316 km^2) of Upper Silesia to Czechoslovakia, while ultimately about one-third of upper Silesia went to Poland. Above all, the famous corridor, splitting East Prussia from the rest of Germany and consisting of portions of Posen and West Prussia, was ceded to Poland to give it access to the Baltic Sea. This was one of the most difficult decisions of the conference and one particularly resented by Germany, but it was probably the least bad solution to an impossible problem, for a clear majority of the inhabitants of the Polish corridor were Polish, despite prewar German colonisation.[26]

Germany, who shared Lloyd George's view of all things Polish, reinforced by a strong sense of cultural superiority, never accepted the 'bleeding border', separation of East Prussia, or loss of any area whose population was 10 per cent German, but other clauses were equally offensive in German eyes. To constrain German aggressiveness and ensure French security, the military establishment was drastically reduced, Germany was largely disarmed, and the vaunted Prussian General Staff was to be disbanded though it soon reappeared under another name. In clauses which proved unrealisable, Kaiser Wilhelm II was to be tried by a special inter-Allied tribunal and other alleged war criminals were to be surrendered on demand for trial in Allied military courts.[*] To ease dislocation, goods from transferred territories could enter Germany duty-free for five years in the West and three years in the East. Because Germany's economy, like that of Britain, was intact and comparatively healthy, and continental victors feared inundation of their devastated areas by German goods or a trade war tantamount to defeat in view of their war-generated economic weakness, similarly temporary clauses restricted German tariff and export policy. In addition, Germany was obliged to pay Allied

* The Kaiser had fled to neutral Holland and the Dutch declined to extradite him. Sally Marks, 'My Name is Ozymandias: The Kaiser in Exile,' *Central European History* XVI (1983), 122–70. The Allies compiled lists of many hundreds of other alleged war criminals but, in the end, only 45, mostly very low-ranking, were charged for trial in a German civilian court at Leipzig. Twelve were actually brought to judgement, of whom the majority were acquitted. Erich Eyck, *A History of the Weimar Republic*, 2 vols (Cambridge, MA, 1962) I, pp. 187–8; Heiber, pp. 41–2.

occupation costs, which in the Rhineland were substantial. Above all, there were reparations.

The reparations clauses were among the least read, most written about, least understood, and most controversial sections of the Versailles Treaty. The basis for reparations arose from Wilson's Fourteen Points, which specified that occupied portions of France, Belgium, Romania, Serbia and Montenegro be 'restored'. During the Armistice negotiations Germany was, on 6 November 1918, notified that this meant 'that compensation will be made by Germany for all the damage done to the civilian population of the Allies and their property by the aggression of Germany by land, by sea, and from the air'.[27] During the peace conference, there were repeated Allied efforts to stretch this statement to cover war costs, but Wilson was adamantly opposed to indemnities; therefore only Belgium, whose violation constituted a crime against international law as well as an act of aggression,* was accorded war costs.

The other Allies, notably Britain, did succeed, however, in stretching reparation for damage done to cover such dubious items as war pensions and medical costs, which appeared at the time to increase greatly the potential total figure. In fact, as the German reparations debt was ultimately established in 1921 on the basis of an assessment of Germany's capacity to pay, inclusion of pensions and other expenses merely gave Britain a larger share but did not affect the total liability. At Paris, the quarrel over reparations was so fraught with political implications that the Big Four eventually decided to make Germany theoretically responsible for all costs but actually responsible for a much narrower but somewhat expanded range of specific categories of largely civilian damages. As a result Article 231 of the Treaty, which was designed to provide the legal basis for reparations (and initially in hopes of limiting Germany's burden), read in full: 'The Allied and Associated Governments affirm and Germany accepts the responsibility of Germany and her Allies for causing all the loss and damage to which the Allied and Associated Governments and their

---

* Under the 1839 treaties, Prussia and later Germany pledged to defend the independence, territorial integrity and compulsory neutrality of Belgium. In the first week of the war, Chancellor Theobald von Bethmann Hollweg acknowledged Germany's guilt respecting Belgium before the Reichstag and promised full restitution. For details, see Sally Marks, *Innocent Abroad: Belgium at the Paris Peace Conference of 1919* (Chapel Hill, NC, 1981).

nationals have been subjected as consequences of the war imposed upon them by the aggression of Germany and her allies.' The potential moral implication escaped the lawyers who drafted the clause.[28]

This article, which makes no mention of war guilt, was not intended to impute it and appears only in the reparations section of the treaty, not that addressing responsibility for the war. On the principle of collective responsibility, the same clause, *mutatis mutandis*, was incorporated in the Treaty of Saint-Germain-en-Laye with Austria (Article 177) and the Treaty of Trianon with Hungary (Article 161); neither interpreted it as imposing war guilt. However, Germany was expecting a war guilt clause and seized on Article 231. The ensuing acrid debate effectively turned it into an unofficial war guilt clause. In later years Germany, knowing that few people would engage in the requisite analysis of three treaties, fulminated to great effect about the injustice of 'unilateral war guilt'.

Article 231 established a theoretically unlimited German financial liability which, however, was restricted by Article 232 to civilian damages, as somewhat loosely defined in an annexe. This arrangement initiated a pattern which held true throughout the history of reparations of a high ostensible German liability and a more realistic actual debt. This sleight of hand suited both sides. Leaders of continental victor states could assure electorates that they would gain far more than was actually asked, and German politicians could garner votes by inveighing against supposedly astronomic demands.

The other difficulty with the reparations clauses was that the total German debt was not set. This stemmed partly from Wilson's determination to verify the damages claimed and partly from the awkward political fact that public opinion in most receiver states anticipated amounts far in excess of German capacity to pay. Naming any realistic figure would have caused the fall of several governments; thus deferral and ensuing sleight of hand. It was to Germany's advantage that the reparations debt be left unsettled, for some British figures discussed at the conference were astronomic, ranging as high as 16 times the amount eventually set in 1921, but the absence of a set sum also gave Germany the propaganda advantage of being able to complain about signing a 'blank cheque'.

The capstone of the Versailles Treaty was the Covenant of the

League of Nations. The peace settlement forwarded international law in several ways, notably through the Labour Charter and clauses pertaining to international waterways, but the western world's imagination and Wilson's hopes centred on the Covenant of the League of Nations, which he unwisely insisted upon incorporating in all of the treaties on the assumption that such would ensure approval by the American Senate. Equally unwisely, Wilson accepted other treaty clauses which he considered unjust in the expectation that the League could later remedy such defects. However, the Covenant clause requiring unanimity in all actions of consequence rendered the League an instrument of the *status quo* and severely restricted its ability to engage in any significant activity at all. The Covenant provided for an Assembly of all member nations (at first not including Germany), a Council dominated by the great powers, a Secretariat at Geneva, a Permanent Court of International Justice later established at The Hague, and some rather ill-defined measures to be taken against disturbers of the peace. Despite intense Japanese efforts, the Anglo-Saxon powers would not tolerate any clause, however ambiguous, in support of racial equality. Nor would they accept French efforts to render the League a forceful instrument to maintain the new *status quo*. The resultant organisation did its best work in consolidating the specialised agencies, many of them pre-existing, and to a lesser degree, in alleviating somewhat the lot of the inhabitants of former colonies of the defeated powers. None the less, in its larger role the League foundered on the twin rocks of the unanimity clause and the absence of the United States. Also, the League lacked any substantial enforcement powers, any answer to the fundamental impracticality of collective security, or any solution to the inevitable conflict between a supra-national organisation and the claims of national sovereignty, which had only been rendered more strident by the war and the peace.[29] In the circumstances the League was foredoomed to failure, and its creation constituted one of the dangerously misleading illusions of the peace.

* * *

The Versailles Treaty has been sharply criticised and some of the criticisms are valid although, given the circumstances in which it was hastily patched together, it is remarkable that it was not much more unsatisfactory. It has often been said, and with reason, that the Treaty was too much of a compromise between thoroughly opposed positions, too soft to restrain Germany and yet too severe to be acceptable to most Germans.[30] Either a fully Wilsonian treaty or a fully French treaty might have been better, but even a fully Wilsonian treaty would have been unacceptable to Germany as it would have involved some territorial loss to Poland and a more severe treaty would have been unenforceable without Russian cooperation. In any event the awkward accommodation of Wilsonian idealism and French fright soon proved unworkable, and a powerful, resentful Germany, determined to break the bonds of the Versailles *Diktat*, disturbed the tranquillity of Europe throughout the interwar years. Since the Versailles Treaty together with the east European settlement left this powerful, resentful Germany largely surrounded by smaller, weaker states, most of whose populations contained substantial German minorities, the potential for future discord was obvious to Germany's fearful neighbours. On the whole the peacemakers at Paris did not recognise the danger inherent in a situation where Germany was no longer surrounded and checked by great empires, though their intent had been to curb German aggressiveness. They assumed erroneously that the Weimar Republic would abide by their decisions and accept its new neighbours.

The Treaty is rarely criticised for providing too little security for France. Most of its compensations to France for Germany's inherently greater economic and demographic power were temporary at best, if upheld. French leaders deemed the settlement barely adequate if it were fully enforced. But then France, which accepted a temporary Rhineland provision in order to gain the precious Anglo-American guarantee, soon lost that guarantee and the security it implied. As enforcement quickly crumbled and Paris was pressed for more concessions on matters affecting its security, France became frightened and increasingly legalistic in an effort to salvage key treaty clauses.

The Versailles Treaty was also criticised for lack of attention to economic realities,[31] but in fact care had been taken to preserve economic units at the expense of ethnic coherence. It was an economic reality supported by an ethnic majority which led to the creation of the Polish corridor. Similarly, retention of German-speaking Asch by a reluctant Czechoslovakia was dictated by economic and strategic considerations. A more serious problem was that such enforcement provisions as there were depended entirely upon continuing harmony of viewpoint among the victors. To the extent that it ever existed, this harmony evaporated immediately and, as a consequence, much of the Treaty fell by the wayside. It could be argued that, aside from the territorial clauses and the complex created in the German mind, the peace of Versailles was of relatively little importance because so little of it was enforced.

The real difficulty was not that the Treaty was exceptionally unfair but that the Germans thought it was, and in time persuaded others that it was. Germany complained that the Treaty violated the Fourteen Points, but reserved its sharpest complaints, as with regard to Poland, for clauses most securely anchored on the Fourteen Points – to the extent that Wilson's wartime slogans could be fulfilled with any precision at all. German territorial losses were perhaps greater than they might have been if the Big Four had had time to consider the matter as a whole, but the Versailles Treaty was not exceptionally harsh, compared to the terms Germany intended to impose if it won and in view of how badly it had lost a long, bitter war. However, the German people, who had not suffered invasion and whose war damage was nearly non-existent, rapidly convinced themselves that they had not lost the war. If they had not lost the war, *any* diminution of territory and any restriction was by definition unfair. Having interpreted the Fourteen Points to maximum German benefit, they expected that Wilson would ensure their version of a 'just peace', which in their eyes meant no penalties, no territorial loss, and acquisition at least of Austria and the Germanic Czech borderlands – ensuring the German continental domination which the war had been fought to prevent. However, as one German scholar has pointed out: 'Germany's enemies had not fought a war and made sacrifices only to end up by turning Little Germany into Greater Germany,'[32] Despite the widespread shock when the terms became known, there is clear evidence that the German people and government began reacting intensely to the Versailles Treaty before it was written, and that they were in fact reacting to a defeat which they would not acknowledge.[33] The fundamental difficulty with the Versailles Treaty was that, for the moment, it represented reality. Since this reality was of short duration, so also was the Treaty.

* * *

After the Versailles Treaty was signed on 28 June 1919, the leading statesmen departed, leaving completion of the other treaties to lesser lights. Much work had already been done on the settlement with the other Central Powers, particularly in matters of interest to Italy. As a consequence it was clear that there would be many territorial changes and several new states, but much work remained. It was done piecemeal from July 1919 to August 1920 by a series of steadily less eminent Allied representatives.

The job of writing four more major treaties was simplified by the fact that much material could be carried over from the Treaty of Versailles. The treaties with Austria, Hungary, Bulgaria and Turkey,[34] all signed in Paris suburbs, each incorporated the League Covenant and the Labour Charter. They all called for the surrender of alleged war criminals and contained disarmament clauses which differed from the German model only in detail, in the size of the armies permitted, and in that such restrictions were more enforceable against small states than against a major power. Each treaty contained financial and economic clauses and customs restrictions similar to those of the Versailles settlement and, while the geographic particulars varied, the principles of the German model regarding ports, international waterways and rail transit carried over. Each treaty contained reparations clauses which, despite variance in detail, owed much to the reparations section of the German treaty, though Austria was too impoverished to pay any reparations except credits for state properties transferred. All Central Powers were to assume occupation and commission costs as a prior charge on their payments. Beyond this the four treaties, unlike the German one, acknowledged the transformation of a much enlarged Serbia into the Kingdom of the Serbs, Croats and Slovenes (hereafter called Yugoslavia though this name did not become official until 1929) and contained a series of clauses designed to protect the rights of ethnic minorities within their territories. All the small states of eastern Europe were soon required to undertake similar obligations toward minorities. To their indignation, the great powers were not afflicted with such restrictions. These were originally designed to protect Jewish minorities, which in the east were usually culturally distinct, but they insured that all minorities could remain or leave, retaining their property in either event, and were guaranteed schools and court trials in their own tongue. These well-intended provisions aggravated divisions.

The eastern treaties, combined with the ultimate settlements along the Russian borderlands, created a string of new or greatly enlarged states from Finland on the Baltic to Yugoslavia on the Adriatic, none of which had any prior experience with democracy and few with self-rule in any form. In part these territorial decisions derived from intense nationalistic pressures and from an effort to redraw the map of Europe along ethnic lines. Beyond that, France, for obvious strategic reasons, supported the creation of sizeable states on Germany's eastern and southern borders. Another important factor was fear of communism.[35] Thus, the Baltic states were finally allowed to be when the Soviet triumph became evident, and Romania, abysmally defeated in the war, roughly doubled in size. Ethnic factors played a part, but the string of successor states known as the *cordon sanitaire* was also designed as a bulwark against the revolutionary virus. In the north, these decisions awaited the outcome of the Russian civil wars and were not included in the Paris settlement, but the territorial changes in central Europe were made at the expense of the defunct Habsburg Empire and were delimited in the treaties with its heirs.

* * *

The Austrian and Hungarian treaties followed the German model particularly closely and were very similar. It was originally planned to present the two treaties simultaneously to the twin heirs of the Habsburg Empire, but the advent of Bela Kun's communist regime in Hungary caused a delay until Hungary had a government which the great powers were willing to recognise. As a result the Treaty of Saint-Germain-en-Laye with Austria was signed on 10 September 1919, while the Treaty of Trianon was held in abeyance until 4 June 1920. Both states were obligated to preserve their independence and to abstain from any act compromising it. Austrian *Anschluss* (union) with Germany was forbidden, though both Germanic states desired it, for the peacemakers realised that if Germany sat astride the Danube, its dominance of south-eastern Europe would be complete. Austria and Hungary each renounced the Habsburg monarchy and all Habsburg rights, privileges and properties overseas. Both treaties contained reparations sections similar to that of the Versailles Treaty. And both states suffered exceptionally severe and damaging territorial losses which rendered them ethnically homogeneous after having long presided over a multi-national empire.

The truncation of Austria was acute. To Italy went the Istrian peninsula, the Trentino, and the predominantly Germanic South Tyrol. The Treaty of Saint-Germain also created the state of Czechoslovakia, the Czech portions of which comprised the most productive of the former Austrian domains. Galicia went to Poland and Bukovina to Romania, while Yugoslavia gained Slovenia, Bosnia-Herzegovina, the Dalmatian coast and a number of coastal islands. What remained to Austria was a land-locked little mountain state with nearly a third of its population concentrated in Vienna and the rest scattered around an unproductive Alpine hinterland. The capital of a vast empire remained, but the empire to support it was gone. Interwar Austria was to prove an economic disaster. Indeed, acute deficit financing and colossal inflation led to bankruptcy in 1922. After financial reconstruction under League auspices, the Austrian economy limped through the 1920s on the crutch of foreign loans.[36]

Hungarian territorial losses were even more severe but left a more economic, if also more irredentist, state which lost 70 per cent of its territory and 60 per cent of its population. Hungary had to cede much of the Burgenland to Austria, while Slovakia and Ruthenia went to Czechoslovakia. Yugoslavia took Croatia-Slavonia and part of the Banat. The rest of the Banat, along with Transylvania and part of the Hungarian plain, went to Romania. The one remaining outlet to the sea, Fiume (Rijeka), was also surrendered, although its disposition was unsettled despite a tense battle at Paris between Wilson and the Italians. Acute postwar economic and political dislocation led to financial crisis and financial reconstruction by the League in 1924, but the surviving remnant of Hungary was none the less economically viable, thanks to its fertile plains. However, three million Magyars were left outside the contracted frontiers,[37] a fact which Hungary neither forgave nor forgot as it blamed the peace treaty for all social and economic problems.[38]

Bulgaria's territorial losses were also very bitter. It saw the First World War as a third Balkan War, and its struggles from 1912 to 1918 had gained it nothing. Under the Treaty of Neuilly of 27 November 1919, Yugoslavia received several small strategic border salients, Romania regained the southern Dobruja's valuable granary, most of Macedonia went to Greece and Yugoslavia, and

Greece took western Thrace, thus blocking Bulgarian access to the Aegean Sea and the Mediterranean. Bulgaria's reparations debt was specifically limited to 24 milliard gold francs (£90 millions or $450 millions) payable in semi-annual instalments over 37 years. This comparatively modest-sounding sum, of which Bulgaria paid about a third, has been estimated at one-fourth of its national wealth.[39] Significantly, Bulgaria emerged substantially weaker in relation to its neighbours, all of whom were much enlarged and with whom it was on poor terms.

* * *

Of all the eastern treaties, that with Turkey was the most complicated, the last signed and the shortest lived.[40] Under the Treaty of Sèvres of 10 August 1920, the Straits from the Black Sea to the Mediterranean were opened in peace and war to the merchant and war ships of all nations, and control of the Straits was vested in an international commission. The prewar capitulatory regime of extraterritorial rights for Westerners was extended to those Allies which had not previously participated in it. In view of the severity of Turkey's territorial losses, reparations were waived except for narrowly defined civilian damages, to the extent that funds were available after service of the prewar Ottoman debt and payment of occupation and commission costs.

Turkish territorial losses were indeed severe, though Ottoman prewar control of some areas had been ephemeral and several clauses merely confirmed pre-existing situations. Thus Turkey renounced all rights in the Sudan and Libya and recognised the French protectorates in Morocco and Tunis, the British protectorate in Egypt, and the British annexation of Cyprus. In the Middle East the Hedjaz (now part of Saudi Arabia) was to become an independent kingdom, while Syria, Mesopotamia (Iraq) and Palestine would be mandates under major power control. Mandate was the new term applied to former German and Turkish colonies transferred to the victors under nominal League supervision. For the Middle East, the mandatory powers were not enumerated in the Treaty of Sèvres but in fact had been decided at the San Remo conference in April 1920. France took Syria and Lebanon, while Britain gained the rest, namely Palestine, Transjordan and Iraq.[41] Finally, in a British and Zionist triumph, the Balfour Declaration of 2 November 1917, endorsing 'a national home' for the Jews in

Palestine, was imposed there as an obligation upon the mandatory power (Britain), notwithstanding prior pledges first to the Arabs and then to the French, and expert advice to the contrary.[42]

In partial fulfilment of the Treaty of London, Turkey ceded a number of Aegean islands to Italy. In a decision related both to the tangled history of the Treaty of London and to the Fiume quarrel, the Smyrna district in Anatolia went to Greece.[43] As a result of a dubious Anglo-American manoeuvre in response to Italian insistence on Fiume, to which Italy was not entitled under the London Treaty, Greece was already in possession of Smyrna. Turkey retained sovereignty over the area, but the exercise of this sovereignty was given to Greece for five years, after which the local parliament could petition the League Council for incorporation into Greece, with a plebiscite to be at the discretion of the Council. Greece also received some of Turkey's Aegean islands and, from European Turkey, the substantial territory of eastern Thrace. In addition, Kurdistan was to become either autonomous or independent, according to the preference of its inhabitants, and Armenia was to become an independent state with boundaries to be set by Wilson (but, in the end, Armenia was absorbed by the Turks and Soviets, and Turkey retained Kurdistan).

The Treaty of Sèvres, an unenforceable nineteenth-century imperial scheme, was never ratified. Before it was completed, Sultan Mohammed VI's subservience to the Allies, coupled with the Greek landing at Smyrna, generated a nationalist revolt led by Mustapha Kemal. His success, particularly against French troops, led Britain to occupy Constantinople (Istanbul) in March 1920, rendering the Sultan a virtual prisoner. In response the national movement swelled, and in April created a new National Assembly in Ankara. There ensued a two-year Greco-Turkish war, expulsion of Greece from Anatolia, the fall of the Sultan and the eventual proclamation of a republic under Kemal, and, in the last stages of the war, a dangerous Anglo-Turkish military confrontation late in 1922 at Chanak (Canakkale) on the Dardanelles. As a consequence, after protracted negotiation, the Treaty of Lausanne, to replace that of Sèvres, was signed on 24 July 1923.[44] By its terms Turkey regained Smyrna, eastern Thrace and some of the Aegean islands. It was relieved of all capitulations, reparations and military limitations except the demilitarised zone of the Straits. A Greco-Turkish convention authorised a forced population exchange which proved ruthless in its execution, but which at least eliminated the minorities problems which plagued central and eastern Europe. Aside from a Kurdish minority, Turkey was now homogeneous; Kemal abolished the caliphate, focused on secular modernisation, and abandoned the ambitious pan-Turkish policy of his predecessors, confining the state to Turkish territory which it could defend alone.[45]

* * *

The creation of an unending series of minority problems is only one of many grounds upon which the Paris peace settlement as a whole has been sharply criticised, though the treaties reduced by half the number of people living under alien rule. Minorities remained all over eastern Europe as frontiers based on ethnic lines proved impossible of realisation, especially in areas of mixed nationalities. Estimates of minority populations vary widely, and official censuses are unreliable because governments tried to minimise minority totals, but even the roughest statistics indicate the immensity of the problem. Poland, a country of 27 millions, contained 18 million Poles by Polish count, but far fewer by other estimates. There were between 3 and 5 million Ukrainians, a million White Russians, and 2 or 3 million Jews, most of them culturally distinct, and at least a million Germans. A border incorporating fewer Germans (at the expense of economics and more Poles in Germany) would have been possible but would not have assuaged German bitterness. Czechoslovakia's population of 14.5 millions included 3.25 million Germans – equally a cause of bitterness, three-quarters of a million Magyars, and half a million Ruthenes. Romania's 18 millions contained at least three-quarters of a million Germans, 1.5–2 million Magyars, half a million Ukrainians, 360,000 Bulgarians, and perhaps a quarter of a million Russians. The surviving remnant of Hungary, despite its drastic truncation, still encompassed in a total population of 18 millions, about half a million Germans, half a million Ukrainians, half a million Jews, and a quarter of a million Slovaks. Yugoslavia's 12 millions included, in addition to its three major native ethnic components, half a million Germans, half a million Magyars, half a million Albanians, and a quarter of a million Romanians. There were also about 600,000 Macedonians whom Yugoslavia counted as Serbs, although Bulgaria, with some reason, insisted that they were

Bulgars.[46] While these startling east-European minorities could have been reduced somewhat by different boundaries, generally at the expense of economic considerations, it is clear that nothing short of massive population transfers could have resolved the problem.

A contradictory complaint about the Paris peace settlement has been that economic factors were ignored in favour of ethnic considerations. On the contrary, it was the effort to reconcile ethnic groupings with economic and strategic necessities which led to the creation of so many minorities. The peacemakers acknowledged that when the language line crossed a vital railway five times in 26 miles, ethnicity had to yield to economics. The difficulty of drawing boundaries was further compounded by the cagey east-European peasant's refusal to commit himself lest he later find himself on the wrong side of the frontier and part of a persecuted minority. Thus enquiries into ethnic allegiance often evoked the reply: 'I am an inhabitant of this place.' Beyond that, language was not the sole criterion of nationality; race and religion were also important, and personal nationality did not necessarily equate with political nationality.[47]

One of the more common criticisms of the settlement, apart from those made by interested parties such as Italy, Hungary, China, and the Arabs, was the argument that the Allies should have restored the Austro-Hungarian Empire, which was an excellent economic unit, if not a successful political entity.[48] While the central European settlement had economic disadvantages, particularly for Austria itself, the Habsburg Empire had dissolved of its own volition and could not have been restored without sustained use of force. More valid perhaps is the argument that Wilson's insistence on self-determination for all nationalities led to the fragmentation of Europe into too many small states, some of them neither democratic nor economic nor by any standard very satisfactory.[49] Often this fragmentation had already occurred, and the problems arose from what came before the peace settlement or after it. The peacemakers recognised that the disintegration of the Habsburg Empire and the fragmentation of eastern Europe would generate economic problems when raw materials fell on one side of a new boundary and processing plants on the other, for sometimes a given manufacturing process of the Habsburg Empire was now spread among as many as three states. To alleviate this problem the peace treaties had provided for a substantial measure of economic integration among the succession states. But intense political nationalism engendered an economic nationalism which prevented economic cooperation.

While the east-European settlement created new difficulties, an acute observer and student of interwar Europe remarked that probably more people were reasonably satisfied with their governments then than at any time before or since [to 1989],[50] and this comment cannot be disregarded. It has been argued that the fragmentation of Europe fanned a dangerous nationalism, and certainly the history of interwar Poland's squabbles with its neighbours tends to confirm the thesis. Yet one must ask whether the nationalist pressures which had been building for a century and which reached fever pitch during the First World War could have been denied in the aftermath of Armageddon and whether the dangers were not perhaps more apparent than actual, since small states can rarely launch large wars. When one contemplates the conflicting claims of ethnicity and economics, one must conclude that the most balanced judgement was that of King Albert I of the Belgians: 'What would you have? They did what they could.'[51]

However, the peacemakers did not examine certain fundamental issues. Since Wilson forbade mention of the balance of power, which he deemed an evil European device, they never dealt with the fact that the war had shattered Europe's classical balance of five great powers or asked what (aside from the League of Nations) should replace it. Though the war had been fought to preserve that balance and to prevent German domination of the continent, there was no discussion of Germany's role in Europe now that it was somewhat cropped but still Europe's greatest power politically and economically – and potentially militarily if it could evade a treaty with few enforcement clauses. Nor did the Four face the fact that Germany was no longer bordered by three great powers but by a much weakened France and by smaller new states preoccupied with quarrels among themselves. Other problems arose because the authors of the settlement were children of the late nineteenth century, Eurocentric, nationalist, imperial, liberal far more than democratic, and imbued with the belief that the West was superior to the rest of the world, including eastern Europe, and therefore should lead.

At a more specific level, there were serious inadequacies in the settlement, some of which could not have been avoided except perhaps by greater injustice. One of the difficulties was that, while so much had been done, so much remained undone. So many questions were unresolved. Perhaps fortunately, none of the reparations debts except that of Bulgaria had been established, but the ensuing uncertainty further strained war-battered economies in defeated and victor states alike. Nor were the frontiers definitively set. All over Europe boundary commissions went forth, some of them armed with considerable latitude, to delimit the borders with precision. Some of their difficulties dragged on for years, and one part of the Belgo–German frontier was not settled until 1931. Moreover, from Schleswig to Kurdistan, there were a series of plebiscite zones where the inhabitants were to determine their own future. With the exception of the Saar, these decisions were completed by the end of 1921, but there had been two years of uncertainty in the interim. The fate of Fiume had not been determined.* Nothing involving Russia had been settled. When the Paris conference ended, Finland had become a state, but its Karelian borderlands with Russia were a battleground; the Baltic states still did not know whether they were to be; and Poland did not have an eastern boundary. Only in October 1920 was the Finnish frontier defined; only in 1921 and 1922 were the Baltic republics of Lithuania, Latvia and Estonia formally recognised; and only after a Russo-Polish war with a degree of French involvement was the Russo-Polish frontier set in the Treaty of Riga of 18 March 1921.[52] In remarking that the peacemakers at Paris in most respects did what they could, one must also remember how much they could not do.

Another difficulty with the settlement was that it was based on assumptions which proved unsound. One such assumption was that all states would approve the treaties. Not only Turkey refused but also China, enraged by the Shantung decision. Germany and Hungary were only brought to ratification by extreme pressure, a circumstance which rendered the binding effect of the settlement

* The Fiume settlement was protracted. In September 1919, freebooters under the Italian poet Gabriele d'Annunzio occupied the city. In November 1920, by the Treaty of Rapallo, Italy and Yugoslavia agreed that Fiume would become a Free City, and Italian forces expelled d'Annunzio. However, the Italian troops remained, finally taking full control in September 1923. In January 1924, by the Treaty of Rome, the Yugoslavs recognised the *fait accompli* and the award of the city to Italy, while the remainder of the Free State went to Yugoslavia.

questionable. Furthermore, by the time the first treaty, that of Versailles, took effect on 10 January 1920, American approval of the settlement appeared doubtful. The peace structure was based upon the premise of full American participation, and the erratic American withdrawal over a period of four years caused first great uncertainty and then acute dislocation of the entire settlement.* The settlement was further dislocated by disagreement among the remaining victors. The elaborate peace structure, which contained remarkably little provision for enforcement, was predicated upon continuing and increased identity of Allied viewpoint but – as the United States withdrew, as Italy pursued its own concerns and showed little interest in much else, as Britain and France quarrelled about everything from submarines to Silesia, from Turkey to Tangier, from reparations to Russia and to the Rhineland – decisions became increasingly difficult to reach and tended to ineffectual compromises. Instability ensued, thanks to American withdrawal, German revisionism, Anglo-French deadlock, and east European failures of cooperation.

The peacemakers had not only assumed that they could agree upon the implementation of their treaties. They had also assumed that the affected peoples would abide by their decisions. Yet several nations, including Poland, Turkey, Hungary and, above all, Germany, did not. During 1920 the peacemakers completed their peace treaties, and the elaborate optimistic structure of commissions to carry them out came into being. Yet the French at least were painfully aware that winning the peace would prove as arduous as winning the war. The battle was joined without delay.

---

* The American Senate twice rejected the Versailles Treaty: on 19 November 1919 and 19 March 1920. Therefore, the United States never joined the League of Nations. In August 1921, it signed separate treaties with Germany, Austria and Hungary, which confirmed it in its privileges but not in its responsibilities under the Treaties of Versailles, Saint-Germain and Trianon. Senate approval was contingent upon the reservation that the United States would not participate in any treaty commissions without Congressional consent. To all practical effect this ended official American participation in the peace structure, although American troops remained in the Rhineland until January 1923 and unofficial participation continued in financial matters.

2 The Effort to Enforce the Peace

Although the Paris peace settlement dealt with the entire globe, it was a peculiarly European peace, written largely by the European victors to their own benefit. Despite nominal Japanese participation and Wilson's efforts toward a new world order, the treaties reflected Europe's view of the world and of its own role in it. Most of the assumptions upon which European leaders operated had, however, been rendered obsolete by the First World War. In this sense the settlement was anachronistic.

Since the West-European states emerged victorious in the struggle with Germany, thanks in part to the contributions of Russia, the United States and Japan, they did not recognise that they had lost their pre-eminence and their position as rulers of the world. Civil war in Russia and China, together with self-absorption in the United States, obscured the extent of the shift in the power balance, as did the distribution of additional colonies to Britain and France. The assumption that it was Europe's absolute right to rule the world clouded the picture further and helped Europeans of all classes to overlook hard economic realities.

Before the war Europe had, along with the United States, taken over the globe, easily subjugating the non-white races, thanks to a wide technological gap, ample capital, military superiority and division among indigenous peoples. In justification of its rule, Europe cited its 'white man's burden' to civilise, Christianise and modernise – often without doing so to any great degree. The peace settlement continued this acquisition as the colonies of the foe were distributed among the victors. True, Japan had to be conceded the north Pacific islands it already occupied, but this unhappy fact was mitigated by the thought that Japan was much the most Westernised Asian nation, the occidental of the Orient. For the rest, the sun still never set on a much-enlarged British

Empire, nor on a larger French Empire. London remained the great pulsing heart of 'the Empire' and Paris of 'France indivisible'. Imperialism appeared triumphant, despite the disguise of mandates. In reality it was on the wane, and the spotlight was starting to move away from Europe as power dispersed, particularly to the United States and Asia.

Europeans, especially Western Europeans, did not recognise this fact. Large or small, European states shared a common but outdated world view, assuming Europe was the centre of the world, of civilisation and of culture. What happened there was what mattered. Tension between France and Italy seemed far more significant than tension between Japan and China, although which nations were on the rise and which on the wane was no secret to the far-sighted. Except for Europe's American offspring (whose sheer power in several senses, especially financial, commanded attention on the rare occasions when it insisted) and the 'white Dominions', the rest of the world consisted of 'wogs' to be economically exploited for European profit and to be gradually – very gradually – civilised into imitation of European systems of government, law, religion, industry and culture. While eschewing additional colonies, Americans expressed similar attitudes in more forthright language. A midwestern senator once exulted: 'With God's help, we will lift Shanghai up and up, ever up, until it is just like Kansas City.'[1]

The bases of Western rule were mainly economic, technological and psychological. One of the most potent and least costly weapons had been the absolute conviction of inherent superiority. The European club had divisions within itself, but its members stood above all others. Lord Curzon, the prewar British Viceroy in India and postwar Foreign Secretary, once remarked that Frenchmen 'are not the sort of people one would go tiger-shooting with'.[2] Yet despite his grandiosity, Curzon hunted tigers before the war with Indian princes and tried to curb British arrogance in the sub-continent, but in this he was hardly the norm. For many Westerners, the racial divide was determining. Indians, along with other Asians and Africans, were *Untermenschen* (subhumans), often regarded by Englishmen and other Europeans in much the same light that Nazi Germans later viewed Slavic peoples.

When Curzon ruled India, a few thousand Britons easily held that vast, teeming subcontinent in thraldom and in security against all comers. No longer. Inherent white superiority was increasingly challenged by newly restive subject peoples, while nascent nationalism made the old policy of divide and conquer decreasingly effective. The cost of maintaining European domination had sharply escalated while European resources were on the decline, largely as a result of the war. Debt-ridden European governments could not afford increased military expenditures to compensate for the evaporation of inherent superiority. Beyond that, moral debts were falling due for the substantial African and Asian contribution to the carnage of Flanders fields. So European overlords made concessions as slowly as possible to peoples who seemed not quite real and who clearly did not matter, while themselves intending to hold as much as possible as long as possible. The implications of their own attitude escaped most Europeans.

The political balance was also shifted by economic change. Imperialism, technology and changing tastes had created an interlocking world economy. The United States was more self-sufficient than any other highly developed nation but, even so, as canned vegetables, automobiles and Coca-Cola became commonplace, its imports of African kola nuts along with Asian tin and rubber soared. Despite the most balanced of major European economies, France also lacked tin and rubber, along with oil and several minerals vital to modern technology. Britain, Italy and Japan were all heavily dependent on imported raw materials and food as well. All traded substantially with the United States, which added to the pattern of interdependence, as did the fact that the industrial powers were dependent on each other's colonies for basic resources. Colonies existed to be exploited to European benefit but, as subject peoples increasingly rejected this assumption, the threat to Europe's long-term future grew.

The war had also shifted the economic balance. Europe had squandered its treasure, in money as well as in blood, and was seriously impoverished. As the European victors were deeply in debt to the United States, the world's financial capital moved from the City of London to Wall Street. During the war, as Britain concentrated upon survival, its lucrative oceanic carrying trade was pre-empted by Americans, while its traditional Asian and Latin-American markets were taken by Japan and the United States. After more than four years of total war, economic as well as military, European industry was either utterly ravaged, as in

Belgium and northern France, or utterly exhausted, as in Britain where production had been maximal and maintenance minimal. Moreover, since Western Europe had industrialised before all others, it now had the oldest, most inefficient mines and factories, which could not compete with new, modern facilities elsewhere. Much of Western Europe's industrial structure was obsolete.

The economic organisation of Europe was equally obsolete. An old Spanish saying declares, 'Wide is Castile'.[3] So it was in the fifteenth century and so also was Spain in the sixteenth century. But by the early nineteenth century, Spain was merely an impoverished little appendage to a Europe dominated by five great and glittering powers. Now, after an orgy of destruction multiplied by modern technology, the glitter was gone and there remained an impoverished small continent cut into some 30 competing little states. As inadequate domestic markets could not consume the yield of mass production and tariff barriers inhibited exports, businessmen soon saw the need for a larger economic unit and began to advocate various forms of European economic union, chiefly to compete with the United States. But most politicians and ordinary Europeans paid them little heed, focusing instead on the traditional European national rivalries. After all, that was what mattered.

The obsolete European assumption that Europe constituted the civilised world and that its quarrels were what counted could be found all across the continent. This view of most of the rest of the world as inferior and unimportant (except as to the strategic position and economic power of European states) transcended centuries-old European rivalries and hatreds. While Franco-German tension was not necessarily the single most serious problem of the interwar world, all Europe thought it was. It completely eclipsed events in Palestine, where tiresome 'natives' misbehaved so often. Almost without exception the European imperial states, large or small, assumed that it was their mission to rule the world according to their interests and to bring it into conformity with their values, while the European non-imperial states assumed that Europe *was* the world.

* * *

This outdated European view was reflected in the organisation created to preserve the new world order. In most respects the

League of Nations was a European club, largely dominated by
European statesmen, assumptions and issues. Japan was the only
non-European state ever to hold a permanent seat on the Council,
and in the early years Europe monopolised most of the non-
permanent seats as well. Of the 63 states belonging to the League
at one time or another, 29 (including Turkey) were European. A
Latin-American bloc of 20 states was entitled to no permanent seat
and one non-permanent seat on the Council. There were six Asian
members of the League (three Middle-Eastern and three East
Asian) and three from Africa, representing *all* the independent or
quasi-independent nations of those two continents in the interwar
period. Finally, the British Empire held five seats (later six) occupied by India and the white Dominions (including South Africa,
where only the white minority was represented, often by an
Englishman).

Without exception the prominent figures in the halls of the
League at Geneva were European. The great powers dominated,
but the most conspicuous devotees of the League were representatives of the smaller European nations, especially those which had
benefited from the peace settlement. These states, frightened of
Russia or Germany or both, tended to cling to the League and to
the illusion that it could protect them and their gains. They were
the leading champions of collective security, knowing that their
smallness ensured that they would never be called upon to provide
it. Generally they viewed the world as bounded by the Urals and
the Azores, unless they were imperial overlords themselves, as were
Belgium, Denmark, Holland and Portugal.

The great powers were less enthusiastic. If collective security
materialised, they would have to ensure it, and no state was eager
to accept such an unlimited, universal military commitment.
Since they were among the world's strong nations, the European
great powers were not attracted to a system intended to protect
the weak against the strong. This new system was rendered palat-
able, however, by the fact that it enshrined the old order, giving
the haves a privileged position *vis-à-vis* the have-nots, and bestow-
ing moral sanction on all aspects, cultural, economic and political, of the existing Darwinian imperial structure of European
domination. The League system helped to disguise the transfers
of power taking place in the world and reinforced Europe's view
of its role.

After centuries of experience in statecraft and great power politics Europe had developed a certain cynicism, which led its leaders to recognise that many of the premises upon which the League rested were naive. The theory of collective security assumed an astonishing amount of agreement and altruism among men and nations, an unfailing willingness to sacrifice and die for strangers. The structure of the new world organisation also assumed, despite the historical record, that men and nations naturally and consistently would prefer conciliation and peace to competition and war. Should a nation deviate from such beatific behaviour, world opinion would deter its transgressions. This extraordinary assumption rested in turn upon four others: that world opinion necessarily existed at all on a given issue; that it was united; that it was unfailingly on the side of the angels; and that it would provide an effective counter to force. Their wartime experience told Europe's leaders that guns were more reliable.

Yet guns and gunboats now cost more than European powers could afford. Besides, the old Concert of the great states was in disrepute, along with the traditional balance of power mechanism. In its place in part was the League of Nations, supposedly a new order, but in fact, even officially, one preserving the special position of the great powers. Europe's leaders quickly recognised that decisions would continue to be made in Berlin, London, Paris and Rome, or by consultation among their representatives. That being so, they contributed to the oratory of Geneva and paid lip-service to its tenets, although always with extreme caution concerning collective security.

The leaders of the European great powers also recognised what ordinary men often did not: that the League was a limited agency of limited functions and effect. It could persuade and conciliate, but little more. Since its Covenant did not ban the use of force and the League had no force of its own, it could not ensure any nation's security, particularly when threatened by a major power. There was no real prospect that the League could fulfil its chief function of enforcing and preserving the peace. That could only be done by the great powers, if they were in agreement or in precarious balance.

* * *

As the new League turned in 1920 to its assigned task of enforcing and preserving the peace, it discovered that the great powers had largely reserved enforcement to themselves or their agencies and that, in many areas, before peace could be preserved, it must first be established. To the dismay of many, peace did not obligingly 'break out' when it was officially declared. During the peace conference, General Sir Henry Wilson, Chief of the Imperial General Staff, remarked that 21 wars were then in progress, and in March 1920 he wrote, 'This Peace Treaty has resulted in war everywhere.'[4] While exaggerated, his judgement was essentially sound. The advent of peace was highly relative. The major powers were no longer in bloody collision, but civil war raged in Russia, Ireland, China, Turkey, and briefly in Germany's Ruhr valley. Foreign troops remained in Russia; the Baltic area was a battleground; and Poland invaded Russia while Hungary marched briefly on Poland, Romania and Slovakia.[5] There was fighting on the Finnish frontier and in Fiume; in Silesia Germans and Poles waged an undeclared war; most Balkan borders were aflame; and in Anatolia Turks fought Greeks, backed by Britain. Yet the world was officially at peace.

In time the little wars fizzled out. In 1922 the last Japanese troops left Siberia, and Lenin was in firm control of a Marxist government which no major power yet recognised. By then the Red Army had marched on Warsaw, Poland had sharply counter-attacked, and after much difficulty, Russia's Western frontiers had finally been set well east of where Western experts had recommended.[6] In 1921 the last Polish–German boundaries, including that in Silesia, were settled by plebiscite and Allied decree, while the creation of the Irish Free State in 1922 as a reluctant Dominion led to the end of the civil war in 1923. Late in 1922 an armistice silenced the guns in Turkey. By then the world had learned that peace treaties are easier to write than to implement.

The peace treaties provided for numerous commissions to execute their provisions until the conditions of peace were fulfilled, after which the League would undertake supervision. Depending on function, the commissions were located in Paris or on the spot. Membership varied. Boundary commissions included the interested parties plus one or several of the great powers. The Rhineland High Commission consisted of the four occupying powers, Britain, France, the United States and Belgium. The composition of military control commissions to supervise disarmament varied but always included France and Britain. The important Reparations Commission in Paris included the three major European powers and initially the United States, plus a fifth seat occupied by Belgium on German matters, Yugoslavia on east European issues, and Japan on naval questions. These and other commissions were supervised by a Conference of Ambassadors in Paris representing the five great powers (although the American soon became an 'intermittent observer'[7] and Belgium was occasionally added on German issues). The Conference was charged to oversee the implementation of the peace and resolve any tag-end problems which might arise.

The commissions encountered many difficulties. Some lacked sufficient authority. The Conference of Ambassadors soon collided with a council of the great powers, found its decision overturned, lost what authority it had possessed, and subsided into inconsequence. Most commissions were ill-equipped to enforce their decisions; they lacked automatic sanctions, especially any applicable by majority vote. As disagreements developed among commission members or major powers over interpretation of treaty clauses, there was no authoritative independent body to render a decision. Worse yet, the membership of several commissions shrank from five to four as the United States withdrew, and so the potential for deadlock increased.

Washington pursued no consistent course regarding the commissions during its erratic withdrawal, but the remaining American members soon ceased to vote. The resultant dislocation of the peace structure was acute and so this structure never functioned as planned. The chair of the Saar Commission, intended for an American, passed to France, to the dismay of German-speaking Saarlanders. Distortion at the Reparations Commission was even greater. As American reparations claims were minuscule and it was the least interested party, it was supposed to chair a five-member commission where deadlock would be impossible since abstention counted as a negative vote. Upon American withdrawal, France, the most interested party, claimed both the chair and the casting vote in case of deadlock accorded to chairmen of other commissions. Thus France could control the commission with the support of one other member. As Britain offended Belgium regularly and Italy usually supported the stronger side, the vote was often three to one, and the second, casting vote was never used on a German issue, but its presence in reserve bolstered France's position. Moreover, whenever Britain refused to participate, the Reparations Commission found enforcement of its decisions difficult.

The United States was the only nation with sufficient power (through use of the war debts issue, if in no other way) to serve as referee and force clear-cut decisions. In its absence, implementation of the peace or a systematic revision of it might still have been possible had there been any agreement among the other victors, but there was none. Britain and France agreed on almost nothing. As a League official observed: 'it is not altogether impossible to bring the French and the British to see eye to eye – only their eyes are so different.'[8] France and Italy came to terms with Turkey, while Britain backed Greece virtually to the end. France supported Poland against Russia and in Silesia, but Britain emphatically did not. Anglo-French interests in Russia were competitive, not complementary. In late 1921 Lord Curzon declared:

> the Foreign Office is only too painfully aware that in almost every quarter of the globe, whether it be Silesia or Bavaria or Hungary or the Balkans – Morocco or Egypt or Turkey or Mesopotamia – the representatives of France are actively pursuing a policy which is either unfriendly to British interests or, if not that, is consecrated to the promotion of a French interest which is inconsistent with ours.[9]

Beyond that, the British were distracted by Ireland and Empire while French interests centred primarily in Europe. Paris was nervous about the patent British desire to restore prewar trade patterns with Germany and Russia, while London worried about the French Air Force and submarines.[10] Britain seriously debated whether the next war would be against France, and when a French alliance was considered late in 1921, the chief argument in its favour was that: 'If, as some think, the most likely enemy is France herself, then, as long as the alliance lasted, such a danger would indeed be eliminated.'[11]

* * *

In addition, the true continental power balance soon ceased to square with the peace settlement. Japan had no interest in Europe and the United States largely withdrew, as did Britain as much as possible. That left the continental states on their own. Of these, Italy, lacking resources and torn by internal strife, was not truly a great power but a regional one with little interest north of the Alps. Its long exposed coastline inclined it toward Britain, the Mediterranean's dominant naval power; its desire for reparations inclined it toward France; and its tactics often amounted to selling itself to the highest bidder. Soviet Russia, which presented the world with its first modern female diplomats and head of mission, was ostracised, isolated and self-absorbed. Despite lingering hopes in the early 1920s that revolution would spread, Lenin was a realist, as was Josef Stalin after him; both wanted to end Moscow's isolation and avoid a possible capitalist combination against Bolshevism. But reconstruction in every sense combined with European hostility to Bolshevism to exclude Russia from the power equation for some years. Its exhaustion, together with that of Germany, gave the 'frail and mutually hostile'[12] east European states a respite from threatening pressure of which they did not make the most, quarrelling instead with each other though each of them abutted at least one great power, Poland two. These states were intended to be buffers against Bolshevism, but the existence of the *cordon sanitaire* separating Germany and Russia facilitated their rapprochement, which affected the power balance.[13]

However, whether Europe stabilised into genuine peace depended primarily upon the triangular relationship of Britain, France and Germany. Of these, Britain was edging back to the middle, trying to resume its nineteenth-century role as the fulcrum of the power balance, which it badly misread, looking at the short term and superficial, not the long-term underlying reality. Thus it saw France as too powerful and Germany as a weak underdog, though Lloyd George also feared potential German revenge. That concern, desire to redress the presumed power balance, and hope that if Germany were given its own way, it and Europe would settle down, enabling Britain to focus on its economy and Empire, led him to early appeasement, which London saw as pacification.

Britain appeared to be Europe's and the world's greatest power, but other powers were only temporarily in eclipse or preoccupied. In reality Britain was over-extended, with ageing industries and its markets and carrying trade partially lost. It slashed defence expenditure drastically[14] until its army was miniscule and its Empire largely patrolled cheaply by the new Royal Air Force. In Europe, it wished to take the easiest course and then disengage; what was easy soon came to be seen as right and moral as Britain swallowed its own propaganda, which was nearly as assiduous as that of Germany and often similar.

Except for Aristide Briand, who was often Foreign Minister, French leaders lacked any talent for propaganda, which cost them dearly in a new era when international affairs dominated the attention of European headlines and electorates. Britain and the United States saw France as too strong when actually it was weak and dependent, a fact underlined by loss of the Anglo-American guarantee. French leaders knew it had not won the war but had been rescued, and it had 'the psychology of a defeated nation';[15] it emerged from the peace settlement dominant on the European continent and possessed of the world's second greatest empire, but its European predominance was based on Europe's largest fully equipped modern army, a temporary absence of competition, and equally temporary Versailles Treaty clauses to compensate for economic and demographic weakness as 40 million Frenchmen faced 62 million Germans. But demobilisation and sharp cuts in the term of service shrank the army quickly, ageing equipment was not replaced, other powers revived, and the demographic differential would only worsen, owing to France's older population and low birth rate. Alliance with Soviet Russia remained politically unthinkable for most of the interwar era; east European substitutes meant that France became over-extended in Europe without feeling secure. French policy was driven by fear and dependence on an aloof Britain, both for its own sake and for its ties to the United States. As Balfour remarked, France was a 'second rate power' whose leaders 'were so dreadfully afraid of being swallowed up by the tiger, but would spend their time poking it'.[16]

What France feared was Germany as both countries assessed the long-term power balance realistically. Like France's Third Republic, Weimar was born of defeat and therefore unpopular, but it never stabilised, partly because defeat was not faced realistically. The army claimed that it had not lost in battle but suffered a stab in the back (*Dolchstoss*) by the home front; this widely credited myth reinforced belief that Germany had not lost the war and bitterness over the hated *Diktat*, almost unanimously rejected by a populace which had assumed that German expansion could continue indefinitely without a reaction from others and that justice meant the Greater Germany.[17] The electorate forgot the severe treaties Berlin had imposed on Russia and Romania in 1918 and its plans to levy heavy war costs on the Allies, psychologically could not accept the reality of the Versailles Treaty which it thought could be escaped by 'passive noncompliance',[18] and did not understand that defeat meant fewer policy options and limited room for manoeuvre. Unrealistic popular expectations were fed by demagoguery, especially from right-wing parties.[19] As Weimar's first and most genuinely democratic governments received the onus of the actions of their predecessors and became 'November criminals', they were impelled, as any politicians would be, to prove their patriotism by endless demands for treaty revision. The fact that a society which was deeply divided socially agreed only on foreign policy reinforced this tendency.

Weimar's revisionism mattered far more than that of smaller states because Germany remained a great power; though absolutely weaker than in 1914, it was now relatively stronger, owing to partial withdrawal by three great Allies, debilitation of a fourth, and creation of weak neighbouring states. As a great power in Europe's centre, its policy options, though restricted more than its people realised, provided opportunities, if not for immediate success, at least for destabililisation of the peace. An inexhaustible and effective propaganda campaign orchestrated by the Foreign Ministry reinforced its revisionism. Beyond that, it tried to widen Anglo-French divergence, focusing on Britain, the key power after American withdrawal, in its effort to undo treaty clauses.

* * *

As the peace settlement crumbled, the fear-driven French became sticklers for enforcing key treaty clauses, while the British, who were having second thoughts about much of the settlement, encouraged the crumbling process. Germany made the most of the resulting deadlock. The small states, many of them beneficiaries of the treaties and fearful neighbours of Germany, were dismayed but helpless. In terms of the peace structure, Belgium was the most important of these, and since it shared some aspects of both British and French views, it struggled to achieve the awkward compromises in German matters which followed. These only papered over the rift and postponed the breach which soon transformed many of the commissions and much of the settlement.

Beyond these difficulties lay others. Many inadequacies of the enforcement system derived from the false assumption that the treaties would be honoured and largely self-enforcing. But Holland refused to relinquish the Kaiser, and Germany did not surrender alleged war criminals. Nor did it disarm on schedule or meet reparations quotas. Austria could not and did not pay reparations. Poland did not accept its frontiers; Italian troops did not evacuate Fiume; and Turkey did not accept the Treaty of Sèvres. Nothing much happened. The will to enforce the treaties was lacking or at best divided. While Britain supported Greece, France would not detach troops from the Rhine to force Turkey to honour the Sèvres Treaty. Similarly, Britain would not support Poland in Silesia or stop its seizure of Vilna (Wilno, Vilnius) from Lithuania. Even when some agreement existed the basic problem remained. One boundary decision was six to one, but the dissenter was Germany, who kept the disputed territory because no power would enforce the transfer. The overriding difficulty was that the only effective means of enforcement was force and, after four years of war, nobody would risk the possibility of more war.

As the treaties crumbled, the commissions grew. Special missions were sent to the trouble spots of eastern Europe and, as plebiscites were postponed and tensions rose, supervisory teams became larger. German refusal to permit inspections often left military control commissions with little to do, but they remained in place. Its rejection of border delimitations gave boundary commissions a new lease on life as precise frontiers remained undefined for years. A vast structure developed in the occupied Rhineland, and revision of the Turkish treaty generated new agencies. Above all, the Reparations Commission swelled. As Austria reached financial collapse, Allied reparations claims were abandoned, but agencies subsidiary to the Commission proliferated in Paris and Vienna to supervise the loans which kept Austria alive. As Germany defaulted steadily, Turkey was substantially relieved of reparations and others paid in part, the Reparations Commission became an army retreating steadily into Never-Never-Land and emitting a bewildering barrage of highly technical documents, with which the statesmen had neither the competence nor the desire to cope. Yet as the reparations question was fraught with political consequences, cope they did after a fashion.

The statesmen did desire to deal themselves with the main

issues which soon came to include many secondary matters. In creating an elaborate peace structure, the leaders delegated much. Then they took a good deal back into their own hands. Many apparently minor problems involved national prestige, strategic alliances, imperial factors or the future pattern of international relations. Accordingly, the Premiers and Foreign Ministers met so often together that the immediate postwar period is sometimes called the era of international conferences. So many of these took place at expensive resorts that the French politician Raymond Poincaré spoke disparagingly of 'la politique des casinos'.[20] Officially termed Supreme Councils, these meetings of Allied ministers with or without their German counterparts revived the nineteenth-century Concert of Europe in a new form but also in new circumstances, for now these gatherings were subjected to the glare of intense press publicity including newsreels, propaganda wars and statesmen playing constantly to their electorates by leaks and public pronouncements.

Less conspicuous but also important, especially in the late 1920s, were unofficial meetings, usually in conjunction with League sessions. The League came into official being in 1920 and wandered from place to place (again, often resorts) until its buildings in Geneva were completed. While most statesmen soon recognised that the League's powers were illusory, their electorates often did not, and so many European Foreign Ministers faithfully attended the regular meetings of the Assembly and Council. These afforded opportunities for quiet diplomacy outside the formal sessions. Foreign Ministers whose countries were officially on poor terms arranged to have rooms in the same hotel and met privately, safe from the pressures of public opinion. Perhaps this informal consultation was one of the League's larger contributions to the unsuccessful effort to create an enduring peace. Looking back after ten years of experience, a British official acknowledged that the League had few major achievements to its credit but remarked: 'If Monsieur A. has Herr B. and Signor C. to dinner – even a bad dinner – several times a year, the tone of the diplomatic correspondence between those three statesmen (to say nothing of their conversation) undergoes a change. Before the war this curious and general trait was never properly exploited.'[21]

While unofficial diplomacy was usually narrow in scope, especially at first, Supreme Councils were far ranging in agenda. These large-scale deliberations began in December 1919 and continued until their culmination at Locarno in October 1925. At first they were largely devoted to completing the Treaty of Sèvres and the Middle Eastern settlement, discussing the many problems arising from the fluid Russian situation, and attempting to repair the treaties already in effect. By the time the last treaty was completed, the earlier treaties were unravelling.

Apart from Turkey, the chief centres of revisionism were Hungary and Germany. Hungary occupied Slovakia in March 1919, but was brought to withdrawal by an Allied ultimatum. There was nervous talk in Paris of what to do if Hungary ignored Allied commands, but the crisis passed without need for resort to force. Then Hungary invaded Romania in July 1919, but a vigorous Romanian counter-offensive in August swept the Magyars back into Hungary, toppled the Communist regime of Bela Kun, and led after elections to restoration of the monarchy with Admiral Míklos Horthy as Regent. Hungary threatened Slovakia again in 1920 during the Russo-Polish war, and twice in 1921 ex-Kaiser Karl tried to return to the Hungarian throne. These moves were defeated by energetic action, including military mobilisation, from Hungary's neighbours, led by Czechoslovakia. Thereafter Hungary subsided into truculence, implying that it hoped to march against one neighbour or another to regain lost territory at the first favourable moment. Continuing Hungarian irredentism together with the events of 1920 and 1921 led to the completion in 1921 of the Little Entente consisting of Czechoslovakia, Yugoslavia and Romania. This bloc had ties to France, Poland, Austria and Italy (despite continuing Italo-Yugoslav friction in the Adriatic), but its core was the three states immediately threatened by Hungarian revisionism.[22]

The Little Entente was a success, though lacking much else in common, and Hungarian revisionism failed because the three countries had agreed views on a single opponent, were energetically led by Czech foreign minister Édouard Beneš, had armies totalling half a million men compared to Hungary's treaty level of 35,000, and were prepared to use force if necessary. The name 'Little Entente' arose from a derisive Hungarian analogy to the greater Entente trying to cope with German revisionism. Beyond the names, the two groups had little in common. What became known as the Western Entente in the interwar years derived from the Anglo-French Entente Cordiale of 1904 and the wartime alliance. In the postwar era, it consisted of Britain and France with intermittent involvement of Italy and Belgian participation as junior partner. The Entente powers did not have agreed views, were not energetically led, and in the main were not prepared to use force. For these reasons and because of its greater power, German revisionism was far more successful than that of Hungary, and during the 1920s much of the Versailles Treaty was progressively dismantled.

* * *

German resistance to the Treaty, especially the reparations clauses, began before it was written and continued without cease.[23] On the rare occasions of Entente unity, Germany had no success, but, more often, Anglo-French deadlock provided manoeuvring room for German efforts to modify the settlement. As Weimar failed to fulfil disarmament and reparations terms, military intervention was discussed at Entente conferences from March 1920 onwards, but Germany was a great power and Britain was increasingly unwilling to contemplate any threat which might have to be made good. As early as April 1920, France occupied Frankfurt and three neighbouring towns in response to an unauthorised German Army incursion into the demilitarised zone in the Ruhr valley. While the French action was effective, Britain protested loudly. Thereafter through conference after conference as German recalcitrance was discussed, France advocated a Ruhr occupation and Britain resisted. As treaty enforcement without such sanctions became more problematic and the question of an occupation thus became immediate, London became even more resistant and the Entente deadlocked.

Few conferences of the postwar years, whatever their formal agenda, concluded without a discussion of reparations or German disarmament, or both. The disarmament question dragged on for years, as Berlin simply did not meet the stringent treaty terms. Similarly, the reparations question poisoned the air through the 1920s. The Versailles Treaty specified interim payments of 20 milliard* gold marks in cash and kind (coal, timber and chemicals)

---

* A British milliard or thousand million is the equivalent of an American billion. The exchange rate was approximately four gold marks to the dollar and 20 to the pound. After 1918, the gold mark was no longer in circulation but remained a necessary legal fiction for accounting purposes because the paper mark fluctuated widely and depreciated rapidly.

until the total liability could be set by the Reparations Commission. However, Germany did not meet its coal quotas. They were revised downward and still it did not meet them. Finally, at the Spa Conference in July 1920, the first postwar German meeting with the victors (at which a Ruhr occupation was seriously considered), the coal quotas were again revised and the shipments partially subsidised. At Spa, the Entente powers settled the distribution of reparations (France 52 per cent, Britain and Empire 22 per cent, Italy 10 per cent, Belgium 8 per cent, Yugoslavia 5 per cent, and 3 per cent for the rest)[24] – when and if they could agree on the total liability.

The Entente reparations haggle moved back and forth across the Channel for many more months. France and Italy wanted as high a figure as possible while Britain, eager to restore its prewar trade with Germany, fought for minimal payments. Eventually a Belgian compromise figure of 132 milliard gold marks plus the Belgian war debt was accepted and announced by the Reparations Commission on 27 April 1921 as the total liability of all the Central Powers combined. Public opinion in most receiver countries was dismayed by the smallness of the figure, but economists and statesmen knew it was far more than Germany could pay and knew also that other Central Powers could pay little. Accordingly, at the London Conference of May 1921, another elaborate sleight of hand nominally preserved the 132 milliard figure but actually reduced the German debt to 50 milliard gold marks (including the unpaid balance of 12 milliard on the interim 20 milliard) to be paid over 36 years according to complex schedules for delivery of cash and kind.[25] The London Schedule of Payments was presented to Germany on 5 May 1921 in the form of a unanimous Entente ultimatum with a Ruhr occupation threatened.[26]

Faced with Entente unanimity and threats, Germany accepted the London Schedule. The first cash payment was met in full (chiefly in borrowed monies) in the summer of 1921, partly because Entente sanctions imposed in March in an effort to evoke a satisfactory German reparations offer were still in effect. To gain the specified foreign currencies, Germany chose to dump paper marks on the market, causing a sharp depreciation which it blamed on reparations. With the cash payment, controls on customs ended but Entente occupation of Düsseldorf continued, despite British objections. German payment was economically but not politically feasible, so there were few further cash payments until after the Dawes Plan went into effect late in 1924. While coal and timber quotas were repeatedly revised downwards, they were never met in full after 1920. Thus the reparations quarrel continued. Instead of arguing over how much, the victors now debated whether to make Germany pay. Through conference after conference, plan after plan was debated without any resolution of the issue.

In the interim France had reacted to German intransigence and British resistance to sanctions. Most Frenchmen had always believed that the Versailles Treaty was barely adequate to ensure French security. Now that its erosion was evident, France sought allies. In July 1920 it badgered a reluctant Belgium into a limited military agreement and in February 1921 it signed a full alliance and military convention with Poland. These arrangements provided some security on the traditional invasion route into France and also a connection to a substantial army to Germany's east. Beyond that, French ties with Czechoslovakia had been close since the wartime efforts of Czech *émigrés* in Paris and these provided an informal link to the Little Entente, which was formalised by a Franco-Czech treaty in January 1924,[27] thus affording France an ally on Germany's south as well as its west and east. Such allies were of some military value, but they were not great powers, nor did they compensate for loss of the prewar Tsarist tie. France had long recognised that the Anglo-American guarantee was defunct and had shown only sporadic interest in any bilateral Anglo-French arrangement. However, increasing German intransigence together with yet another squabble with Britain heightened French fear of isolation and thus its interest in a British tie.

* * *

The United States triggered the renewed attempt at Anglo-French *rapprochement* by returning briefly to the international scene and sponsoring the Washington Conference from November 1921 until February 1922.[28] Its purposes were several. One was to disengage Britain from its prewar alliance with Japan. Canada in particular feared that some future Japanese-American clash in the Pacific would precipitate Anglo-American conflict. Another aim was to extract Japan from the Shantung peninsula and to settle a variety of Sino-Japanese questions pending since the war, including the Twenty-One Demands forced upon China by Japan in 1915. Both goals were achieved in negotiations parallel to the conference by sweeping new arrangements for East Asia and the Pacific. While Japan was a major power and China was in a state of anarchy with three competing regimes, China had Entente support not available to it during the pressures of war but now developing as Anglo-American concern grew over increasing Japanese power in the Pacific. Thus the Chinese were relieved of many Japanese infringements, and the Nine-Power Pact of 6 February 1922 affirmed – without commitment to defend – the independence and integrity of China along with an 'Open Door' for the trade of all nations and debarred future special concessions there, as Washington wished. But existing concessions continued, including the privileged Japanese position in Manchuria, and China was not restored to full sovereignty. The Anglo-Japanese alliance was submerged in an anodyne Four-Power Pact of Britain, France, Japan and the United States designed to preserve the *status quo* in the Pacific and to avoid isolating Japan.

The other major goal of the Washington Conference was naval disarmament. While the peace settlement had forcibly disarmed the defeated powers, it had also implied that universal disarmament should follow. The United States, potentially the world's greatest naval power but entering on fiscal conservatism and alarmed at Japan's rising strength, took the lead to limit the world's major navies. In the end the Five-Power Treaty of 6 February 1922 followed the American plan in most respects. Naval tonnage for capital (large) warships was limited to 525,000 for Britain and America, 315,000 for Japan, and 175,000 for France and Italy. Thus Britain accepted equality with the United States and the mistress of the seas reigned no more though it retained naval hegemony in Europe, while France accepted humiliating parity with Italy, the only power able eventually to increase its navy under the scheme. The three greatest naval powers had to scrap existing vessels to meet the limits. There was to be no construction of capital ships for ten years, then only replacement of ships more than 20 years old with strict limitations on tonnage and armaments, and in a national ratio of 10:10:6:3.5:3.5. The American desire to extend these limits to lesser ships ran foul of French intransigence on auxiliary vessels, particularly submarines. The

Five-Power Treaty also banned further fortification of potential island bases in the Western Pacific, a decision benefiting Japan, given its local superiority, lesser distances to cover, and disregard of this provision. Washington hoped the treaty would end naval rivalry and imperial competition and create in their place a new system of international relations in East Asia and the Pacific complementary to the European-oriented Western system of the League. This arrangement, like its European counterpart, foundered on the fallacy that all nations, whether dissatisfied, incarcerated in inferiority, or non-signatory, would abide indefinitely by self-denying ordinances.

In particular, though Japan was now dominant in the Western Pacific and had little interest in other waters, it was mortified by its lack of formal equality with Britain and the United States. London, eager to avoid a costly naval race with Washington, accepted restrictions which deprived it of the means to defend its Empire. The startling parity of Italy, largely a Mediterranean state, and France, possessor of a global empire, which was imposed at Anglo-American insistence, revealed the hostility of both powers to France, meant permanence for its existing naval weakness and ensured that it could not even reach much of its Empire in wartime. Yet revealingly, France, which could not afford new battleships, emerged relatively satisfied because it could still build destroyers to use against Italy in the Mediterranean.[29] This was not the mentality of a great power.

But Paris was less satisfied in other respects. Throughout the conference, France was isolated and disgruntled. The quarrel with Britain over submarines was especially bitter, revealing substantial British distrust of France. Briand took alarm and upon his return home pursued a defensive alliance with Britain. While cautious, Lloyd George agreed that the matter could be added to the already crowded agenda for the Cannes Conference, opening on 6 January 1922. This Supreme Council would deal with several issues, including German reparations defaults and a British plan for a world-wide economic conference. During the Cannes meetings, however, Briand suddenly resigned in response to press and political charges of subservience to British policy.[30] The Cannes Conference came to an abrupt end and in time experts concocted yet another reparations plan which papered over German default and avoided declaring it, for if it were declared, something would have to be done and there was no agreement on what to do.

As a consequence also, the negotiations for an Anglo-French alliance proved abortive. *En route* for home Lloyd George stopped in Paris to see Poincaré, the Premier designate, who was as rigid as Briand was flexible. The ensuing stormy discussion of the proposed pact revealed clashing mentalities. Lloyd George argued sweepingly that the pledged aid of the British Empire should suffice, while Poincaré demanded to know how many British divisions France would receive in how many days.[31] After this impasse, negotiations dragged on for some months. Britain offered a broad but unspecific guarantee against Germany in return for French concessions all over the globe. Poincaré found both the price and the ambiguity unattractive and eventually let the matter drop.

* * *

The one item settled at Cannes before Briand's resignation was a plan for a major economic conference, eventually held at Genoa. This had been pressed by Lloyd George, and Poincaré was unenthusiastic, but the commitment had been made and plans proceeded apace. Lloyd George's concern arose in part from the chaotic condition of European trade. Prewar trade patterns had been disrupted by both war and peace, as new borders, tariff barriers and currencies inhibited the flow of goods. Inflation was rife across the continent and exporters were reluctant to exchange goods for increasingly valueless money. In Western Europe reconstruction generated inflation and government deficits. In France alone 80 milliard francs (i.e., 64 milliard gold marks, $16 milliard, or £3.2 milliard) were expended by 1926 to repair the wartime ravages to its ten richest departments and restore industrial production. In eastern Europe currencies were unstable and economic nationalism rampant, as each new country sought self-sufficiency and protected infant industries, thus pricing its goods out of international markets. As Czechoslovakia had an industrial surplus and Hungary an agricultural surplus, an exchange of products would have made economic sense but their mutual hostility rendered that politically impossible, and Hungary launched its own steel industry. In most east-European countries, economies were stagnant and underdeveloped, while land reform broke up vast estates into small, less efficient farms, thereby reducing the agricultural surplus available for export and raising its price, often above that of New World competition. Further east, Russia coped with rampant inflation, the ravages of civil war and political stabilisation. It did so in political isolation, and its involvement in international trade was scant.

As the war had done much physical and financial damage to Europe as a whole, European-wide industrial capacity had decreased sharply, non-European competition in world markets had increased markedly, much foreign exchange had been lost, and governments were burdened with huge domestic and foreign debts along with heavy expenses for reconstruction and pensions. In addition, the impoverished continent had now to support more people on less production as restrictive American laws choked off the swollen prewar stream of European emigrants to the United States. Overpopulation became acute in eastern Europe, depressing the economy of the region and rendering it less able to buy Western Europe's industrial goods. Signs of stagnation quickly appeared in the West. Clearly Europe's economic circulatory system needed restorative measures.

Lloyd George was even more concerned about the parlous economic condition of Britain. Its industry could not compete in world markets or even in British markets; foreign trade languished; unemployment was high and strikes frequent. In 1920 American iron was underselling Scottish iron on the Glasgow market, while Belgian iron sold at about half the price of the local product. At the same time, most west-European countries and the British colonies were reducing purchases of high-priced British goods. Worse yet, in 1911–13 on average Germany absorbed 8.3 per cent of British exports, but in 1920 only 1.5 per cent and in 1921 2.4 per cent.[32] Faced with such figures Lloyd George hoped that restoration of prewar patterns of European trade would alleviate some of Britain's economic distress. While badly in need of a foreign policy success to bolster his sagging coalition, Lloyd George was genuinely eager to bring Russia and Germany back into economic circulation and also afraid that those two political pariahs might join together in an anti-western bloc.

A limited 1921 Anglo-Russian trade treaty already existed, but re-entry of Russia into the European family had been sharply limited by unwillingness of most states to grant *de jure* recognition to Lenin's government, by Soviet repudiation of Tsarist debts to

Western countries, and by Russian nationalisation of foreign private property. Lloyd George hoped to resolve these difficulties in a widely representative conference which would so revitalise European trade that the Franco-German clash and the unresolvable reparations issue would shrink into insignificance. Exclusion from the agenda of reparations and war debts, two issues affecting the economies of most European states, had been the price of French participation, but none the less Lloyd George remained optimistic. Russia was less hopeful but delighted to be included in European diplomacy for the first time since 1917, while Germany was happy to participate in something other than an adversarial relationship to the Western Entente.

Lloyd George's fears of Russo-German *rapprochement* proved justified. During the first week of the Genoa Conference, which opened on 10 April 1922, Lloyd George assiduously courted the Soviets. Germany took alarm and on Easter Sunday, 16 April, signed the previously drafted Treaty of Rapallo, a resort near Genoa. Its publication the next day told a startled world that the Russophiles had won over the Westerners in the German Foreign Ministry. By its terms, Germany granted Russia *de jure* recognition and cancelled all debt claims, provided Russia did not compensate other claimants, a proviso with major implications for the conference itself. The treaty provided for close economic relations and mutual most-favoured-nation treatment.[33] There were immediate rumours of secret military clauses. These did not exist, as a secret Soviet-German military collaboration had begun in 1921, but the Rapallo *rapprochement* led to its expansion. It was a marriage of enormous convenience. Russia had the raw materials Germany needed, while Germany had the technological sophistication Moscow craved. Russia also had the space Germany wanted. On the Russian plains, far from the prying eyes of military control commissions, Germany built factories to produce prototypes of the airplanes, poison gases and tanks forbidden by the Versailles Treaty, tested them and trained military personnel, both German and Russian, in their use. While this mutually beneficial arrangement had its ups and downs and was always small-scale, it flourished throughout the 1920s and to a lesser degree until the advent of Adolf Hitler.[34]

In the short run the Treaty of Rapallo, which was also an anti-Polish pact, wrecked the Genoa Conference. Lloyd George struggled on for five more weeks, trying to find a way to reintegrate

Russia into the European economic structure. The chief stumbling block was the substantial prewar Western investment in Russia. The Soviet government had nationalised all foreign enterprises without compensation. No government had done this before; the rights of private property remained sacrosanct throughout the Western world, so shock and outrage were intense. At Genoa Western leaders, prodded by infuriated investors, still sought restitution, while Russia offered only a hazy possibility of some compensation. The British tried to bring others at least part way to the Russian view, but when the Paris press floated reports that British interests were negotiating to obtain prewar Franco-Belgian oil concessions in Russia,[35] Poincaré had the excuse he sought to stand adamant. The Conference concealed its failure by delegating its problems to an expert committee at The Hague, which achieved nothing.

* * *

With Genoa's failure, the German problem returned to the fore. The twin issues of reparations and disarmament remained unabated, but the focus was on reparations, for the postwar became what a German official called 'the continuation of war by other means'[36] as Weimar tried to use the reparations issue to undo the Versailles Treaty and to reverse the military verdict of 1918. It knew that if Germany, with no foreign war debt, escaped reparations while the victors faced reconstruction costs as well as war debt payments to Washington, the economic effects would shift the balance of power and be tantamount to a German victory. Thus Berlin's efforts were unflagging.

The arrangements patched together after Cannes had relieved Germany temporarily of most cash payments for the rest of 1922 and reduced coal and timber quotas, but, unless something was done, the London Schedule of Payments would resume effect on 1 January 1923. In mid-July 1922 Germany requested a full moratorium (legal authorisation to postpone payment) on cash payments for the remainder of 1922 and all of 1923 and 1924. British experts felt that Germany needed a longer and more sweeping moratorium, covering kind as well as cash, while the French were unwilling to consider any extended moratorium without seizing something – customs revenues, state forests or tax receipts – to ensure that Germany would eventually resume payment. A technical device deferred the 1922 cash payments, but some more substantial arrangement would be necessary before 1 January 1923. There was no agreement on what it should be, so the dispute over reparations dominated the remainder of 1922.[37]

By this time, the reparations question was entangled with several others. One was German economic and monetary health. Successive German governments claimed that reparations demands were destroying the German economy and currency. Few scholars now agree.[38] While Germany, which emerged from the war and the peace with most of its industrial strength intact, was economically healthy, its monetary ailments were serious. It had ended the war with the mark worth half its prewar value. Thereafter the inflation of prices and depreciation of the currency had continued at a rapid if erratic rate. An apparent conjunction had developed between Entente reparations demands or payment deadlines and sudden dramatic inflationary lurches of the mark. Berlin claimed that reparations demands caused the dismaying depreciation. Both British and French experts at the time thought the reverse was true: that Germany was deliberately destroying its currency to escape reparations as well as for domestic political and economic reasons. However, they drew opposite conclusions. The British felt that since Germany had succeeded in destroying its currency, it must be granted a long moratorium and an extended opportunity for financial reconstruction.[39] France objected to awarding the requested moratorium as a bad conduct prize and feared that reparations, once halted, would never resume. In the autumn of 1922, after cash payments had ceased, Germany entered upon hyper-inflation as the value of the paper mark plunged from 100 per one gold mark to 2500 per gold mark.[40] It seems unlikely that reparations which on the whole were not being paid could have caused so much.

By this time also, the conjunction between reparations and war debts had become almost absolute. Originally there was no connection between the reparations Germany owed for the damage done in France, Belgium and elsewhere and the enormous debts owed to the United States by the wartime Allies either directly or through the agency of Britain, who had served as Allied broker for American loans. Moreover, most Allied countries carried huge domestic debts as a consequence of the war and some were incurring further large debts to repair the wartime ravages.

Though the Versailles Treaty called for commensurate taxation, the European victors were taxing their citizenry far more heavily than Germany. On top of that loomed the American debts. The American people took the view that a debt is a debt and must be repaid in full with interest. Accordingly, the Congress took the same view and, by 1922, it was clear that formal war debt relief was not likely. The money had to come from somewhere, and the only available source was German reparations. In one of many Allied efforts to pressure Washington into assuming the debts, on 1 August 1922 Britain issued the Balfour Note urging all-around cancellation of reparations and war debts, but, since the American attitude made that impossible, declaring that Britain would ask from its debtors only what it must pay to its American creditors. This proposal met with a hostile reception from London's City bankers, Washington and Paris. Both the latter rejected the connection between reparations and war debts, while Poincaré indicated that, for France, more was involved in reparations than money.

Another factor which sharply exacerbated the reparations crisis of late 1922 was that the British were distracted and gave it little thought. French interests were firmly centred on Germany and Germany's immediate neighbours. Britain was interested in everything, and everything was happening at once. The British economic situation, unlike that of France, remained grave and gave impetus to British desires for reconstruction of the German economy. Germany was in fact a competitor in such sickly British industries as steel, shipbuilding and coal export, and German distress redounded to British benefit. But the British held fast to Lloyd George's nostalgic belief that a healthy Germany in a healthy Europe would alleviate Britain's deep-seated economic problems.

There were also Lloyd George's own problems. His Greco-Turkish policy was winding to its disastrous close and a triumphant Kemal, having expelled the Greeks from Smyrna and having persuaded France and Italy to withdraw, was on the brink of open warfare with British forces. An armistice was eventually arranged on 11 October, but the long crisis distracted Britain from the European scene and led to the fall of Lloyd George's coalition. Andrew Bonar Law replaced him with a Conservative government. An election ensued, providing further distraction, along with a strenuous but successful effort to arrange payment of the American debt – on Washington's terms, though with sleights of hand implying larger sums than were actually required.[41] Above all, a new Prime Minister was pitched into the height of the reparations crisis.

This crisis was predictable in advance, but British Cabinets, distracted by Turkey and domestic politics, never substantially discussed the issue through the autumn and early winter. Bonar Law, lacking Lloyd George's long experience in such matters, failed to see the opportunities open to him. He ignored Belgium's frantic appeals to avert a collapse of the Entente and a Ruhr occupation, overlooked signs that Poincaré was seeking a solution short of marching into the Ruhr, as indeed he was,[42] and disregarded the possibilities offered by the end of a long Italian political crisis with the advent of Benito Mussolini, who ardently wanted attention on the international scene. He failed to see that France never acted against Germany when the rest of the Entente was firm in opposition, and he unnecessarily offended Belgium and Italy, sending both to France's side. British leaders similarly failed to see that Berlin never resisted when the entire Entente stood together against it, only when Anglo-French clashes provided room for manoeuvre. The British reasoned that nothing should be asked of Germany because it would refuse and then something would have to be done. The only thing that could be done was a Ruhr occupation, and Britain by definition opposed that. So Britain insisted on a four-year moratorium without guarantees, while France, thinking the Versailles Treaty at stake, demanded both Entente unity and substantial guarantees.

Through Entente conferences and Reparations Commission wrangles, the crisis deepened. At the end of 1922 Germany was in massive default on timber deliveries, and the default was formally declared over strenuous British opposition, although the Reparations Commission took no further action. Germany was defaulting regularly on monthly coal quotas,[43] and that question would loom in January for perhaps the last time as France decided that enough was enough. Also in January there must be a new reparations plan – and there was none.

On 2 January 1923 the Entente powers and Germany converged on Paris. All except Belgium brought a plan and each of these was published at once, inflaming opinion everywhere. The German proposal, foreshadowing Locarno, offered a Rhineland pact as a diversion from reparations default. Poincaré declined to be diverted. The French and Italian plans stressed Entente unity and limited economic sanctions, although France indicated that, lacking unity, it would take more drastic action. Bonar Law brushed these aside and insisted that the British plan[44] was the sole basis for discussion. This was a new version of a plan previously rejected by France. It would have destroyed all Belgian benefits from reparations, given Germany a four-year moratorium on cash and kind without any guarantees, required open cancellation (a politically difficult act) of the more ephemeral portions of Germany's ostensible debt, reduced and reconstructed the Reparations Commission to destroy France's preponderance there, given Britain a veto over punitive measures against Germany in the event of future default, and given Britain a free hand to dictate Entente policy in non-German reparations. As this plan would have meant the practical end of reparations, no continental politician could accept it and survive in office. None did, and the conference dissolved in deadlock.

On 9 January 1923 the Reparations Commission declared the coal default by a vote of three to one and, on the strength of it, by the same vote decided to occupy the Ruhr. On 11 January French, Belgian and Italian technicians charged with procuring the coal encircled the Ruhr and entered Essen, protected by small contingents of French and Belgian troops. At the eleventh hour Britain, which voiced its disapproval of the action openly, debated whether to let France mount it on railways through the British Rhineland zone to the Ruhr. Though it could have been accomplished in no other way and thus London could have blocked the occupation, consent was given. Bonar Law dreaded a breach with France, and sought to avoid enlarging it. Later, as both the occupation and British opposition to it swelled, London altered Rhineland zonal boundaries to transfer a key railway to French control so that France could handle its increasing Ruhr traffic.[45]

Throughout the long Ruhr crisis, Poincaré misjudged the Ruhr operation and Britain misjudged Poincaré. Both errors exacerbated and prolonged the crisis, to the cost of almost all nations concerned. A timid, reluctant Poincaré had struggled to avoid drastic action, but had been driven to it by the French right and inadvertently by Britain.[46] A man of much ability but little imagination, he thought he could simply send in a few engineers and collect the coal, though Belgian leaders told him otherwise. As Berlin called for passive resistance and financed it – paying both wages and lost profits – from the empty German exchequer[47] to the utter ruination of the mark since costs far exceeded those of reparations, France and Belgium sent more troops and sealed the Ruhr off from the rest of Germany. Its industrial heart ceased to beat while Frenchmen and Belgians ran the railways and collected what coal they found above ground. Italy and Belgium soon lost heart and sought a way out, but Poincaré hung grimly on.

British leaders never saw why. They did not understand French fear of Germany and thought Poincaré was being vindictive. They did not accept that France needed coal, its demands having greatly increased owing to German destruction of its mines in 1918 and reacquisition of the Lorraine iron fields, a need only partially filled by the Saar output, much of which was unsuitable for steel production. They failed to recognise that France urgently needed money as reconstruction was being financed by borrowing and the franc was becoming precarious. Beyond that they failed to see that what was at stake for France was survival of the Versailles Treaty and the wartime victory. Poincaré well knew that in occupying the Ruhr he had played the last trump and that there was no other. He had to win on this card or go down to defeat to a larger, industrially stronger, more populous Germany with a higher birth-rate, boding ill for the future. Equally fearful of defeat or of new decisions, he clung stubbornly to his stance.

The Ruhr battle was prolonged by two additional factors beyond Germany's dogged resistance. First, Poincaré lacked brutality. Instead of cutting off the flow into the Ruhr of money and food from Germany which sustained that resistance, he allowed both to enter and created soup kitchens for the Ruhr's poor.[48] In addition, had Britain committed itself firmly to either side, the crisis would have ended quickly, but it balanced in the middle, unwilling to break with France or to discipline Germany, and kept trying futilely to bring the warring giants together. Lost in technicalities, British leaders never realised that they were watching a costly extension of the First World War.

In the short run nobody suffered financially from the Ruhr crisis except the German people. The British economy improved as the chief competitor disappeared from European markets, although the British never admitted their profits even to themselves. British officials, blinded by their assumption that the Ruhr occupation was an economic disaster to Britain, insisted that there was no connection between the occupation and a significant drop in unemployment. They saw no correlation between employment figures and a total increase in exports, especially in coal and pig iron, along with heavier demands on British shipping, as continental buyers, denied the Ruhr's products, turned to British substitutes.[49] France and Belgium profited also, slowly at first and then very considerably, although the British denied that reality by comparing the Ruhr receipts to the London Schedule of Payments, ignoring the fact that the London Schedule was defunct and that the choice had been, at British insistence, between the Ruhr receipts and nothing. The German government and state enterprises paid off all their domestic debts as well as the Reich's war debt of 153 milliard gold marks[50] with worthless inflation paper marks at no cost, leaving a grand total worth less than 1¢.[51] Leading German entrepreneurs, such as Hugo Stinnes, who had close ties to the business cabinet of Wilhelm Cuno, took advantage of the situation to buy up failing firms and corner a startling percentage of German national wealth. While the working class suffered from the runaway inflation, the middle class suffered more, both financially and psychologically. However, the demoralisation of the German middle class, paving the way in part for the advent of Hitler, is another story outside the scope of this book.[52]

After an increasingly bitter struggle Poincaré's trump won. In August 1923 Gustav Stresemann became German Chancellor briefly and Foreign Minister until his death in 1929. Knowing that neither the hyper-inflation nor the resistance could endure through another winter, he officially called off the passive resistance in late September 1923 while reverting to the *status quo ante* as slowly as possible. Franco-Belgian profits soared[53] and their forces remained in the Ruhr. The more stringent aspects of the occupation were gradually relaxed as Germany complied, but there remained the problems of reforming the German currency (rapidly accomplished by Stresemann despite extreme circumstances), extracting the French from the Ruhr, and creating a new reparations plan. The latter two tasks took nearly two years. When the job was done, Poincaré was in eclipse and his victory appeared hollow indeed.

After September 1923 the battle continued, but now Britain and Germany joined forces to minimise the effect of the Ruhr occupation, while Poincaré struggled to preserve France's victory. Bound by his legalism, concern to preserve the British tie and fear of decisions, he did not seize the opportunity to gain important economic benefits. As American and Belgian pressure was added to Anglo-German efforts, Poincaré's isolation increased, the franc sagged dangerously, and France's moment passed, especially since American bankers were in a position to impose conditions for both the loan France urgently needed and the loans to Germany essential to any new reparations plan. None the less Poincaré held out stubbornly, in turn delaying an easement of the occupation, precipitously backing Rhenish separatism, and trying to stave off a comprehensive reparations settlement which was bound to lead to a less satisfactory situation for France.

Poincaré's slowness in easing the rigours of the occupation was one of several factors leading to separatist outbreaks in the occupied Rhineland in late 1923. He had little regard for Rhenish separatist leaders and had hoped that the rail regime he had created in 1923 in the occupied territories would be the lasting gain from the crisis, one affording France a good deal of security, but others, as in 1919, sought to detach the Rhineland from Germany altogether. Thus French agents in the Rhineland supported a ragtag batch of incompetent and unimpressive separatists. However, a premature separatist outbreak at Aachen in the Belgian zone in October 1923 was easily suppressed by the Belgian authorities, demonstrating that separatism had little popular support. But Poincaré, taken by surprise, panicked and plunged into support of a Rhenish republic at Coblenz which had a short and squabbly life, while an autonomous government in the Palatinate lasted until February 1924 when British threats of public exposure forced withdrawal of the conspicuous local French support which kept the movement alive.[54]

As separatism collapsed, Poincaré tried to delay a reparations settlement, but pressures from all the powers were too much for him. President Calvin Coolidge indicated in October 1923 that American citizens could participate unofficially in a committee of experts, thus making possible the American financial support vital to the success of any new reparations scheme. Poincaré soon bowed to the unavoidable; a committee under the chairmanship of

Charles G. Dawes, an American banker, began work in January 1924. The Dawes Report, written largely in its technical aspects by Sir Josiah Stamp of Britain and Emile Francqui of Belgium and in its political arrangements by Owen D. Young of the United States, was issued in April 1924. The Plan operated at two levels: technically it was very precise and politically it was totally ambiguous, largely because political factors would determine its fate. No government liked the Dawes Plan much, for widely varying reasons, but each accepted it in full, the French and Germans only after intense British pressure, because there was no alternative.

The Dawes Plan[55] called for reorganisation of German finances with some foreign supervision, a large international loan to Germany, and an agent-general for reparations in Berlin to oversee a complex administrative structure bypassing the Reparations Commission. An American, S. Parker Gilbert, held this key post throughout the history of the Dawes Plan. It also called for commensurate taxation but, in the usual sleight of hand, ensured that this would not happen, for such taxation would raise ample funds for reparations.[56] By including commission expenses, occupation costs and miscellaneous charges in German payments, the reparations total was effectively reduced, although by how much was unclear because the duration of the plan was unspecified. Germany would pay little for two years (with the first year covered by the international loan), increasing amounts for two years, and 2.5 milliard gold marks for one year. Thereafter, it would pay 2.5 milliard marks plus a percentage based on a complex index of German prosperity. Under the Dawes Plan, Germany always met its payments almost in full, thanks largely to a flood of American investment, but by the time the 2.5 milliard mark year was reached, it sought and gained another downward revision. From the start, Berlin viewed the plan as a temporary expedient to remove the French from the Ruhr and keep reparations minimal. Revision as soon as payments became onerous was taken for granted.[57] The French suspected as much but, deep in financial crisis and urgently in need of Anglo-American financial aid, could do nothing.

While the Dawes Plan itself was quickly accepted, there remained reconstruction of the Reparations Commission, extraction of France from the Ruhr, and several agreements needed to put the plan into effect. Since most of these constituted substantial revisions of the Versailles Treaty, an international conference was necessary. Before it was held in London during July and August 1924, Poincaré had fallen, defeated partly as a result of diplomatic isolation but mainly because France's financial crisis had forced tax increases. He was replaced in June 1924 by Édouard Herriot, who was both inexperienced and eager for a settlement. In addition, in January 1924, Ramsay MacDonald had become the first Labour Prime Minister in British history. Also inexperienced and eager for a settlement but more careful, MacDonald took personal charge of British foreign policy, and the 1924 London Conference was his triumph, eased to its conclusion by his engagingly informal style. While Herriot and MacDonald were startlingly different from their predecessors, the shifts in British and French policies were barely perceptible. Both men were bound by national interests and shaky parliamentary majorities. Yet the change of heart and style as both stressed pleasantness helped to provide enough manoeuvring space to achieve a settlement. Another spur to success was the fact that failure would ensure the fall of at least three governments.

In London the Entente powers settled matters among themselves and then negotiated with Germany. Anglo-French disagreement gave the wily Stresemann an opportunity to gain concessions. He achieved much. Arrangements were made to implement the Dawes Plan in full, end the economic occupation of the Ruhr almost at once, and end a reduced military occupation in a year. The powers of the Reparations Commission were sharply reduced with an appeal to arbitration in the absence of unanimity or the presence of German protest, the addition of a private American citizen whenever declaration of default was considered, and provisions to make future sanctions against default virtually impossible.[58] These final terms were needed to gain approval by the American banking firm, J. P. Morgan, of large loans to Germany which would last 25 years, whatever happened to the Dawes Plan.[59] All governments concerned ratified the plan quickly. The only protest, purely *pro forma,* came from Germany, the chief beneficiary.

By the time the last French troops left the Ruhr in August 1925, it was clear that France had won the battle but lost the war. Gone was France's commanding position in a powerful Reparations Commission; gone was any hope of detaching the Rhineland or ever occupying the Ruhr again; gone were the Ruhr receipts, the rail regime, rapid reparations in the future and sanctions against default. Gone also was any hope of a Franco-German trade treaty on French terms when Versailles Treaty economic clauses expired in January 1925. France had not only failed to enforce terms which it deemed minimal to its security; it had to accept substantial revision of the peace to the advantage of its foe. Moreover, as those last troops returned to France, it was evident that the revision of the peace already in progress would continue at an accelerating pace.

3   The Revision of the Peace

The 1924 reparations settlement constituted a major revision of the Versailles Treaty in that the Reparations Commission was reorganised while both its powers and German payments were sharply reduced. By the time this scheme was achieved, there had been other revisions of the 1919 settlement as well. Most of the reparations provisions of the Paris treaties had been jettisoned. Austrian and Turkish reparations had been abandoned altogether. Hungary had been granted a virtual moratorium on all except small coal deliveries, while Bulgarian reparations had been scaled down to a more realistic 550 million gold francs plus a lump-sum payment of 25 million francs for occupation costs. Despite the reduction of reparations to a trickle, European victors were embarking on lengthy negotiations toward settlement of their American debts on long-term payment schemes. There remained a correlation between these plans and reparations schedules as European countries came to view reparations primarily as a means to pay war debts.

There had been territorial revision as well, both *de jure* and *de facto*. The entire Turkish treaty had been revised to the advantage of Turkey, while the Washington Conference had undone one of Japan's two solid gains of 1919 and partially rearranged the East Asian settlement to China's benefit. In Europe, Germany retained some disputed border areas, though not those it wanted most. Poland's Russian frontier had settled well to the east of where the experts thought it should be, and its seizure of Vilna from Lithuania was accepted as permanent since no other state was prepared to use force, while the retaliatory Lithuanian occupation of the valuable German port of Memel succeeded, thanks largely to its timing just as France entered the Ruhr in January 1923. The Free City of Danzig now existed, as did friction over Polish use of its port facilities, and Poland was building its own port at Gdynia. After open warfare and a plebiscite in 1921, upper Silesia had been partitioned on a line displeasing to both Poland and Germany. While Germany retained the lion's share, Poland took the more economically lucrative part.

Further south, by 1924, Italy's seizure of Fiume had been recognised, and Yugoslavia had taken advantage of Greece's defeat by the Turks to gain port rights at Salonica. Yugoslavia lost territory to Austria in the Klagenfurt plebiscite but gained several frontier rectifications at Bulgarian expense. It had also occupied northern Albania, while Greek forces held eastern areas assigned to Albania by the Conference of Ambassadors, but in the end both occupants bowed to threats from the great powers. By the end of 1924, the Greco-Albanian frontier had been delimited and the Yugoslav-Albanian border was in the process of settlement. Greece gained a little over 1913 boundaries but not much, Yugoslavia nothing at all. Here as elsewhere action or the lack thereof by the major powers was decisive. By the mid-1920s the Balkan borders had finally been established except that between Russia and Romania, as the Soviet Union would not recognise Romania's acquisition of Bessarabia despite Romania's continuing occupation.

* * *

In the early 1920s Russia concentrated on ridding itself of foreign troops and civil war, and on reorganising the ravaged country in the communist mode, but by 1921 Lenin opted for a degree of coexistence along with some continuing subversion[1] After its debut at the Genoa Conference, Russia reappeared on the international scene as Western states reluctantly accepted that the Marxist experiment would survive. Until 1924 the Soviet Union had gained *de jure* recognition only from countries abutting it (except Romania), invariably through treaties delimiting the common frontier, and from Germany in the Treaty of Rapallo. In 1924 the barrier broke. Mussolini, whose state had few prewar investments in Russia to consider, opened negotiations in 1923 but his desire to lead the way was frustrated by MacDonald's precipitous recognition of the Russian regime on 1 February 1924. Italy followed within a week, France in October. During 1924 Scandinavia and most central European states followed suit, abandoning many claims of prewar investors. In other countries the capitalist creed and the claims of private property proved strong enough to prevent recognition. At the end of 1924, Belgium and

Holland still held out, as did the United States until 1933. The Bessarabian issue prevented Romanian recognition, while Japan delayed until 1925 out of reluctance to evacuate northern Sakhalin until guaranteed oil concessions there. Embarrassing incidents ensured that Switzerland, the citadel of finance, and the Vatican, citadel of religion, stood aloof.

As the Soviet Union resumed diplomatic relations with many states and comrade envoys appeared in Western capitals, Russia's diplomatic re-emergence was distinctly partial. Its own concerns were mainly domestic: reconstruction, economic development, and the internal power struggle after Lenin's death in January 1924, leading to the dictatorship from 1927 on of Joseph Stalin who saw the era as a truce between wars. He also thought moves toward European pacification were intended as threats to Russia and saw capitalist anti-Soviet plots where none existed. Still, capitalist states remained wary and there was little talk of inviting Russia to join the League of Nations. Even more than Germany, whose possible entry was discussed occasionally, Russia remained a pariah. None the less, some Western states wanted trade treaties as the harmony between Russian resources and Western technology seemed evident. Several such treaties were signed, to mutual but limited benefit as Western engineers aided the modernisation of Russia and Soviet raw materials flowed West. Yet the country which had tried hardest to reintegrate Russia into the European economy failed to achieve a sweeping trade treaty, thanks to the alleged activities of a new entity on the international scene.

Britain, plagued with deepening economic depression, had tried to revive the Russian trade since 1920,[2] and MacDonald pursued this goal as doggedly as Lloyd George had done. A treaty had been agreed but not ratified when on 25 October 1924 the Zinoviev letter appeared in the British press. This purported to be a directive from Gregory Zinoviev, head of the Comintern (Third or Communist International, so-called to distinguish it from the continuing Second or moderate socialist International led by Emile Vandervelde of Belgium), to British communist leaders, ordering them 'to stir up the masses of the British proletariat, to bring into movement the army of unemployed proletarians' to assure ratification of the treaty.[3]

The Comintern, formed in March 1919 to further world revolution, had fostered the Berlin and Bavarian communist movements of 1919, backed Bela Kun's short-lived Hungarian regime, tried to create a real 'red revolution' in the Ruhr in 1920, and contributed to the forced inclusion of the Armenian republic in the Soviet Union. It created a communist party in China in 1921, apparently involved itself in an uprising in the Rand of South Africa in 1922, took over some anti-colonial liberation movements, and engaged in a Bulgarian revolution in 1923. The Comintern tried to take advantage of the Ruhr crisis of 1923 by planning a German national uprising and by seizing brief control of Saxony and Thuringia but failed to achieve a broad revolution. It had also taken the direction of most national communist parties in the world.[4] While ostensibly an independent organisation of like-minded groups as the Second International actually was, the Comintern was widely recognised to be an agency of the Russian Communist Party charged in the early 1920s with undertaking the propaganda campaigns and rough work attendant upon world revolution while the Narkomindel (foreign ministry) led by Georgi Chicherin, who did not set foreign policy, tried to pursue traditional Russian goals and posed as the model of propriety in its quest for diplomatic recognition.

By 1924 the Comintern had largely abandoned immediate world revolution in favour of infiltrating moderate socialist parties and dictating the policies of foreign communist parties according to Russian needs – usually to the detriment of the popularity of communism in the countries concerned – but, by then, most Westerners were prepared to believe anything of it. Zinoviev's earlier exhortations to peoples to launch a holy war against British imperialism[5] lingered to strengthen British suspicions. The Zinoviev letter may have been a forgery as both Zinoviev and the Soviet government claimed, but its publication helped to ensure the defeat of the Labour government in the British election of 29 October 1924, the advent of a Conservative ministry under Stanley Baldwin with Austen Chamberlain as Foreign Secretary, and abandonment of efforts to enlarge the Russian trade until MacDonald returned to power in 1929 and completed a more limited Anglo-Russian treaty in 1930. In the Russian power struggle after Lenin's death, the Comintern subsided as well, except in China where it remained influential until 1927.

* * *

It was the Fascist Mussolini, an ex-socialist and a conservative anti-communist, who led the way to recognition of Soviet Russia despite the problems of private property and Comintern activities. It was Mussolini as well who revealed that another aspect of the peace had already been revised or, more accurately, had always been an illusion. He faced Italy's perennial problem of trying to be a great power while lacking the wherewithal, particularly in industrial resources. Thus he had a penchant for dramatic escapades where some glory could be collected on the cheap, but no heart for major ventures where much had to be risked. Grabbing Fiume and imposing a virtual protectorate in 1926 on hapless Albania made him a hero in Italy, but his erratic course in the 1923 Ruhr crisis and later at Locarno revealed his nervousness. In 1923, in the Corfu incident, Mussolini engaged in an adventure precisely to his taste and, at the same time, demonstrated the helplessness of the League to enforce the peace when even an intermediate power objected.

In August 1923, a boundary commission sent forth by the Conference of Ambassadors was delimiting the Greco-Albanian frontier when several of its staff, including its Italian head, were mysteriously murdered on Greek soil. Mussolini, who had been seeking an excuse for action, sent an ultimatum to Greece reminiscent of that from Austria to Serbia in 1914. Greece, battered by the Turkish defeat, flooded with refugees from Anatolia equivalent to 25 per cent of its population and bankrupted thereby, and in the midst of a cabinet crisis, accepted the more reasonable Italian demands, rejected the rest, and proposed that the matter be referred to the League. Mussolini's response was to bombard and occupy the strategic Greek isle of Corfu commanding the entrance to the Adriatic Sea. Greece appealed to the League Council. Before it could act, the Conference of Ambassadors demanded an inquiry into the death of its agents. Athens indicated willingness to accept its decisions as well. Mussolini threatened indefinite occupation of Corfu if the League intervened in response to the request of its Greek member; he much preferred the Conference of Ambassadors where the decision would be taken by three powers, of which Italy was one and France, in need of continued Italian support in the Ruhr, was another.[6] Led by smaller states who were beneficiaries of the peace settlement and who thus wanted to maintain both it and as much League protection for small powers as possible, the League made a genuine effort to deal with the Corfu crisis, but Mussolini held firm. When the League produced a compromise solution, it was overridden by the Conference of Ambassadors, a puny body of itself but an instrument of the great powers. The Ambassadors imposed heavy financial penalties on Greece, whose culpability was never established; Italy then evacuated Corfu. While Mussolini's original intent had been permanent occupation, fear of British naval action led him to take the profit and pacify European opinion, partly to forestall support to Yugoslavia on the eve of his Fiume coup.[7]

The League Council considered the implications of the Corfu episode and concluded that the League need not investigate a serious dispute 'likely to lead to a rupture'[8] in response to a member's request and could not act at all if settlement through other channels was being attempted. Further, measures of coercion not intended as acts of war need not necessarily be considered violations of the Covenant. *Force majeure* was given a free hand. Mussolini was well pleased, but the League had failed its first test and had paved the way for future failures.

* * *

These came quickly in another sphere but for the same reason: the League was so much weaker than the powers which dominated it. In 1923 and 1924 the League made two attempts to achieve real peace by linking security and disarmament. Few further steps toward general disarmament had followed the Washington Naval Conference, and French fears regarding its security were an obstacle to reductions of military and air forces on the European continent. In July 1922, when negotiations toward an Anglo-French pact were lapsing, Lord Robert Cecil (who generally represented either Britain or South Africa at Geneva but who was a power unto himself, impervious to Foreign Office direction) proposed a scheme to provide the security to make disarmament possible. Out of this grew the Draft Treaty of Mutual Assistance laid before the League Assembly in September 1923. The Draft Treaty obligated all members to come to the aid of a victim of aggression (though military action was not required on another continent) with the Council allocating specific responsibilities. Regional arrangements to keep the peace were authorised under League supervision and provision was made for an elaborate disarmament scheme to follow, including quotas.[9] Most European states, led by France, approved the Draft Treaty, some with reservations, but Britain, partly in response to pressure from the Empire, rejected the plan on 5 July 1924. Australia and New Zealand knew nobody would aid them, and Canada feared an obligation to wage war on the United States, or even to engage in economic sanctions against its southern neighbour upon whom its economy depended heavily.

This episode indicated clearly the conflict in British policy between continental interests and imperial ties. To complicate matters, while the Dominions nominally had no control over their own foreign policies, they had obtained *de facto* control by 1919, as their presence at the 1919 peace conference and their sometimes strident pursuit there of their own interests indicated. This situation was not formalised until the Statute of Westminster of 1931, which transformed the Empire into the British Commonwealth of Nations, but through the 1920s the Dominions had their own seats at Geneva and British treaties specified that they would not be bound without their consent. Since British military manpower was limited without Dominion support, they could and did influence the extent of British commitments.

With the onus for the defeat of the Draft Treaty on his shoulders, MacDonald sought a new scheme. He and Herriot devised the Geneva Protocol for the Pacific Settlement of International Disputes of 1924. This was an ingenious plan to link security and disarmament *and* compulsory arbitration to determine the aggressor in disputed cases, but, by the time it reached its final form, the Protocol was so freighted with loopholes and reservations that it would be virtually inoperable.[10] Still the Dominions objected and the Conservatives campaigned against the Protocol in the 1924 election, which they won. Thus, to French dismay, Britain rejected the Geneva Protocol in March 1925.

* * *

With the failure of two League efforts to bolster the peace, European diplomats fell back on the traditional approach of defensive alliances. As Germany faced the prospect of a network of opposing alliances, it reacted and, as a result, a west-European security pact emerged. Envisaged by some as a means to reinforce the peace, it was intended by others as a device to revise the peace settlement. On balance it did the latter, as a plan initially intended to enhance French security and thus pave the way for pacification redounded to the advantage of Germany and to the detriment of France and its east-European allies.

The 1924 reparations settlement had defused a major issue and thus, in a sense, it paved the way for further pacification. But it had intensified French fears as Frenchmen looked across the Rhine and saw a larger, more populous, industrially stronger Germany rapidly returning to economic health and prosperity. When the new Conservative government in London noted the brooding concern over security in Paris, the francophile Chamberlain sought to allay French fears by an Anglo-Belgian-French security system. However, his policy was soon turned to another path toward peace by Stresemann, abetted by the British ambassador in Berlin, Lord D'Abernon.

Stresemann was dismayed at the prospect of an Anglo-French-Belgian combination against Germany tied through France to Warsaw in the east and Prague to the south. Further, while he had laid the reparations issue to rest for the time being, he had not solved the disarmament question which threatened to delay the scheduled evacuation of the first (Cologne) Rhineland zone on 10 January 1925. Under the Versailles Treaty, the Rhineland was to be evacuated in three stages in 1925, 1930 and 1935, but the occupation could be prolonged if Germany had not fulfilled its obligations. Several specific grounds existed but, with the reparations settlement, the issue had narrowed to disarmament. The Inter-Allied Military Control Commission (IMCC), which had been unsuccessfully trying to supervise German disarmament to treaty levels, had been inactive during the Ruhr occupation because Berlin refused to guarantee the safety of its members. However, in August 1924 Herriot, partly as the price for French agreement to the London reparations settlement, prevailed upon MacDonald to join in telling Germany that the Cologne zone would not be evacuated until the IMCC had investigated to establish whether Germany had honoured its disarmament obligations. This would be a final investigation by the IMCC and upon Entente satisfaction, Cologne would be evacuated and further supervision of German disarmament would be transferred to the League, whose inspections – as Germany hoped and France feared – would probably be ephemeral.

After much foot-dragging, Stresemann conceded and the IMCC

returned to Germany. It was unable to complete its labours by January 1925 but in December 1924 issued an interim report indicating large-scale German default on most military clauses of the Versailles Treaty. Accordingly Germany was notified that the Cologne zone would not be evacuated on schedule. Thus Stresemann faced the problem of achieving evacuation without disarmament. His solution, to submerge the issue in a Rhineland pact, succeeded. By the time the IMCC's Final Report of 15 February 1925 announced Germany's failure to disarm in 160 pages of damning detail,[11] negotiations toward the Locarno treaties were under way. While satisfaction was requested but not always obtained on a few key points, the IMCC report fell by the wayside. German failure to disarm did not become a major issue because that could jeopardise the Rhineland pact, which was linked to evacuation of the Cologne zone and a smaller occupation in the remaining zones. The juridical link between disarmament and evacuation was direct; there was no legal connection between evacuation and the Locarno treaties, but it was understood that evacuation was the price Stresemann demanded for the Rhineland pact he offered.

His first overture to Chamberlain in January 1925, similar to the plan proposed in December 1922 in an effort to prevent the Ruhr occupation, made the connection clear. Stresemann had been prodded to his offer by D'Abernon, who was operating outside his instructions and contrary to Chamberlain's policy of Anglo-French entente. Stresemann thought the initiative had British blessing and approached London.[12] Apart from informing Paris and urging Germany to do the same, Chamberlain did little at first. Until early March both he and the Cabinet were torn by political manoeuvring, consideration of the Geneva Protocol, fear of French military might (especially air-power), desire to link Britain to France's army, which was the largest on the continent, and interest in the German offer. In Paris Herriot, whose hopes rested on the Geneva Protocol, also took no action. But in early March, Chamberlain told him that Britain would reject the Protocol and thought the German offer provided an appropriate route to peace and security.

A hiatus ensued until May while France underwent a Cabinet crisis and Belgium had a general election, the British Foreign Office reorganised after the sudden death of the permanent under-secretary, Sir Eyre Crowe, and Germany elected elderly

Field Marshal Paul von Hindenburg to fill the vacancy created by the death of President Friedrich Ebert.[13] Hindenburg's past had been ultra-conservative, monarchist and militarist, but Stresemann assured Western leaders that his accession would bring right-wing support to the cabinet's policy of detente. Election to the German presidency of the pre-eminent symbol of the Kaiser's militarism was not allowed to disrupt negotiations, so greatly was the advent of true peace desired.

When negotiations resumed in May, the men of Locarno were all in place. Foremost among these were Briand, Chamberlain and Stresemann. These three controlled their nations' foreign policies until 1929, and Briand until 1932. They were each awarded the Nobel Peace Prize for their labours at Locarno in 1925, and collectively they dominated European diplomacy for the remainder of the 1920s. They became very well acquainted, but in 1925 they were taking each other's measure for the first time.

Of the three, Stresemann had been in power the longest. When he took office in 1923 and called off the Ruhr resistance, Stresemann enunciated a policy of fulfilment of the Versailles Treaty. Few, even in Germany, recognised that the object of 'fulfilment' was to dismantle the treaty as rapidly as possible. Stresemann substituted conciliation for truculence to achieve a goal which had never changed, using reconciliation to gain treaty revision. He had substantial political difficulties, as the German left distrusted his conservative past and the German right thought he was conceding too much to the Entente; Stresemann made the most of these to gain foreign concessions and at Locarno bent his instructions very considerably.[14] Entente leaders, anxious to keep in office this 'good European' – who was in fact a great German nationalist dedicated to restoration of the Reich's power – generally gave way. Stresemann invariably had a list of concessions to Germany necessary to achieve the pacification of Europe. As he achieved one concession from the top of the list, two or three more were always added at the bottom. With immense skill, Stresemann gained most of his list, and no man in the Weimar Republic did more to destroy the Versailles Treaty. Unfortunately, his last great achievement, the full evacuation of the Rhineland five years ahead of schedule in 1930 (after his death, but his achievement none the less), burst the bonds of pent-up German nationalism and paved the way for Hitler.[15]

Stresemann's adversary was Briand. The most flexible of French Foreign Ministers and the most of a 'good European', he dominated foreign policy through successive coalition Cabinets, as did his counterpart across the Rhine. Briand was accused, especially by the French right, of being easily duped by Stresemann. However, he knew he had inherited a situation where France had already played its last trump and had not won. As Stresemann wanted to keep Briand in office, Briand pleaded his own political difficulties to forestall concessions, but with less success than Stresemann since France was increasingly isolated whenever it tried to enforce any part of the Versailles Treaty. Briand soon recognised Stresemann's goals and saw that they would be achieved, given the international climate of opinion. Thus he sought to impose new bonds on Germany through European economic and diplomatic integration. He became an advocate of all forms of European union in an effort to enmesh Germany so deeply in all-European economic, political and diplomatic ties that it could never make war on France again. Since the old sanctions were gone or going, this seemed the only remaining route toward French security. Briand pursued it with energy as the alternative was too frightful to contemplate.[16]

If D'Abernon was perhaps the true father of the Locarno settlement, Chamberlain was its midwife. Through the spring, summer and autumn of 1925 he persevered, although often infuriated by Stresemann's mounting demands. In the end he brought France and Germany warily together, with helpful nudges from Washington. Locarno was his triumph and he exulted in it. He was also the one true believer at Locarno, thinking he had achieved genuine peace.[17] What he had really achieved was an improvement in Britain's power position, making it the temporary arbiter of European peace from the middle ground. Chamberlain considered Locarno the peak of his career and developed a great fondness for all the men of Locarno except Vandervelde. He was particularly grateful to Mussolini for his participation. This attitude led him in later years to be more indulgent of Italian escapades than he might otherwise have been.

The other two men of Locarno were the Fascist Mussolini and the socialist Vandervelde, whose 1925 tenure at the Belgian Foreign Ministry brought the security arrangements so long sought by his predecessors. This was an accident of timing and

Vandervelde had little to say about the Locarno scheme. He also had nothing to say to Mussolini, to whom he was not speaking as a result of incidents in their mutual socialist past and Mussolini's Fascist present, notably the recent murder of the Italian socialist Giacomo Matteotti.[18] Mussolini also had little to say about the Locarno pact, thanks to his own vacillation. When first asked if Italy would join Britain in guaranteeing German treaties with France and Belgium reaffirming the Rhineland frontiers, Mussolini angled for a guarantee of the Brenner frontier between Italy and Austria. Stresemann allegedly said this could occur only if *Anschluss* were allowed, for Germany was not at present on the Brenner Pass, and that ended that.[19] Thereafter Mussolini showed only intermittent interest, torn between his desire to avoid commitments north of the Alps and his equal desire to seize the glory of joining with Britain to guarantee the peace of Europe. Much disliking international conferences where he had to share the limelight, he half hoped that no treaties would materialise and so stayed away from Locarno at first. When it became clear that success was in sight, he roared up Lake Maggiore in a speedboat, arrived with his usual noisy panache, and initialled the agreements with the rest.[20]

There perhaps should have been two or three other men of Locarno. Stresemann originally offered only a mutual guarantee of the permanence of the Franco-German frontier and the demilitarised zone in the Rhineland. Entente pressure extended the guarantee to the Belgian border and there was talk of a guarantee of Germany's other frontiers with Austria, Czechoslovakia and Poland. Austria was soon dropped, but Chamberlain made one effort and Briand several to extract a reaffirmation of the Polish and Czech frontiers from Stresemann, who said he could not guarantee these borders in perpetuity and could only promise that they would not be altered by force (though frontiers are rarely altered in any other way). In the end he would not even put this promise in writing. As Britain decided that its efforts to keep the peace could go to the Rhine but not the Vistula, Briand yielded to get the British guarantee and sought a way to reaffirm France's guarantee of Poland and Czechoslovakia, embodied in alliances with both countries. Even that proved difficult and had to be done indirectly. The Polish Foreign Minister of the moment, Count Alexandre Skrzynski, and the perennial Czech Foreign Minister, Édouard

Beneš, who dominated interwar Czech foreign policy, were allowed to attend the closing days of the Locarno conference to collect the few small crumbs allotted to them but, as Stresemann accurately and openly boasted, 'Herren Beneš and Skrzynski had to sit in a neighbouring room until we let them in. Such was the situation of the states which had been so pampered until then, because they were the servants of the others, but were dropped the moment there seemed a prospect of coming to an understanding with Germany.'[21]

* * *

Before the men of Locarno could gather in that small Swiss town to rearrange the peace of Europe, there was much negotiating to be done through normal diplomatic channels during the summer of 1925.[22] The shape of things to come soon became clear. Germany on the one hand and France and Belgium on the other would mutually forswear war against each other and reaffirm both the absolute permanence of their existing frontiers and the inviolability of the Rhineland demilitarised zone, while Britain and perhaps Italy would guarantee these pledges, committed to aid against any violator of them.

It was also clear that Germany must enter the League of Nations as part of the bargain. Stresemann wanted to join the League, and had in fact applied for membership in 1924, but also wanted maximum rewards for doing so. Pointing to German hostility to anything linked to the Versailles Treaty, he indicated that Germany must receive all its prewar colonies, a permanent seat on the League Council, and full exemption from Article 16 of the Covenant calling for sanctions against aggressors – because of its exposed geographic position and alleged disarmament. The colonies were a bargaining counter and Stresemann gained the rest. Whenever negotiations became sticky, he would murmur that Germany would never undertake sanctions against Russia,[23] raising the spectre of greater Russo-German rapprochement to scare the Entente into concessions.

It was agreed as well that the Rhineland pact should be tied to the League and that the League Council should determine violations of the treaties, but there was much difficulty over mechanics. Britain insisted that there should be no obligation to act until the Council had declared a violation. Given French, British, Italian and German permanent seats on the Council and the unanimity requirement, such a proviso could have rendered the guarantee a nullity. French protests led to a distinction between violations and 'flagrant military violations' involving troop movements across frontiers or into the demilitarised zone, which required immediate aid in advance of Council deliberations.

With this, the scheme moved toward achievement. Neither Stresemann's demands nor a strident German denunciation of the 'war guilt clause' deflected the course of events. At the start of September, a meeting in London of German and Entente jurists ironed out many details.[24] After a pause while all the Foreign Ministers except Stresemann attended the annual League Assembly meetings in September, the statesmen gathered on 5 October at Locarno in southern Switzerland to solemnise what they had arranged. Locarno had been chosen by Stresemann as a neutral site, a small town with fewer gawking bystanders than a city, and a location convenient for Mussolini should he decide to come.

The prevailing ambiance at Locarno was public amiability. There were smiling strolls through town, a cosy chat between Briand and German Chancellor Hans Luther in a nearby *albergo,* a famous boating expedition on Lake Maggiore, and a hilarious press luncheon where Entente and German leaders broke bread together for the first time.[25] This was a far cry from the grim tension of earlier conferences with Germany. There had been no Entente gathering prior to Locarno and private Entente sessions there were few. Clearly Stresemann had brought Germany a long way on the road to diplomatic respectability and had done much to weaken the Western Entente.

Behind the scenes hard and bitter bargaining continued as he tried to extract further concessions. On the boating excursion, sea, sun and champagne yielded the '*texte de bateau*', which essentially promised that Germany would be exempted from the Covenant Article 16 obligation to engage in sanctions, either economic or military, against aggressors. The wording, declaring that each League member should 'resist every act of aggression in a measure compatible with its military situation and which takes account of its geographic position',[26] suggested that each country could decide for itself whether it had any obligation to participate in any agreed sanctions, but only Vandervelde displayed concern about the implications for the future of the League and he was overridden.

The five-hour trip of the good ship *Orange Blossom* yielded a second German triumph. France abandoned any explicit guarantee of the arbitration treaties to be signed between Germany and both Poland and Czechoslovakia, though retaining an implicit right to come to their aid in case of attack. Thereafter progress was swift and the treaties took shape. Within a few days Stresemann demanded virtual cancellation of the Versailles Treaty including drastic changes in the Rhineland as the price of German ratification. He got nothing except what he wanted most: a French promise that once agreement was reached on disarmament and a start made, Germany's word would be taken about execution without inspection and the Cologne zone would be evacuated. By this time Briand was entirely committed to the pact and prepared to give Stresemann what he needed to ensure its approval. Besides, with a sickly franc he could not alienate the Anglo-American financial community, and he could not afford to fail once more to gain the British guarantee of France, even in an inferior form.[27]

Stresemann continued to angle for further concessions while the jurists tied up loose ends and the statesmen solved a thorny question. They all wanted to append their names to the historic documents being prepared, but none had full powers to sign. Thus they decided to initial the treaties of Locarno *at* Locarno, and Chamberlain invited them to London for a signing ceremony later. The British delegation had conspired to ensure that the closing ceremonies at Locarno would fall upon 16 October, Chamberlain's sixty-second birthday. So the men of Locarno gathered for the last time that Friday evening at the little mairie of Locarno, initialled their pacts, and spoke their speeches. Then they came forth on the balcony to show the historic treaties to the crowds gathered in the dusk. Briand bussed Luther on the cheek; old women knelt in the dust to cross themselves; church bells rang out over the lake; fireworks erupted in the evening sky; and the normally staid citizens of Locarno celebrated the advent of peace until daybreak.[28]

Chamberlain's birthday present came in several packages. Germany signed arbitration treaties with France, Belgium, Poland and Czechoslovakia, while France signed new treaties of mutual assistance with Poland and Czechoslovakia to compensate for the absence of any German guarantee of the eastern frontiers. Above all, the five-power Rhineland Pact guaranteed the maintenance of the existing Belgo-German and Franco-German frontiers and the demilitarised zone, committed Britain and Italy to act against any violation of this territorial *status quo*, and provided for arbitration to resolve future disputes. The Rhineland powers forswore war with each other except in narrowly defined circumstances which would permit France to aid Poland in the event of German attack. Violations of this treaty, which would take effect when Germany joined the League, would be referred to the League Council with elaborate procedures for its actions and for arbitration of disputes to avoid violations and war.[29] The clear intent of the Locarno treaties was to freeze the Rhineland frontiers in perpetuity in order to remove a major impediment to permanent peace. Treaties, however, may be read in many ways. Within a few days of the ceremony at Locarno Stresemann, using a German-induced textual ambiguity, unsuccessfully sought retrocession of Eupen and Malmédy from Belgium, claiming that he had only promised not to alter the frontier by military means.[30]

* * *

Since on that October evening the treaties of Locarno gained an instant sanctity normally accorded only to motherhood and no politician in power dared speak against them, it is hard to know what the men of Locarno really thought of what they had wrought. Mussolini was unhappy, having gained a commitment he did not want and nothing he did want. Chamberlain was euphoric. Like the people of Locarno and most ordinary Europeans, he thought he had made peace. Stresemann, while not euphoric by nature, knew he had gained a great victory with more to come. He had restored Germany to equality and diplomatic respectability, dissolved the disarmament deadlock, forestalled an Entente alliance against Germany and weakened the Entente in the guise of a greater detente with Germany, resolved the Rhineland evacuation (for he would not enter the League and bring the treaties into force until Cologne was evacuated), conceded little, and gained much. More could be gained as the price of German ratification and League entry, and surely the spirit of Locarno would yield opportunities for further treaty revision. Stresemann well knew that all was now possible as the price of fulfilment so long as he did not send troops across a Western frontier or into the demilitarised zone. The implications did not escape French and Belgian leaders; privately they were pessimistic, but the long-sought British guarantee had to be taken in the only form in which it was offered and there was naught to do but accept the changed situation. Polish and Czech leaders also had no choice but to accept, but they did so in fear. As leading beneficiaries of the Paris settlement, they had wanted to see it preserved, not undermined, and they knew they were the losers of Locarno.[31]

In negotiating the Rhineland pact, Germany stressed that it was now offering voluntarily to affirm what had been imposed upon it by *force majeure* in the Versailles Treaty. Stresemann emphasised that the voluntary affirmation was considerably more binding than the Versailles *Diktat*. Chamberlain so badly wanted peace, while France and Belgium so deeply craved security that the argument was accepted. However, reaffirmation of some treaty clauses not only implied a need for such action but also cast doubt on the validity and binding force of others. Stresemann intended this effect regarding the Polish frontier which he flatly refused to mention in the treaties. Locarno was widely interpreted as a green light for Germany in the east. Well before the treaties were completed, a German diplomatist remarked: 'I am a poor German but I would not wish to be Polish, for there would not pass a night when I would sleep tranquilly.'[32]

Even in the West much had changed. French troops had left the Ruhr and could never return, for if they did Britain and Italy must go to Germany's aid. France could not even seize customs revenues without facing, at a minimum, a ruling from the League Council, in which the veto was now abandoned by interested parties in disputes arising out of the Locarno pacts, probably in support of Germany. France's powers of enforcement were gone and, while the Locarno treaties nominally strengthened the League by giving it supervision of execution, in fact the reinterpretation of Article 16 meant that the League had lost what little power of enforcement it had ever possessed. To gain this pact so unfavourable to France and its allies, Briand had promised to end the disarmament dispute without further ado, to release German prisoners held by France and Belgium on charges stemming from both the war and the Ruhr occupation, to evacuate Cologne shortly, and to reduce the occupation in the two remaining zones. The instruments of coercion embodied in the Versailles Treaty had all but disappeared. Germany could default with impunity if it chose on disarmament and reparations, France's two greatest concerns, and France would be helpless to act.

Briand had accepted this situation to get the British guarantee and because diplomatic isolation stemming from the Ruhr occupation and the continuing weakness of the franc made any policy contrary to Anglo-American diplomatic and financial interests impossible. Briand knew that France's position was fundamentally untenable and that the alteration of the power balance implicit in Locarno was now unavoidable. He was trying to salvage what he could, and the British guarantee was his consolation prize. However, he gained an illusory security, for the Locarno guarantees were from the start inoperable. London quickly realised that having guaranteed both sides of the Rhenish frontier it must make military arrangements with all three countries or with none, so it made them with none.[33] Given the speed and complexity of modern military operations, a guarantee of immediate action against flagrant military violations without detailed preparations was a nullity; a country could easily be engulfed before help arrived.[34] Further, the British army was small and much of it was stationed in Palestine, India, and the other outer reaches of Empire. What was available to Europe was militarily laughable.

Yet Locarno made Britain briefly the arbiter of Europe's peace and restored it to the fulcrum of the balance of power, able not only to tip it against the evil-doer but largely to determine who the evil-doer might be. In the meantime its hands were free. It seems incongruous that a largely disarmed Britain became the primary instrument for the enforcement of peace. Yet Briand and Stresemann both knew that, should another Franco-German collision be protracted, the British navy, Empire and ties to Wall Street might again be decisive. In the long run, as the Treaty was further dismantled, the power balance would tip toward Germany, but for the moment Britain held the balance. Neither Briand nor Stresemann seriously considered crossing the Rhineland frontier.

The Rhineland pact was unpopular in Germany precisely because it guaranteed the Western frontier and thus precluded reversion to the 1914 boundaries[35], which most Germans still considered their birthright. Stresemann could not enunciate the extent of his triumph to the German electorate without creating acute political difficulties for the other men of Locarno, especially Briand, whom he wished to keep at the Quai d'Orsay, so he used his own political difficulties to extract further concessions as the price of German ratification. Most of what he gained had been foreshadowed at Locarno itself. Germany's word that such disarmament as was being required had been carried out was hastily accepted and IMCC agents were told not to haggle over details. The Entente powers announced that evacuation at Cologne would commence on 1 December, the date scheduled for the London signing ceremonies of the Locarno treaties, and later that evacuation would probably be completed by 31 January 1926, as it was. The Entente further promised to reduce the IMCC to a token level, to overlook German police quartered in barracks – a substantial, seasoned military force outside the limits imposed by the Versailles Treaty – to reduce the Rhineland occupation, and to make a long list of changes there, all ardently desired by Germany and tending to give the occupation a less permanent character. With that, the Reichstag approved the treaties of Locarno.[36]

Yet still Stresemann sent word that he wished to talk business when he came to London for the signing ceremonies. For the first time, a German move did not evoke any Entente consultation, even through ordinary diplomatic channels. It was already evident that as the Versailles Treaty was progressively dismantled, there would in future be fewer occasions when Germany would ask and the Entente would be obliged to answer in unison. But the absence of Entente consultation before the London meeting raised the larger question of the future of the Entente. It had come into being as a result of the war and its function was to enforce the peace, particularly in regard to Germany. Yet it had abandoned this task and was now seeking peace through detente with Germany. If this detente became actual, the Entente would lose its *raison d'être* and cease to exist.

At London detente was less than total. After the public signing ceremonies on 1 December 1925 and speeches hailing both peace and the spirit of Locarno which would make peace real at last, the men of Locarno met privately once more. Stresemann demanded and got further troop reductions in the remaining Rhineland zones and an end to billeting on the population there. He complained that the IMCC was 'over-punctilious' and, while he did not obtain full withdrawal of the IMCC, he gained further reduction to two small detachments. He obtained other concessions as well, but Briand indicated that more changes were not possible overnight and Chamberlain was emphatic that the colonies would not be returned.[37] As usual, Stresemann went home with most but not all of his lengthening list accomplished or developing nicely.

As the year turned and Entente troops came home from Cologne, Europe celebrated the advent of true peace. Henceforth the spirit of Locarno would reign, substituting conciliation for enforcement as the basis for peace. Yet for some peace remained a desperate hope rather than an actuality. A few men knew that the spirit of Locarno was a fragile foundation on which to build a lasting peace. After all, the real spirit at Locarno behind the façade of public fellowship was one of confrontation between a fearful France flanked by the east Europeans, trying to hide their humiliation and panic, and a resentful, revisionist Germany demanding more alterations in the power balance to its benefit. Since it was potentially the strongest continental power, the private fears of its neighbours only deepened. As a French official noted, the spirit of Locarno, *l'esprit de Locarno*, and *die Locarno Geist* were three different things, signifying Britain's reversion to the middle ground, France's defeat and dependence, and Germany's continuing revisionism.[38]

Yet the public faces remained serenely smiling, and ordinary Europeans did not know about the clashes behind closed doors. They knew only that Germans and Frenchmen had gone boating together and had chatted of peace at a small inn. The public façade at Locarno and the treaties themselves had created an illusion of peace, and ordinary folk rejoiced. Misled by a false front Europe thankfully entered the Locarno years, thinking real peace had arrived at last. Of all the interwar years these were perhaps the best years, thanks in part to a patchy prosperity and to reduced German truculence, but none the less they were years of illusion.

4 The Years of Illusion

Before the euphoria engendered by the Locarno meetings had time to fade, another episode heightened the illusion that peace had arrived and that henceforth conciliation would reign. Scarcely a week after Locarno concluded, skirmishes on the Greco-Bulgarian frontier erupted into a Greek military invasion of Bulgaria, who appealed to the League of Nations. Ensuing events gave the League a much-needed but illusory success.

Briand, to whom the rotating presidency of the Council had fallen, convoked an emergency session and demanded that both countries end hostilities and withdraw their forces. A further Greek offensive was cancelled but skirmishes continued. Under Briand's firm leadership the Council refused to hear arguments on the issue until each army was behind its own frontier. As the great powers made concerted démarches in Athens, sent observers to the area, and threatened naval demonstrations and sanctions under Article 16 of the Covenant, the Greeks withdrew. Thereafter the League investigated the episode, established responsibility (finding some Bulgar provocation) and levied an indemnity, which Greece paid. It appeared that pacific settlement of international disputes was a reality.[1] Actually resolution of the Greco-Bulgarian clash arose from rare unanimity among the European major powers, their energetic action including threats of force, the internal weakness of the Greek regime which made the bluff easy to call, and the fact that the parties to the dispute were small states susceptible to great-power pressure. What had occurred was an almost Metternichean manoeuvre reminiscent of the early nineteenth-century Concert of Europe condemned by proponents of the League.

There was much rejoicing and optimism about the growing importance and success of the League at the December Council meeting where the Greco-Bulgarian dispute was settled. While this satisfaction was self-delusive, those few months after Locarno were perhaps the League's brief heyday, the one moment when the League's future seemed bright. It had halted a shooting war (or seemed to have done so) and had precariously managed to delimit the disputed Turko-Iraqi boundary despite involvement of Britain as mandatory power in Iraq. By this time the League Council met in quarterly sessions which most European Foreign Ministers attended, turning the spotlight onto Geneva. Further, Franco-German tension, the greatest threat to European tranquillity, appeared misleadingly to have been entombed at Locarno, and Germany's entry into the League was anticipated in the new year. Nobody expected the United States or Russia to join soon, but all other powers of consequence would belong. The League's proponents predicted that henceforth its role in European matters would be enlarged, with decisions made in the League halls at Geneva, not by treaty agencies in Paris or the Entente powers in conference. Few foresaw that German entry into the League would transform it, while the activities of the Locarno powers would undermine it. Most hailed Locarno and awaited German entry eagerly. However, by February 1926, when the German application arrived, it was becoming clear that such optimism was premature, while the unseemly squabble which ensued demonstrated that brotherly love did not yet reign in Geneva.

* * *

Since the Locarno treaties would not take effect until Germany entered the League, its application was anticipated and careful preparations had been made in Berlin and Geneva. These preparations had overlooked one problem, however. Under Article 4 of the Covenant, there was no way to grant Germany the permanent Council seat – demanded in its earlier 1924 application without objection from other members and clearly promised to it at Locarno – without opening up the larger question of the composition of the Council in general. There was no disagreement about either Germany's admission or its claim to a permanent Council seat, but German entry was jeopardised and delayed by the heated controversy caused by the additional claims of existing members. Some of these were of long standing, and the difficulty should have been foreseen. Tension over the composition of the Council had been rising for several years, and the German application provided an occasion for it to erupt. The claims of Spain to represent the

Hispanic powers and of Brazil to represent the Americas in the absence of the United States, both with permanent seats, had been seriously discussed at Geneva in 1921 and 1923. For several years China had argued for both a geographic distribution of seats and its own claim to great-power status. Poland's claim, the most explosive politically, was more recent but predictable as soon as German entry was seriously considered since Berlin could be expected to use its Council seat to press for treaty revision at Poland's expense. Yet at Locarno the clear understanding had been that Germany alone would be granted a permanent seat in recognition of its undoubted great-power status. In his insistence that this implicit promise be honoured without modification, Stresemann was on solid footing.

When Germany's application for membership arrived in Geneva, Brazil, Poland and Spain filed claims for permanent seats on the Council, thus forcing the issue of its composition. China and later Persia (Iran) each filed a contingency claim that, *if* the number of permanent seats were increased, it should have one. These demands reflected growing dissatisfaction with European domination of the Council, an increasing tendency toward informal groupings to gain regional representation, and the emergence of intermediate powers. The Covenant distinguished only between great powers with permanent Council seats and small powers eligible to compete for temporary seats. Yet even a weak China torn by civil strife clearly outranked Siam, Brazil overshadowed El Salvador, and Poland was more powerful than Latvia.

The claims of the intermediate powers met with little enthusiasm. They created a problem that diplomatists preferred to avoid, which explains in part why nothing was settled before the League Assembly met. Secondly, as a British observer remarked:

> From the West-European point of view it seemed intolerable that the destinies of a region which was the cultural center of the Western World should be at the mercy of outlying countries whose international position was comparatively secure and whose contributions to the common culture of Western society could hardly be compared to those of France, Germany, and Great Britain.[2]

Further, the European great powers, with the customary arrogance of great powers, assumed that they should settle the matter themselves, preferably in a private gathering of the Locarno signatories. Finally, the smaller European states, led by Sweden, announced sharp opposition to any enlargement of the number of permanent seats beyond that for Germany. Sweden, Denmark, Belgium, and other less vocal European members had a clear stake in the pacification of Europe implicit in rapid German entry, disliked any dilution of the European representation on the Council, and were alert to the threat to themselves in any distinction between small and intermediate powers. Thus they vociferously backed the great-power inclination to resist the new claims, which were pressed with mounting publicity in advance of the Assembly meeting.

On 8 March 1926, the special session of the Assembly called for the express purpose of German admission convened without any solution in sight. Since Stresemann and Luther had arrived in a special train crammed with diplomatists and documents,[3] some were hopeful that the problem would soon be solved. Disillusionment came swiftly. As the technicalities attendant on German entry were trivial, they were completed quickly. Thereafter the delegates sat idle in humiliating ignorance while the Locarno powers tried to arrange matters behind closed doors.

Pressures on the three principal claimants were initially unavailing while Sweden reiterated opposition to any enlargement of the Council beyond Germany, whether by permanent or non-permanent seats. Despite that, an attempt was made to resolve matters by awarding a permanent place to Germany and creating an additional non-permanent seat for Poland, but Germany rejected this scheme. Finally, in a move which was less altruistic than it appeared to be, Sweden offered to vacate its present seat in favour of Poland.[4] Stresemann agreed, provided that Czechoslovakia would also vacate in favour of Holland in order to reduce the pro-French cast of the Council. But Brazil balked. Since it indicated its intention as occupant of a temporary seat to veto Germany's permanent place on the Council unless it also received one, there was naught to do but refer the matter to a committee and postpone German entry. At the final Assembly session to approve this solution, the Netherlands and Norway bitterly denounced the closed-door gatherings (which were already known as 'Locarno tea parties') and the damage being done to the League's structure of committees, which remained unused during the special session.

German nationalists reacted to the delay by concluding that since Council seats were so hard to get and so widely desired, they must be more valuable than hitherto supposed. Thus Stresemann's political difficulties were diminished, not increased. Still, he made the most of the moment. On 24 April 1926 in Berlin, he signed a treaty of neutrality and non-aggression with Moscow to reinforce the Treaty of Rapallo, quiet Soviet apprehensions about the Locarno alignment, maintain the Russian tie (which for Moscow provided a bridge to the West and a barrier to feared Western attack), appease the Russophile element within Germany, counter-balance Locarno, and encourage Entente concessions. While the text of the Treaty of Berlin was innocuous,[5] France and its east-European allies were alarmed. Moreover Stresemann claimed that Hindenburg was objecting to League entry and that three conditions would be necessary to pacify the 'Old Gentleman': (1) a sharp reduction in the number of occupation troops; (2) an agreement on the duration of the Rhineland occupation, thus implying early evacuation; and (3) an end to the work of the IMCC. As usual Stresemann sought new concessions as a reward for accepting concessions already gained. But this time Chamberlain, who had defended the Russo-German treaty, sharply told Stresemann not to bargain.[6] None the less, the special Committee on the Composition of the Council renewed its efforts.

In the late summer it found a solution of sorts. Germany would gain a permanent place, but the number of non-permanent seats would increase from six to nine. Of these, six or more would carry three-year non-renewable terms, creating a long-desired rotation system, but a maximum of three intended for Brazil, Poland and Spain could be specified as eligible for re-election, creating a class of semi-permanent seats for some intermediate powers. Poland accepted this scheme, but Brazil and Spain declared their intention to withdraw from the League. Before the mandatory two-year period of notice expired, Spain returned to Geneva, but Brazil did not, becoming the first state to leave the League (except for Costa Rica, which could not meet the annual assessments). Poland took its semi-permanent seat, and an informal understanding about geographic allocation of the other eight temporary seats soon developed. European domination of the Council became some-what less obvious, but, as European dominance of the League itself increased, the non-European states were left with the illusion of power, not the reality.

Nobody much liked the Committee's solution but, as there was no other, everybody except Brazil and Spain accepted it to facilitate German entry into the League. That long-heralded event took place during the regular annual Assembly session. It was a grand occasion, only somewhat dampened by the thunderous squall which had gone before. On 10 September 1926, the twelfth anniversary of the battle of the Marne, the German delegation formally entered the Assembly Hall at Geneva and Stresemann accepted membership in an address with only muted revisionist and nationalist overtones. Briand, chosen to speak alone for the League as Europe's most fluent orator and as the leading apostle of Franco-German conciliation, replied in a soaring oration assuring the world that the long history of bloody Franco-German conflict had ended. To delirious applause, he cried: 'Away with rifles, machine guns, and cannon! Make way for conciliation, arbitration and peace!'[7] The spirit of Locarno appeared to have triumphed.

In a sense it had, although not as the smaller states had hoped. To their delight Briand's speech deplored the secret diplomacy of the special session, but his actions soon belied his words. A week later came the famous interview at Thoiry, a secret luncheon meeting between Stresemann and Briand, their first private session together. At first Thoiry was regarded as an omen of conciliation, but in time such meetings evoked dismay, especially since the Locarno tea-parties at Geneva continued unabated, despite cries of secret diplomacy from the excluded smaller states.

* * *

One effect of Locarno and German League entry was that the leading revisionist state was admitted to a position of power in an organisation largely designed to uphold the *status quo*. The smaller European states most dedicated to maintenance of that *status quo* took alarm, especially since at Thoiry Stresemann again sought retrocession of Eupen and Malmédy. Another effect of German diplomatic rehabilitation was that Germany was now admitted to the hotel-room diplomacy of Geneva, and so that diplomacy changed, signalling a shift in the balance of power and an alteration in the character of Geneva's closed-door deliberations. While in the past hotel-room negotiations had served for quiet resolution of disputes between two states and for regional caucuses of the Little Entente and the Latin American bloc, Locarno tea-parties had a different character, extending to the full range of European problems and sometimes beyond. Meanwhile the agenda of the League was reduced to trivia. A League official later remarked that the Council 'listened to brilliant but interminable speeches on the claims of Hungarian landowners to be compensated by the Roumanian government for their properties distributed among the peasants of Transylvania. But of the greatest questions it heard nothing.'[8]

These questions were settled in the hotel rooms of the Locarno powers, who continued the '*politique des casinos*' at Geneva, obviating the need for international conferences to settle the leading issues of the day. Sometimes these issues properly fell under the Locarno pacts although, even so, Poland and Czechoslovakia were excluded. Often they did not. In 1927, when Italy accused Yugoslavia of preparing an invasion of Albania, Mussolini prevailed upon Chamberlain and Briand to block a Yugoslav appeal to the Council, and the matter was discussed only in a Locarno party without Yugoslav participation.[9] Such episodes evoked constant protest from small states but to little avail. The most conspicuous figures of Geneva, such as Beneš of Czechoslovakia, Hymans of Belgium, Fridtjof Nansen of Norway, Östen Undén of Sweden, and Guiseppe Motta of Switzerland, found themselves helpless in the face of the reality of great-power politics.

When the composition of the League Council was originally debated in 1919 in terms of great-power representation only, Paul Hymans had shouted: 'What you propose is a revival of the Holy Alliance of unhallowed memory!'[10] Now it had revived in another form, less official but equally forceful. And Stresemann was surely the Talleyrand of this twentieth-century alliance. As the nineteenth-century Concert against France had rapidly been converted into a Quintuple Alliance including France, so the Entente against Germany had welcomed Stresemann to its hotel-room deliberations. While Belgian and Japanese representatives were usually in attendance, the Locarno tea-parties constituted a Concert of the four great European powers although, given Mussolini's lack of enthusiasm for both Locarno and the League, more often the new Quadruple Alliance was reduced to the Locarno triumvirate of Britain, France and Germany.

This system derived partly from the natural arrogance of great powers and their habitual tendency to reserve decisions to themselves. In part it derived from Stresemann's conviction that rapid revision of the peace settlement could best be achieved through cultivation of Briand and from Briand's desire to perform his foot-dragging in private, not in public. Then, too, Chamberlain had a great fondness for France in general and Briand in particular. He saw Locarno as his finest achievement and displayed a natural tendency to prolong its rosy glow. He wished to limit British commitments and considered Locarno that limit. Thus Chamberlain preferred Locarno tea-parties to League Assemblies, even referring revealingly at Geneva to 'your Council' and 'your Assembly'.[11] He was more than pleased to escape from the universal commitments embodied in League membership into cosy meetings of the European Concert he had created at Locarno.

* * *

The nineteenth-century Metternichean Concert of Europe foundered on the hard rock of diverging interests of the great powers. The same problem caused the Locarno triumvirate to falter and eventually to fail. Signs of the basic difficulty appeared as early as that first private meeting between Briand and Stresemann at Thoiry just after they had proclaimed conciliation to a jubilant Assembly, blissfully unaware of what lay ahead for the League.

We shall never know precisely what occurred at the famous four-and-a-half-hour lunch at Thoiry, a French village near Geneva. Stresemann's account differs in many details from that of Briand's interpreter, the only other person present.[12] Who offered what and who agreed to what are in dispute, but there is no doubt that both men were seeking a settlement of all major Franco-German issues. Stresemann apparently proposed complete evacuation of the Rhineland within a year, immediate return of the Saar, prompt withdrawal of the IMCC, and repurchase of Eupen and Malmédy. In return he offered the possibility of commercialisation of part (or possibly eventually all) of the

German reparations bonds under the Dawes Plan so France could receive prompt payment of a substantial amount.* This extraordinary scheme has an aura of unreality. Normally Briand would not have listened to talk of immediate Rhineland evacuation and return of the Saar, while normally Stresemann would not have considered any action rendering future reduction of the reparations debt harder. But Stresemann was using a French financial crisis in hopes of purchasing Germany's freedom from the Versailles Treaty in return for a probably very limited debt commercialisation.

The opportunity arose because the French franc had collapsed, along with the Belgian franc and the Polish zloty, while the German mark was stabilised and American investments were flooding into Germany. In France years of heavy reconstruction costs, slipshod and deficit financing, and shrinking reparations had contributed to a débâcle so acute that in July 1926 Poincaré had been returned to power as Premier and Finance Minister to restore the franc. Poincaré himself had authorised Briand to investigate commercialisation of reparations bonds as a route to some quick cash to save the situation. Stresemann seized the moment not only to treat with Briand but also to try to buy Eupen and Malmédy from Belgium and to announce that German participation in Poland's financial reconstruction required immediate return of the Polish Corridor and Upper Silesia.[13] Somehow, Berlin had funds for what it really wanted. Of its proposals the Franco-German plan alone did not entail outright territorial transfer from a victor power, but it did involve reparations, a matter of concern to other states, notably Britain.

In the end the Thoiry scheme came to nothing as Poincaré

---

* Bonds payable over 37 years representing mortgages on the German state railways and industry were on deposit at the Reparations Commission. To commercialise these would be to effect a technical change in their status so that they could be marketed on the world's stock exchanges to private investors, chiefly American. Of the proceeds from any such sale, France would receive 52 per cent under the Spa Protocol of 1920. But despite any future reductions of Germany's reparations liability, it would still owe the face value of the bonds to the private holders. For this reason and others, it seems improbable that Germany would have accepted even gradual commercialisation of any appreciable amount. For the key role of the German state railways in Dawes Plan reparations, see Alfred C. Mierzejewski, 'Payments and Profits: The German National Railway Company and Reparations, 1924–1932', *German Studies Review* XVIII (1995) 65–85.

briskly stabilised the franc through strict fiscal conservatism, while Belgian and Polish leaders did the same for their currencies, aided by a temporary lack of competition owing to the 1926 British coal strike. In addition Berlin explored the drawbacks of commercialisation and London objected strenuously to this prospect, if not to revision of the Polish frontier. Besides, the American market could not absorb enough bonds to provide an appreciable cash yield. There was no real consensus on the terms of the Thoiry bargain and little prospect that French and German opinion would accept any likely scheme. Within two months, as the franc began to recover its value, Briand abandoned the matter. Thereafter Paris and Berlin returned to the more cautious approach of tackling their joint concerns one by one.

Ordinary citizens knew none of this, however. They were unaware that at Thoiry Briand and Stresemann were trying to do an improbable deal born of French financial desperation, that they apparently agreed on none of the terms, or that Briand tackled Stresemann sharply about the many paramilitary organisations prevalent in Germany. The ordinary European knew only that, after the soaring oratory at Geneva, the French and German Foreign Ministers had smilingly wined and dined on rabbit stew together at a simple village inn and had sought to reconcile their national differences amicably. The spirit of Locarno appeared to have worked its magic.

* * *

This illusion was heightened for some when the International Steel Agreement was announced on 26 September 1926, barely a week after Thoiry. This had been under negotiation since 1924 and would have reached fruition in any event, but it was viewed, except in some socialist quarters, as one more Locarno marvel. The agreement established a steel cartel* (called a steel pact to avoid wounding working-class sensibilities) involving Germany, France, Belgium, Luxemburg and the Saar to limit production and thus raise prices. German industry wanted such a scheme, which provided penalties for exceeding agreed quotas and subsidies for underproduction. France, on the other hand, sought extension of

---

* A cartel is a national or international arrangement among producers to control price, production, or distribution of a commodity.

duty-free entry of Lorraine iron ore into Germany (as allowed by the Versailles Treaty until 10 January 1925) in the face of threats of a high German tariff. The two agreements were negotiated concurrently and a Franco-German commercial treaty was signed on Berlin's terms shortly after the steel cartel was established.[14] This, too, was hailed as yet another sign of the advent of true peace.

In the interim the steel cartel established its headquarters in Luxemburg City under the continuing chairmanship of the Luxemburgish members, thereby demonstrating the advantage of petiteness. Other cartels to control metals, other minerals, pharmaceuticals, chemicals and munitions were created in the ensuing months, while in 1927 Austria, Czechoslovakia and Hungary were admitted to the steel cartel *en bloc* with a single bloc quota. Britain and Poland declined to join on the terms offered. The United States, the world's largest steel producer, consumed its own production and so was no factor in European or world markets. Neither was Russia. But now most major continental producers had joined in an international agreement which, as optimists noted, included three former Central Powers and their hitherto hostile neighbours.

The steel producers joined together primarily to increase their profits, but some among them hoped that such arrangements could lay a foundation for a future European economic union. The cartel's first chairman, Emil Mayrisch, was an emphatic proponent of this view, and in its early years the steel cartel was thought by many to have profound implications for the future organisation of Europe. As the American economy boomed in the 1920s, some of Europe's business leaders contemplated the advantages of mass production, mass markets and large free-trade areas without restrictive tariffs, and talked of an economic 'United States of Europe'. They came to recognise that a small continent cut up into some 30 states, each with its own customs barriers, was not good for profits. And so the possibility of European union came to be contemplated seriously by hardheaded businessmen, not only by those whom they regarded as visionary cranks.

There also were the visionaries. Their headquarters was Vienna, their journal *Pan-Europa*, and their leader Count Richard Coudenhove-Kalergi, a Bohemian aristocrat of Czech citizenship and diverse ancestry. By October 1926, his movement had gathered sufficient momentum to hold a successful First Pan-European Congress in Vienna. The four days of meetings were jammed and the event was considered significant enough to evoke detailed reporting by professional diplomatists. Its respectability was indicated by the fact that the Austrian Chancellor welcomed the delegates, the more powerful leader of the Austrian Catholic party opened the session and Briand sent greetings, as did other prominent European politicians.[17]

* * *

Not everybody was among the converted. Mussolini was so hostile that he sponsored a journal titled *Anti-Pan-Europa*. He was equally if less overtly hostile to both the League and Locarno. In January 1926, while Europe basked in the afterglow of Locarno, Mussolini declared that Fascism was embarking on its 'Napoleonic year'.[18] As usual Mussolini's oratory outran his performance, and the outcome in foreign policy hardly surpassed some of Napoleon III's less splendid years.

Mussolini's dislike of Locarno stemmed from the commitment involved and fear that pacification on the Rhine might turn German eyes to the Alps and Austria. Mussolini began his 'Napoleonic year' by an acrid public exchange in February with Stresemann over the rights of the German-speaking South Tyrolese.[19] Mussolini favoured German nationalism if it remained on the Rhine and directed toward France, with whom Italy's relations were strained as the two powers competed in North Africa and south central Europe. The Tyrolean tempest in a teapot, lasting less than a month, enunciated Mussolini's concerns. It also led to the resignation of the Italian Foreign Ministry's Secretary-General and, soon after, of several other key diplomatists. Thus such restraints as had existed dissolved and Mussolini was free to pursue his 'Napoleonic' designs.

The professional Italian diplomatists had sought rapprochement with Yugoslavia in 1925 over both Albania, a bone of contention between them, and relations in general, primarily to forestall a Franco-Yugoslav treaty in the offing. Further they had urged participation in a proposed 'Balkan Locarno' to ensure that it would not be directed against Italy. But Mussolini, who disliked the first Locarno, had no desire for a second. Freed of diplomatic restraint, he pursued another course and in November 1926 signed the Treaty of Tirana with Albania.[18] This, the main achievement of the Napoleonic year, did little more than formalise existing Italian dominance there, thanks to British acquiescence. Having blocked any substantial Italian gains at the expense of Ethiopia and Turkey, Britain allowed Mussolini a little balm for his ego in Albania, which in 1921 had been recognised by the Conference of Ambassadors as an Italian sphere of interest.

The Treaty of Tirana ended efforts toward Italo-Yugoslav rapprochement, as Mussolini intended, and thereafter he intrigued with Croatian separatists against Belgrade. The predictable result was completion of the Franco-Yugoslav friendship treaty in November 1927.[19] As Romania had signed such a treaty with France in June 1926[20] and Czechoslovakia had an alliance dating from 1924, the entire Little Entente were now tied to France. Briand held off the Yugoslav treaty for more than a year in hope of coming to a tripartite French-Yugoslav-Italian arrangement and a resolution of Italo-French tension arising from not only the Mediterranean and Danubian rivalry but also the vocal activities of anti-Fascist Italian *émigrés* in France.[21] Ultimately, however, Briand accepted that Mussolini's hostility to Yugoslavia forced a choice between Italy and the Little Entente. He chose the Little Entente as the more reliable and less contentious partner.

Over the years the Little Entente had regarded Mussolini with a wary eye. His interest in Danubia, domain of the Little Entente, was obvious. At first there had been some attempts at conciliation between Italy and the Little Entente states, but relations with Czechoslovakia, a country too democratic for Mussolini's taste, did not progress beyond a commercial treaty in 1924, while relations with Yugoslavia were strained first by Fiume and then by Albania. Moreover, accommodation with Romania was blocked by Mussolini's refusal to ratify the international accord recognising Romanian acquisition of Bessarabia, as he still hoped for major economic benefits from his early recognition of Russia. Beyond that the Little Entente was pained by Italy's generally good relations with Hungary and Bulgaria and by the latent revisionism in Mussolini's foreign policy.

From 1926 on that revisionism became more pronounced and, as the Franco-Yugoslav treaty finally moved toward completion, Mussolini made a futile attempt to counter French influence, disrupt the Little Entente and reorganise Danubia under Italy's aegis. First he signed a treaty of friendship with Romania in September 1926,[22] close on the heels of the Franco-Romanian pact. The Italian treaty was singularly devoid of content but was designed as a step toward another. In 1927 Mussolini dangled before Romania the prospect of Bessarabian ratification in return for Italian economic penetration of Romania and a new quadruple alliance of Italy, Hungary, Romania and Bulgaria under Italian domination. Romania refused, having no desire to trade recognition of the Bessarabia *status quo* for the ominous threat of revision of the Transylvanian frontier implicit in any rapprochement with irredentist Hungary.

The effect of Mussolini's effort to dismember the Little Entente was to draw it closer together and somewhat closer to France.[23] It also repaired relations with Greece, despite continuing frontier incidents on the Greco-Yugoslav border, as on all Balkan frontiers. Mussolini was left with only the east-European revisionists, Bulgaria and Hungary. Italy and Bulgaria were both hostile to Yugoslavia, though Belgrade's reaction to Macedonian terrorist attacks on the Yugoslav-Bulgarian frontier was restrained. From 1926 on, Italy edged closer to Bulgaria, offering its good offices to settle border incidents and to facilitate the international loan arranged in 1926 to resettle Bulgarian refugees from territories transferred to Greece by the peace treaties.

Mussolini's actions towards Hungary were more dramatic. In April 1927 he signed a ten-year treaty of friendship, conciliation and arbitration, the first bilateral pact Hungary had gained with any of its wartime enemies.[24] This treaty, however, was the sum total of Hungary's diplomatic accomplishments in the era. Hungarian revisionism and hatred of the peace settlement rivalled the intense feeling in Germany, but Hungary had neither a Stresemann nor major-power status and so, even with Italian support, it achieved little. The Hungarian treaty signalled Italian revisionism, inherent in the Fascist stance from the first. In 1928 this revisionism was announced publicly, and Italy was charged at Geneva with smuggling munitions to Hungary in violation of the Treaty of Trianon.[25]

None the less Mussolini's Napoleonic year or years had gained him little, partly because Chamberlain tried to restrain him from major ventures and to appease him on minor issues. After thwarting Italian aims in Africa and the Near East in 1926, Chamberlain entertained Mussolini on his yacht. Lady Chamberlain sported the Fascist insignia and the entire party offered the Fascist salute (except Chamberlain himself, prohibited by his position as a minister of the Crown).[26] This did much for Mussolini's ego but nothing for his foreign policy. Lacking solid achievement, Mussolini was left with little but an alignment with the weaker, defeated nations of the war, a risky commitment to revisionism at the expense of France and the Little Entente, and an obligation in future to fulfil some of the expectations which his inflated oratory had aroused in Italy.

* * *

Mussolini's combination of great expectations and small accomplishments was not unique. It could almost be taken as the pattern of events in the post-Locarno era. Whether on a multinational or a bilateral level, efforts toward genuine detente seemed doomed to disappointment. As peace had supposedly arrived, further disarmament seemed in order, so two attempts were made to build upon the auspicious start of the Washington Naval Conference. On American initiative another naval conference was held in Geneva in June 1927, as the United States under President Calvin Coolidge hoped to extend the Washington limitations on capital ships to cruisers, destroyers and submarines. But tension between France and Italy was so acute that neither came, leaving only Britain and the United States to squabble at Geneva, with Japan futilely trying to play the peacemaker. The Anglo-American quarrel arose in part from British refusal to accept across-the-board American parity in all classes of ships, in part from widely different quota schemes arising from differing national interests and defence needs, and in part from lack of diplomatic preparation. Inexperienced American leaders, misled by the 1922 Washington success, failed to realise that, while it is possible to go the last mile at an international conference provided that much has been settled in advance and the will to agreement is strong, sweeping and fundamental differences can rarely be resolved in the glaring publicity of a short summit meeting. In the end the conferees had to take the unheard of step of disbanding without the slightest shred of accomplishment.[27]

In 1930 they tried again at London. Coolidge and the British Conservatives had gone; their replacements, Herbert Hoover and

Ramsay MacDonald, prided themselves on their pacifism, humanitarianism and internationalism. The will to agreement was stronger, and key issues had been settled in advance. In the autumn of 1929, MacDonald had invited himself to the United States, the first British Prime Minister to make the trip, and Hoover shrewdly took him to his private fishing lodge on the Rapidan River in the Virginia mountains. There, sitting on a log by the waterfalls, they ironed out Anglo-American naval differences, and MacDonald conceded parity in all classes to the United States.[28]

Despite the Rapidan Agreement, the London meetings the next year did not go much more smoothly than those at Geneva, although this time all five naval powers attended. Japan expressed dissatisfaction with the existing 10:10:6 ratio, especially in regard to cruisers. Italy insisted on parity with France over strenuous French objections, while France, in an effort to reinforce its sagging security, angled repeatedly for an American commitment. As Secretary of State Henry Stimson refused any link involving military aid and was equally cool to French proposals for an automatic trade boycott against aggressors, Britain also declined, for boycott leading to blockade and possibly to war against the United States could no longer be contemplated. Accordingly France and Italy refused to sign the naval agreement, which merely extended the building holiday on capital ships five years and established a 10:10:7 ratio across the board, except in submarines, where Japan gained parity, and in heavy cruisers, where Japan reluctantly accepted the actuality of 10:10:7 under the paper appearance of 10:10:6 to a storm of domestic and military criticism boding ill for the future. Further, Britain insisted upon an 'escalator clause' allowing a power to build beyond its quota if it felt threatened by a non-signatory (i.e., France or Italy), thus punching a large loophole in a limited agreement.[29]

Military disarmament fared even less well. From December 1925 on, a League of Nations Preparatory Commission laboured toward a world disarmament conference without making noticeable progress. Moscow's call for an end to all armies, navies and air forces met with resounding silence. Paris insisted upon security but Berlin demanded equality, which France deemed incompatible with its security. Moreover Britain as a sea-power opposed large armies, the core of France's defence, and took issue with the French position on naval disarmament. A 1928 attempt to compose Anglo-French differences at the expense of the American view on naval vessels had to be abandoned in the face of intense Italian and American objections. Meanwhile, at Geneva the experts toiled slowly on toward the disarmament conference finally held in 1932, but even in the optimistic Locarno era, hard-headed diplomatists saw little prospect of accomplishment.

* * *

Attempts at international cooperation in the economic sphere met with similar scant success. By 1925 European agricultural and industrial production had returned to prewar levels. Production continued to increase slowly throughout the remainder of the decade as stabilisation of currencies facilitated the exchange and thus the production of goods. But the increase in Europe's population combined with a sharp decrease in its share of world trade and a slower economic growth rate than on other continents meant that Europe as a whole did not return to a prewar standard of living. In general northern and Western Europe except Britain prospered while southern and eastern regions did not.

Even in the West there were serious economic problems and signs of stagnation. While the Western industrial nations including Germany and Czechoslovakia maintained their technological superiority over the east, they faced severe competition from the United States. The Western-European industrial powers invested heavily in Eastern Europe and exploited the mineral resources of the Danubian region to their own profit, but Western per capita income did not rise as it did in the United States. Investment capital for industrial modernisation was in short supply in the West, and these countries became heavily dependent upon infusions of American capital as their booming economies were increasingly fuelled by a stream of short-term American loans. Cartelisation continued apace, and the large European and American firms came to one arrangement after another, but still the European share of world markets continued to decline as Japan and the United States consolidated their wartime gains. In particular Britain's overseas markets shrank alarmingly as it stagnated through the 1920s with high unemployment. Beyond that European domestic markets were proving too small to absorb increasing production, but tariff barriers all over the continent inhibited exports.

In eastern Europe economic nationalism and high tariff barriers continued, along with growing agricultural distress. Overpopulation, small farms and backward methods yielded inadequate and high-priced agricultural surpluses which could not compete with the endless bounty pouring into Rotterdam from the vast, modernised farms of North America's heartland. While inexpensive river transport on the Danube meant that it was more economic for Austria to buy costly Hungarian or Romanian wheat than to trans-ship American grain from Rotterdam, the big population centres of Western Europe found American wheat cheaper. Yet eastern Europe's chief market for its agricultural produce was Western Europe. As eastern Europe encountered difficulty in selling its crops in Western markets, it was increasingly unable, despite French loans at high rates, to amass the foreign exchange it needed to purchase Western Europe's industrial surplus. Shortsighted French investment in eastern Europe amounted to economic imperialism and benefited economies there little.

Thus, even in the boom years, signs of economic stagnation were evident. Most efforts at international cooperation ran afoul of economic nationalism, but in May 1927 a three-week World Economic Conference was held at Geneva under League auspices. A thousand delegates and observers, mostly businessmen and economists, came from 50 nations all over the globe, including not only the United States but also Russia in its first formal appearance since Genoa. Russia's isolation remained acute, but its economic potential ensured its presence at another economic conference. Despite the Conference's diverse representation, the emphasis was strongly European, though Russia and the United States shared the headlines. The Russian delegation protested vehemently against the heavy Swiss police guard imposed upon it to prevent possible assassination by anti-communist Russian refugees, but, after tense debate and a threat to withdraw, gained formal recognition of the existence of two economic systems, capitalist and communist, and of the possibility of their peaceful coexistence. The American delegates also found the atmosphere uncomfortable as Europeans envied the huge American internal free trade area, railed against high American tariffs, and talked variously of organising cartels against American economic might or of creating a United States of Europe to compete with Anglo-American domination of world trade. The conference had a strong pan-European focus but could not agree on cartels or much else. In the end its final report was a damp squib, containing little more than exhortations to an all-out effort toward tariff reduction and a freer international exchange of goods.[30]

By the time a second Economic Conference met in Geneva in February 1930, optimism about what could be accomplished by efforts toward international cooperation had receded, and the agenda was confined to customs barriers as the chief impediment to trade. Still, the conference produced nothing more than a limited tariff truce, signed by the majority of European countries, freezing bilateral arrangements for one year. As a result of the conference, however, an agrarian bloc of eight east-European *cordon sanitaire* countries organised by Poland met in Warsaw in August 1930 to explore ways to combat agricultural depression and to improve the bargaining position of agricultural nations *vis-à-vis* the industrial giants. This group established a permanent organisation to concert agricultural policies and enjoyed a modest success until the dramatic economic and political changes of the 1930s rendered it a nullity.

* * *

The agrarian bloc was only one of several Polish efforts in the Locarno years to improve its shaky international position and its almost uniformly unsatisfactory relations with its neighbours. Its indifferent success well illustrates the limited options available to even a power of intermediate rank, particularly when the great powers interest themselves in its situation. Despite strenuous efforts by Skrzynski and, after Marshal Josef Pilsudski's *coup d'état* in May 1926, by his Foreign Minister August Zaleski, Poland's relations with its neighbours remained strained while its international position became more precarious. Stresemann had set out to isolate Poland and largely succeeded, but his 1925–6 tariff war against Warsaw in hopes that Poland would collapse failed, owing to the 1926 British General Strike, which benefited Poland economically.[31]

One of the few Polish successes was with Czechoslovakia. As Skrzynski and Beneš both smarted from the sting of Locarno, they hastened to compose their differences. A treaty of arbitration and conciliation resulted, along with a commercial agreement. In addition a 1921 treaty with Romania was successfully renewed in March

1926.[32] As it reconfirmed Romanian possession of Bessarabia, however, it eliminated any faint hope of a Russo-Polish treaty, much to the relief of Stresemann, who had told Moscow that he would not sign the Treaty of Berlin if Russia came to terms with Poland. Skrzynski also made two efforts to reinforce Poland's position, first by a Scandinavian Locarno which Sweden and Finland refused, and then by a Baltic pact which Russia blocked to prevent Polish domination over the small Baltic states.

The advent of Pilsudski in 1926 brought political stability in the form of quasi-dictatorship, financial stabilisation and relatively little reorientation of Polish foreign policy. He relaxed the French tie to a degree, perhaps because its utility was declining as France's construction of the Maginot line of forts on its eastern frontier implied a purely defensive stance and as the Quai d'Orsay from 1927 on spoke of revising the Polish frontier and became extraordinarily vague about the circumstances in which the Franco-Polish alliance would come into force.[33] Significantly the French now saw this alliance as a liability, not an asset. Significantly, too, both Britain and France accepted that the Polish frontier was untenable, for Germany would not accept it and Germany was a great power. Since no other great power would maintain it by force, the Polish frontier was threatened. This trend continued as Germany's power position improved, Stresemann championed German minorities in Poland at Geneva, Britain's small enthusiasm for the existing situation evaporated altogether, and Stresemann skilfully sapped French support. Thus Pilsudski and Zaleski struggled with little effect to find some accommodation between Germany and Russia and to come to terms with other bordering states.

Of these, Lithuania was shrilly intransigent, and relations worsened into a dangerous crisis in 1927. Germany and Russia, not wishing to see Polish influence extended, exhorted Lithuania to stand fast against efforts to resolve the crisis. Lithuania, which hardly needed urging, obligingly informed the League that it was threatened with invasion. Strenuous diplomatic efforts ended the technical state of war which had existed since the birth of both countries, but the border remained closed and diplomatic relations were not established. Further efforts toward pacification failed, thanks to the natural hostility of the two parties and to the efforts of their two powerful neighbours who, as they said, continued to 'bet on the Lithuanian horse'.[34]

These two, Russia and Germany, constituted Poland's dilemma from the moment of its rebirth. The dilemma was deepened by the 1926 Treaty of Berlin, an anti-Polish pact based on the premise that Poland should shrink at the first opportunity. While Russo-German economic and military ties continued through the late 1920s, the two powers were no longer drawn together as outcasts since Germany had received full and Russia partial diplomatic rehabilitation. Their chief common concern now was eastern Europe in general, which Stresemann considered an exclusively Russo-German sphere of interest, and Poland in particular. As neither wished to see Poland settle with the other, in theory Polish diplomacy had a certain field of manoeuvre. In practice it was limited by the fact that Pilsudski could not consider ceding the Corridor and Upper Silesia to Germany nor any close embrace of the communist colossus equally eager to chew off territory.

None the less Pilsudski and Zaleski tried to improve relations with Russia. Some progress had been made when in May 1927 the Soviet envoy in Warsaw was assassinated by a Russian refugee. The ensuing war scare occasioned a Locarno tea-party without Polish participation at Geneva in June. It also increased tension between Russia and Germany as Poland became a bone of contention between them. The difficulty was that, by this time, Russia needed the Russo-German tie far more than Germany did. Russia's diplomatic re-emergence remained limited. Relations with the Western powers, always weak, had worsened. Indeed Britain, alarmed by Soviet propaganda and political meddling in England during the General Strike and throughout the Empire as well as Russian support of anti-imperialist movements in China, had just severed diplomatic relations altogether, leading Moscow seriously to fear invasion by Britain's tiny army. Russia would not consider joining what it deemed to be a capitalist, imperialist League of Nations and it was not showered with invitations, even before it turned inward in 1928–9. In short, Germany was Russia's only entrée into great-power politics, a fact implicit in the Entente suggestion at the Locarno tea-party that Stresemann speak to Chicherin about Poland and reassure him that London was not contemplating invasion.

On the other hand, Germany was a member in good standing of the League and the Locarno club, and thus had other options. Though lacking force, Stresemann skilfully deployed its assets:

economic might, German minorities in neighbouring states, Russia, propaganda and the continuing Anglo-French split. While he appeared to give primary attention to Germany's western frontier, Stresemann never took his eye off Poland, fully intending to regain Danzig, the Corridor and Upper Silesia (and perhaps Memel from Lithuania) at the first chance. After his 1925–6 tariff war failed, however, he concluded that revision of the Polish frontier could best be achieved not through a deal with Russia but rather by extracting France from the Rhineland, thus removing that brake on German freedom of action, and bringing Briand to accept frontier revision in the east. Meanwhile he conceded to Pilsudski in small matters in order to allay his fears, and watched with equanimity a decline in Russo-German collaboration.

* * *

As Stresemann bent himself to his task in the West, he, like Pilsudski and even more like Mussolini, found that the post-Locarno years did not meet his expectations. Despite Mussolini's profound contempt for Stresemann, whom he erroneously considered insufficiently nationalistic, the two men had in common their intense revisionism and concomitant ambitious programmes which failed of rapid realisation. Stresemann's expectations were perhaps more justified and his skill certainly greater, but the fruits of Locarno, which reduced neither French fear nor German revisionism, did not ripen quickly enough to satisfy him. Unlike Mussolini, he gained most of what he sought eventually, but it took longer than he had hoped. One reason for the delay was the fact that Austen Chamberlain's undoubted affection for Mussolini was equalled, if not surpassed, by his admiration for Briand and his frequent exasperation with Stresemann.

Stresemann had counted on British pressure to prod France to new concessions on the heels of German entry into the League. In both Berlin and London, Britain's role was conceived of as an impartial arbiter between France and Germany and, in German eyes, impartiality meant speedy concessions. At the end of 1926, the Entente promised to reduce the size of the occupation forces and to withdraw the IMCC altogether, as was done on 31 January 1927 without any close verification of German claims of fulfilment. There was also the *cachet* of the Nobel Peace Prize announced in December 1926. But that was all, and thereafter concessions came slowly, partly because there was no sustained British effort to hasten them. In part Britain's eyes were turned elsewhere, its chief concerns in the late 1920s being strained relations with Washington (especially after the 1927 Geneva disarmament fiasco), the 1927 break with Russia, and the turbulent situation in China, where civil war and rising nationalism so threatened imperial interests that it massed 20,000 troops at Shanghai in 1927 to defend the International Settlement against Chinese assault. In part too, as Chamberlain admitted, he did 'love France like a woman'[35] and saw Briand as France's finest son. Thus he veered between detente with Germany and entente with *la belle France*. Chamberlain was sympathetic to Briand's domestic political problems and irritated by Stresemann's persistent and mounting demands for more concessions faster.

Like Stresemann, Briand had to contend with domestic opinion and made the most of it. France's craving for security had not abated, and the generals insisted that the protective shield of the Rhineland occupation be retained as long as possible. As it must end eventually, the military leadership, faced with a reduced term of service and a falling birthrate, both portents of a smaller army in future, decided in 1927 on construction of the Maginot line, named for the then Minister of War. This string of massive defensive fortifications along the German border from the Rhine to Belgium reflected French experience in the First World War and was designed to replace the protection afforded by the Rhineland occupation. It signified defeat, acceptance of British policy domination and erosion of the eastern alliances. The long French debate over the costly Maginot project heightened the awareness of insecurity of ordinary Frenchmen and thus gave the generals an opportunity for further pressure on Briand and the cabinet. Henceforth, until the Rhineland was evacuated in 1930, they never ceased to argue that it must be held until the Maginot Line was completed and France secure. They were joined by most of the right wing except Poincaré and by those who prophesied that evacuation would mean the end of reparations. Under these circumstances, Briand, who was committed to pacification but not at the expense of France's safety, had little choice but to delay dismantling the barriers so carefully erected in 1919.

His foot-dragging began at once. Late in 1925 Stresemann had been promised troop reductions in the occupied territory and an early withdrawal of the IMCC. Entente reluctance to take Germany's word without verification of fulfilment of the last remaining disarmament requirements, coupled with many intelligence reports, some exaggerated, about the excellence of the German army and paramilitary formations,[36] delayed the IMCC withdrawal until 1927. Troop reduction in the Rhineland was equally protracted, as French generals resisted and Briand thus could not agree with Chamberlain on the size of the reduction. In this matter Chamberlain leaned toward Stresemann's view, but Briand, capitalising on Chamberlain's annoyance with Germany's 'ever-growing demands put forward almost as ultimatums',[37] succeeded in linking troop reduction to disarmament and in forestalling any reduction until September 1927. Even then, he held the cut to 10,000 men, leaving an occupying force of 60,000, predominantly French.

Stresemann did not consider these grudging concessions adequate recompense for signing at Locarno and joining the League. At Locarno tea-parties, he never ceased to agitate for early evacuation of the Rhineland and return of the Saar. Periodically he would use his Russian weapon or mention the Polish border, preparing the ground ahead. On the Rhenish issues, lack of progress led him to threaten resignation and to try to lure Chamberlain into unilateral evacuation. This effort to split the Entente failed, although it rattled the teacups at Geneva, particularly in the spring of 1927.

Even Stresemann could not prevail against Anglo-French solidarity, and he had to wait. His patience was rewarded in 1928, when events led to agreement at a Locarno tea-party in September that negotiations would begin over a final reparations settlement, an early evacuation of the Rhineland, and an agency of surveillance to ensure continuing demilitarisation there. While a promise to negotiate is a far cry from a completed agreement, it was a startling shift from haggling over the size of a troop cut to a sweeping reassessment of the only real restraints remaining on Germany: reparations and the Rhineland. Yet this shift was accomplished despite the illness of Chamberlain, which sent him off on a long cruise to the New World, and the more serious illness of Stresemann, which kept him away from Berlin and the direction of affairs for several months.

One impetus for the shift from small matters to large was a call in December 1927 from Parker Gilbert, Agent General for Reparations who supervised the workings of the Dawes Plan, for a final reparations settlement. As the Dawes Plan standard year, in which reparation payments would become onerous, would commence in September 1928, Berlin took up the call. There was also concern that Germany was financing reparation payments from the abnormal flood of foreign investment into the country and could not continue to do so at a rising rate. A circular flow of money had developed from private American investors into Germany, from Germany to the Entente powers, and from them to the United States in payment for war debts, though Germany borrowed far more than it paid in reparations, partly to avoid taxes. As some specialists knew, this monetary merry-go-round depended upon continuing American investment, which was beginning to slacken. Further, early in 1928 Stresemann ended his policy of restraint, declared German patience exhausted, and publicly demanded prompt evacuation of the Rhineland, calling the occupation an 'iron curtain' between France and Germany.[38] In response Briand hoped to trade early evacuation for a firm reparations scheme and a Rhineland inspection system to enhance French security. Ultimately he failed. Inspection fell by the wayside, entombed in the Locarno arbitration clauses, and Stresemann successfully demanded evacuation as his price for accepting a reduction in Germany's reparation payments. Briand had been edged on to his path by Entente realisation that the spirit of Locarno was fading, that prolonged occupation meant more bitterness, and that as the 1935 date for final evacuation came closer, the concessions obtainable in return for early withdrawal became fewer. Over the next year, Stresemann made mincemeat of this logic, and the Entente made, not gained, concessions in the course of the Rhineland negotiations.

* * *

One other factor perhaps facilitated the shift back to the concept of a comprehensive settlement. On 27 August 1928, the Kellogg-Briand Pact for the renunciation of war was signed in Paris. While misunderstood by ordinary people at the time, it refurbished the flagging spirit of Locarno, contributed to renewing the illusion that perpetual peace was at hand, and raised false hopes that the United States was emerging from isolation. It also gave Stresemann an opportunity to talk to Poincaré, who, in his concern for France's financial health, was eager for a reparations settlement even at the price of evacuation.

The Kellogg-Briand Pact, one of the great oddities of diplomatic history, arose from Briand's concern for French security. He had forestalled major change as yet, but could not do so indefinitely. Some American commitment, however indirect, would reinforce France's weakening position. In June 1927 Briand made the first of several overtures, proposing that France and the United States bilaterally forswear war against each other. Secretary of State Frank Kellogg was unenthusiastic, viewing Briand's draft treaty as a negative guarantee forcing American neutrality should any of France's allies embroil it in conflict. Pressures from American pacifist groups were strong, however, so in December Kellogg proposed instead a multilateral pact among the principal powers, excluding Russia. But, as France noted, most of these were bound by commitments to the League, Locarno and guarantee treaties to make war in certain circumstances. Accordingly the draft text was diluted to allow for self-defence and fulfilment of treaty obligations and, at British request, the lesser Locarno powers, the Dominions, India, and Ireland were invited to participate. It was understood that all other nations would be invited to adhere later.

After leisurely negotiation, the final text of the International Treaty for the Renunciation of War as an Instrument of National Policy was ready for signature in the late summer of 1928.[39] It was a brief two-paragraph declaration against sin, devoid of any commitment or enforcement clauses. Thus, Kellogg was willing to sign it. In addition to renouncing war as a national policy, the signatories agreed only that settlement of disputes would be 'sought' solely by peaceful means. One American senator sneeringly but accurately termed the Pact an 'international kiss'. Yet it engendered immense enthusiasm among ordinary people without a sharp eye for enforcement clauses. While there are times when politicians gain votes by advocating war, the late 1920s were not among them, especially in Europe. Peace was popular then, and the enthusiasm for the Kellogg-Briand Pact was indicative of a yearning to put the war and the postwar into the past and to enter a long, golden era of peace. Eager advocates convinced themselves that the flimsy foundation of the Pact was firm and that its empty verbiage could provide a basis for peace. In fact the Kellogg-Briand

Pact contributed to the illusion of peace, not its reality, and proved ineffectual whenever it was invoked in years to come. None the less, for all its defects, the Pact constituted the first formal renunciation ever of war as an instrument of national policy and the first step toward the slowly spreading view that war is immoral.

One reason for the Pact's popularity was the mistaken notion that it signalled the return of the United States to world affairs. This illusion was heightened by the fact that Kellogg came to Paris to sign the treaty. Stresemann came too, arising from his sickbed with a nervous physician in attendance. As he was the first German Foreign Minister to visit Paris since the Franco-Prussian War of 1870, his presence added fuel to the flame of hope. On 27 August 1928, in an elaborate ceremony at the Quai d'Orsay dominated by film technicians recording the event for posterity, representatives of 15 nations signed the Pact with a special golden pen. Soon thereafter, 31 more countries adhered. Almost everybody was delighted to declare against sin.

Russia was no exception. It not only signed but seized the moment to compensate for internal dissension and diplomatic weakness by an overture to Poland and an attempt to bolster Lithuania. Chicherin's deputy, Maxim Litvinov, proposed to both states that the Pact be put in effect trilaterally among them without awaiting ratification by other powers. When Poland unexpectedly agreed, asking only for the addition of the other Baltic states and Romania, Stresemann took alarm, scenting Russo-Polish rapprochement to the exclusion of Germany. However, prompt ratification of the Pact by other powers robbed the Litvinov Protocol of 9 February 1929 of what little significance it possessed, and Russo-Polish relations soon deteriorated again, to Stresemann's relief.

* * *

While in Paris for the signing ceremonies in August 1928, Stresemann saw Premier Poincaré, who later noted how seriously ill his old adversary was.[40] After Stresemann assured him that he would not raise the question of *Anschluss* as yet, despite much talk of it in Germany, they discussed Stresemann's most immediate concern, the Rhineland. He sought unconditional evacuation, but Poincaré said evacuation must be contingent upon a reparations settlement.[41] Thus, despite some Anglo-French foot-dragging, the six nations of the Locarno tea-parties announced at Geneva on 16 September, in the absence of the ailing Stresemann and Chamberlain, that separate but parallel negotiations would begin on both issues plus the commission of verification proposed by Briand.

The Geneva communiqué of 16 September[42] called for a six-power commission of financial experts to devise a final reparations plan, as this task was much more complex than early evacuation. This was to be the first but not the last 'final' plan, and henceforth there was much talk of 'final liquidation of the war'. As this meant liquidation of the peace settlement and of the mentality which created it, Germany took the lead in calling for the committee of experts and urged inclusion of American citizens, partly because war debts to the United States were bound to be a factor and partly because Americans, with few direct claims on Germany, might be moderate. While Washington was unenthusiastic about even private American participation, it agreed that Owen D. Young, whose involvement with reparations dated back to the Dawes Plan, could chair the committee, many of whose other members were equally experienced in the intricacies of reparations.

The Young Committee began work early in 1929 and concluded its labours in June. By then the Locarno triumvirate had met together during League Council sessions at Lugano to try to resolve the political issues. Chamberlain had backed Briand's insistence on a verification mechanism, his view that the second (Coblenz) Rhineland zone scheduled for evacuation in January 1930 be evacuated only when negotiations on security and reparations had made real progress, and his demand that withdrawal from the third (Mainz) zone be contingent upon a final reparations settlement. Thereafter Briand's position stiffened and he refused to discuss evacuation at all until the Young Report was received. Instead he came increasingly to Poincaré's opinion that evacuation should be gradual as reparations under the new plan were commercialised and advance payment received by France.[43] This stand became harder to maintain as the experts laboured to draft the plan because, across the Channel, Chamberlain found his foreign policy under mounting attack. The Labour and Liberal parties called loudly for immediate, unilateral, unconditional evacuation of the Rhineland. Chamberlain held firm, but in the May 1929 general election, the Conservatives lost their majority. On 5

June a new Labour government took office under MacDonald, with Arthur Henderson as Foreign Secretary.

The new Cabinet, which quickly restored relations with Russia, found itself faced with the Young Report of 7 June 1929.[44] This document had been achieved with great difficulty as there was no agreement between what the creditors hoped to receive and what Berlin deemed its capacity to pay. The plan enshrined Entente expectations on paper but not in practice. Germany was to pay annuities in varying amounts, all below the Dawes standard-year figure of 2.5 milliard marks, for 59 years, the duration of remaining Allied debt payments to the United States. The paper total, covering all charges including service of the Dawes loan, came to nearly 114 milliard marks, but had a present marketable value of only about 37 milliard marks. If paid in full, the annuities would cover war debts and provide most states except Britain with some indemnity. However, only 660 million marks of each annuity (generally about one-third) were unconditionally payable, and only this portion of the debt could be commercialised. The remainder was postponable under certain conditions of economic or monetary distress. This sleight of hand papered over the gap between expectations and potential economic reality.

While Germany disliked the ostensible total, it had succeeded in keeping the annuities for the first ten years all below two milliard marks. Before that time lapsed, surely there would be an end to reparations or at least another reduction. In the interim deliveries in kind would be sharply reduced and all supervision of German finances would end. Further, the complex structure of treaty commissions and Dawes Plan agencies would be dissolved. In their place a Bank for International Settlements would be established at Basle, Switzerland, charged to receive and distribute reparation payments and to provide a long-needed institution for cooperation among central banks of various countries.* In its second function, the Bank still survives as the sole legacy of reparations.

Germany accepted the Young Plan because the alternative was continuing the higher Dawes payments, but demanded immediate

---

* For example, the Bank of England, Bank of France, Bank of Italy and so on. In the decentralised American system, the Federal Reserve Bank of New York fulfils the functions of a central bank in international monetary matters.

evacuation of the Rhineland and return of the Saar Basin as the price of acceptance. France also accepted the Plan but not evacuation before payment was received, nor any discussion of the Saar. Britain, while backing France on the Saar, threatened unilateral evacuation and refused to approve the Young Plan without modification. Instead of trying to compose these yawning differences, the three powers convened in early August, along with Italy, Japan and Belgium, at The Hague for what they grandly titled 'The Conference on the Final Liquidation of the War'.

The month-long first Hague Conference, as it is usually called, was largely consumed by the successful British effort to modify the Young Plan to British advantage. The extraordinarily acerbic Chancellor of the Exchequer, Philip Snowden, conceded neither a farthing nor a polite word, loudly protesting the revision of the old Spa percentages in the Young Plan, which left Britain with its war debts covered but no reparation for damage done. While this bore some resemblance to the Balfour note of 1922, Snowden was adamant, particularly since Britain's share of the unconditional annuities was to be slight. Agreement on political questions was equally difficult as Briand insisted on verification of demilitarisation and Stresemann demanded the Saar, while Henderson declared that, whatever else happened, British troops would be home by Christmas, but Briand maintained that the French Army must stay another year. On every political issue it was two against one, and the majority won. Briand had to settle for ephemeral verification while Stresemann had to accept later talks on the Saar, which came to nothing. While not conceding fully to Anglo-German pressure, Briand also had finally to agree that the Rhineland would be free of foreign troops by 30 June 1930. On the financial question, however, majority rule failed in the face of Snowden's flinty stance. After weeks of wrangling, the Young reparations receipts were reallocated to British benefit.

When the major disputes were settled, no time remained to draft enabling documents and resolve lesser details, as the diplomatic timetable required that the Foreign Ministers arrive at Geneva within 48 hours for the annual Assembly meeting. Accordingly the conferees hastily organised themselves on their final day, drafted a Protocol of 31 August 1929 accepting in principle the decisions reached, and belatedly chose a chairman, Prime Minister Henri Jaspar of Belgium, who was charged with appointing committees to complete the work of the conference and reconvening it when all was arranged.[45]

Six days later at Geneva, Briand issued a dramatic call for European union, urging not only economic association but also a degree of political and social federation. As the old sanctions were dissolving, Briand attempted to enmesh Germany in a new web of European integration, creating an interdependence which might in time eliminate war as a practical possibility. While German and British press reaction was cool, Stresemann himself was gracious. In what proved to be his last diplomatic appearance, he ruled out the unspoken thought of some that a European bloc could serve as an instrument of economic war against the United States but gave his blessing to steps to bring Europe out of economic obsolescence. It was agreed that Briand would draft a proposal, that the 27 European members of the League would consider and amend it, and that a revised draft would be further discussed at Geneva in a year's time.[46]

Meanwhile the British and Belgians had already begun their withdrawal from the Coblenz zone and the French their retirement into the Mainz zone. Both were completed before Christmas. By then hostility to the Young Plan in Germany had reached disturbing proportions, as seen in a national plebiscite in which 5.8 million voters registered opposition.[47] This raised questions about future German good faith, the sole guarantee of fulfilment embodied in the Plan, but it was insufficient to overturn German ratification. Accordingly the seven committees convened by Jaspar, one of them revealingly termed the 'Committee on Liquidation of the Past', completed their tasks and he issued a call for a second conference at The Hague on 3 January 1930.

In the interim Stresemann had died on 3 October 1929, having literally worked himself to death at the age of 51. As he was dying, he said: 'We are again masters in our house.'[48] In his last months he had recognised the rising tide of strident, belligerent German nationalism and had known that the days of his indirect, patient policy were numbered. Had he lived, he undoubtedly would have tried to stem this clamorous tide long enough to regain the Saar, a task to which no other German leader was equal. None the less, in his six years as architect of German foreign policy, he had liberated the Ruhr and the Rhineland, ended military inspection, twice reduced reparations and transformed Germany from the pariah to the pre-eminent member of the European family of nations. He had further demonstrated the futility of imposing upon a great power a treaty which it will not accept. Germany's absolute refusal to accept had always been the chief difficulty with the Versailles Treaty. Stresemann had broken most of the fetters. His successor, Julius Curtius, bent himself with lesser skill to completing the task.

Fortunately for the inexperienced Curtius, Germany was not the main issue at the second lengthy Hague Conference. As the Young Committee had called for the dissolution of the joint reparations responsibility of the wartime Central Powers, the conference sought a comprehensive settlement of non-German reparations. Since the seven successor states to the old Habsburg Empire had inherited its debts and five of them were entitled to reparation from the other two, the potential for discord was immense and fully exploited. But smaller states, unlike Germany, could be threatened into compliance. After less than three weeks of major power pressure, a huge heap of documents were solemnly signed on 20 January 1930. These formally closed the old pre-Dawes accounts, thus cancelling the reparations clauses of the Versailles Treaty; regulated non-German reparations; provided for the evacuation of the Rhineland; and, along with a variety of special bilateral agreements and annexes, arranged the entrance into force of the modified Young Plan.[49] As the experts had planned for it to go into effect on 1 September 1929, it was made retroactive to that date. In fact by common consent, the Young figures had been quietly applied immediately after the first Hague Conference and Germany was currently paying less than half of what it would have owed under the Dawes Plan. For this reduction, its reward was the Rhineland.

The last French troops left German soil precisely as scheduled on 30 June 1930. The next day President Hindenburg, together with the entire German Cabinet, issued a proclamation in honour of the occasion.[50] In deference to the growing forces of right-wing nationalism, it conspicuously omitted mention of Stresemann, undoubted father of the liberation. Instead, in a document full of nationalist fervour, the proclamation spoke pointedly of Germany's obligation to its war dead, and called for the return of the Saar. At once the paramilitary veteran's organisation, the *Stahlhelm* (Steel Helmet), with which Hindenburg publicly associated himself, engaged in jubilant demonstrations on the French and Belgian borders in the demilitarised zone.[51]

Despite these portents, which led the British ambassador, Sir Horace Rumbold, to write of German 'ingratitude and tactlessness',[52] Briand's plan for European union was under consideration through the summer. In May he had circulated a proposal calling for a federation based on moral union and regional entente reinforced by permanent legislative, executive and secretarial institutions.[53] Briand noted that he was placing political matters before economic, as economic union depended upon security which in turn was linked to political union. In brief he was trying to reinforce the political *status quo*. Briand called for a general European system of arbitration, security and Locarno-style international guarantees. He briefly urged the creation of a European common market with free circulation of capital, goods and peoples, but suggested that detailed economic plans, along with the possibilities of intellectual and parliamentary cooperation, be deferred for later study. Curtius privately said: 'For Pan Europe, read Pan Versailles.'[54]

Briand's proposal, designed to substitute a new peace structure for the old, was being debated by European members of the League at Geneva for the annual Assembly meeting when on 14 September 1930 Adolf Hitler's National Socialist (Nazi) Party scored a smashing victory in the German Reichstag election, coming from nowhere to gain 107 seats and become the second largest party. With rare realism, the League Assembly referred Briand's plan to a committee for quiet interment. While the illusion of permanent peace was not yet shattered, it had developed a conspicuous crack and henceforth those charged with guarding the security of European states watched with dismay as this crack spread across the entire fragile façade, portending disintegration to come.

5 The Crumbling of Illusion

Decades rarely provide convenient historical dividing lines, but 1930 was something of a watershed year. It would be an oversimplification to suggest that the 1920s looked back to the First World War while the 1930s looked ahead to the Second World War. None the less the diplomacy of the 1920s had centred on the postwar settlement and attempts to uphold or undo it, with a mounting desire to consign the postwar bitterness to history. The Hague Conference's Committee on the Liquidation of the Past was only one of many signs of a widespread belief that old problems could be solved, reinforcing peace and prosperity. As the decade turned with many of these issues unresolved, Europe entered an era of new problems, economic and political, including fear of a new war. The 1930 German election led a French politician to remark, 'We've been outwitted',[1] and the Belgian Foreign Minister expressed 'great fears of an imminent fresh outbreak of war'.[2]

Hope had been widespread that 'liquidation of the past' meant the end of all problems. Henceforth peace, prosperity and international harmony would reign. The late 1920s had seen surface harmony and apparent economic prosperity. Except in Britain, whose economic ailments seemed incurable, the Western industrial world had enjoyed an economic expansion and, in some areas, a rising standard of living. These trends had been pronounced in Germany and the United States, fuelled in both instances by American investment. Why should not these good times continue? The Young Plan was based upon the premise that German and Western expansion would continue indefinitely. Similarly it was widely believed that, with the Rhineland evacuation and a 'final' all-European reparations settlement, there would be little future occasion for international tension, at least in Europe. After all, Russia had adhered to the Kellogg-Briand Pact, Mussolini had not engaged in any escapades for several years, the Balkans and the Baltic were less turbulent than usual, and the greatest single source of Franco-German strife had been removed. Surely after so much tension, one could expect that true peace had come.

Yet warning signs had been flashing for several years for the shrewd to see. In many Foreign Ministries it was recognised that the postwar settlement had been based on a particular power balance and that the more the balance shifted the more the settlement would be revised. Hence growing Polish nervousness. Moreover the clamorous voices of revisionism and of intense nationalism were rising higher, both in Europe and in Asia. In general the dissatisfied powers were becoming stronger and more aggressive, leading the thoughtful to wonder what lay ahead.

One of the few dissatisfied powers which was not becoming stronger was China, and its weakness created a dangerous situation. The Chinese nationalist, anti-imperialist and anti-foreign movements continued unabated, but so did the multi-faceted Chinese civil wars. These became more complex, particularly after the leading Nationalist general, Chiang Kai-shek (Jiang Jieshi), broke with the Communists in 1927, expelled the numerous Russian advisers and seized key cities, but could not maintain much control on the outer fringes of the roiling Chinese mass. This situation tempted a powerful and aggressive neighbour, Japan, which feared that Chiang might gain effective control in Manchuria (Dong Bei).

Japanese revisionism was becoming pronounced. In an era when further disarmament was the watchword, military leaders in Tokyo were incensed at the outcome of the 1930 London Naval Conference, whose results, so favourable to Japan, did not satisfy it. Japan needed mainland markets and raw materials in areas nominally controlled by China, and its economy, so dependent upon international trade, was highly sensitive to world market fluctuations. Further, tension was mounting between the military authorities and civilian governments. Should the military win the *sub rosa* struggle in progress, Japan's policy would become aggressive.

Russia kept a wary eye on both these Asian neighbours but, after its expulsion from China, an even warier eye on Europe. Stalin devoted the late 1920s to tightening his control of Russia and to headlong industrialisation. As his grip on power became more secure, some wondered how long he would accept the boundaries forced on a prostrate Russia at war's end. Stalin was among the first to react to the warning signs in Germany. Even before the 1930 election he recognised that Russo-German collaboration was in jeopardy and signalled a policy switch in July by appointing Litvinov as Foreign Commissar to replace the ailing Chicherin. Litvinov pursued a policy of cooperation with the West-European powers and with Geneva. While Russia did not as yet join the League, Litvinov attended conferences held under its auspices and cultivated Western leaders. As Hitler's electoral successes swelled and his anti-Semitic oratory evoked wide response in Germany, Litvinov, who was Jewish, remained in office and, from 1932 on, Stalin situated Russia's new factories in or east of the Ural mountains, beyond the range of German bombers. In 1932 as well, Russia signed non-aggression pacts with France and with four of its north-European neighbours, including Poland. Having mended his diplomatic fences, Stalin consolidated his power in Russia and watched.

Mussolini also watched and consolidated, both at home and in Albania. In the late 1920s he eliminated most political opposition in Italy and reinforced his dictatorship. He also enjoyed his greatest diplomatic achievement, which proved to be his sole important legacy. By the Lateran Accords of 11 February 1929,[3] he ended the cold war between the Italian kingdom and the papacy dating from the unification of Italy in 1870. These three treaties established the sovereign state of the Vatican City in Rome (area 108.7 acres), provided financial compensation to it for the seizure of the Papal States by Italy in 1870, and defined the special status of the Roman Catholic religion in Italy. While Mussolini's success in ending an absurd situation arose largely from being in power at the right moment and – unlike his predecessors – having a government strong enough to negotiate, the Lateran Accords brought him new popularity and facilitated a firmer grip upon Italy. In the international arena, Mussolini's respectability quotient, already high, soared higher,[4] and much twaddle was written about a spiritual renaissance in Italian fascism.

Otherwise, after his failure to disrupt the Little Entente, Mussolini's foreign policy was largely confined to distinctly unspiritual sabre rattling and to an attempt at economic penetration of Ethiopia. Relations with France remained poor, and Mussolini scarcely bothered to conceal his contempt for Briand's moves toward international conciliation and European union. Despite Britain's best efforts, France and Italy could not be brought to any agreement on naval limitations as Mussolini insisted on parity. Since France had a much larger fleet in being, along with north and south Atlantic coastlines and Asian colonies to defend, all of which Italy lacked, Mussolini's determination to enlarge his navy implied aggressive plans for the future. By 1930 this quarrel and Mussolini's bellicose oratory had generated a widespread belief that Italy was the leader of the revisionist states.[5] Still Il Duce did little. Like Stalin he watched, alert to any German threat to Austria and to the possibility that this vital buffer might be erased by *Anschluss*.

* * *

The fact that *Anschluss* was being discussed in 1930 was one of many signs of greater German revisionism. Throughout the year, the German appetite grew, unslaked by the Rhineland evacuation. Hindenburg's proclamation on that occasion indicated sharper revisionism, as did the intense protest against the Young Plan. In addition, the weakness of the Weimar political system was becoming glaringly obvious as, from July 1930 on, the Reichstag seldom met because the Cabinet of Chancellor Heinrich Brüning could rarely command a majority and resorted to rule by presidential emergency decree. Then too, German military and naval expenditures were rising sharply and continued to rise, although Berlin claimed that its army and navy remained within the stringent Versailles Treaty limits. Western military attachés consistently doubted these claims and noted that the German Army, whatever its exact size, was being trained as the cadre for a much larger army.[6] Foreign observers were less likely to notice the organisational development and quiet growth of the Nazi party in the late 1920s, as it spread from Munich throughout Germany and acquired a solid base for future expansion.

The economic scene also provided warning signs, particularly in Germany, and a few of these were heeded. The Young Plan, with its sharp cutback in annual payments, recognised that American investment was slowing as more lucrative opportunities developed in the United States. In the late 1920s, Germany borrowed to pay reparations and repay debts but also to live lavishly. Germany borrowed nearly twice as much as it paid in reparations and much of the balance, often lent to municipalities, was expended on football (soccer) stadia, swimming pools with artificial wave-making apparatus,[7] and blocks of workers' housing with the unheard-of extravagance of private bathrooms in each family unit. Some sarcastic grumbling emanated from Britain and France, where such luxuries were rare among the working classes, along with an envious desire to emulate the German boom. But this boom, despite Germany's fundamental economic strength, rested on a fragile base of borrowing and more borrowing, largely in the form of short-term loans which could be recalled on 90 days notice or on demand. The debts mounted, but the danger of using short-term loans for long-term building projects was blithely ignored. By 1928 American investment slackened and, after the New York stock market crash in 1929, slackened more. Then came the 1930 German election.

As the American crash, heralding the advent of a global depression of unprecedented severity, occurred in the autumn of 1929, world trade shrank 40 per cent in 1929–30, and the German election with the smashing Nazi victory occurred in the autumn of 1930, some have assumed that the Depression was responsible for Hitler's triumphant march to power. This assumption is comforting, implying that only in extraordinary circumstances of overwhelming calamity could a civilised European nation embrace such unparalleled barbarism. Alas, it is inexact. Despite the sudden drama of the New York crash, the Depression was a slowly creeping miasma, which arrived gradually over several years. Even in the United States where it all began, rock-bottom was not reached until March 1933, two months after Hitler became Germany's Chancellor.

During the summer of 1930 as the electoral campaign progressed, the German economy was in a recession but not yet a depression. Nobody was suffering much except the workers, who remained true to their traditional parties.[8] Fear of a depression probably induced some members of the middle class, so badly traumatised by the 1923 inflation, to vote Nazi, especially since the economic misery of 1923 was generally blamed on France and the Versailles Treaty, and the Nazis proclaimed that they alone had never endorsed anything done under that *Diktat*. Even so, one must conclude that, while the Weimar Republic had economic ailments in 1930, its mortal illness was virulent nationalism.[9]

Foreign policy dominated the electoral campaign. In a celebrated dispatch, Rumbold, a shrewd and moderate observer, surveyed the German political scene and remarked that calls for repeal of the Young Plan, ratified only in March, came from clear across the political spectrum. In part this rare unanimity reflected popular belief that the reduced Young annuities were responsible for the recession, and in part it reflected the view, widely evident in 1929, that any further reparations were an insult to German honour. Rumbold also noted demands from left, right and centre for immediate return of the Saar, prompt revision of the eastern frontier at Polish expense, return of the prewar colonies, and rearmament. He concluded:

> The snowball of 'revisionism' continues to roll down the electoral slopes, and, as it rolls, it is gathering speed and size. It may now indeed be said that the first electoral campaign which has taken place in Germany without the shadow of the Rhineland occupation has brought out into the open, through one party or another, all that Germany hopes for and intends to strive for in the field of external affairs.[10]

Rumbold spotted the key factor: the Rhineland evacuation. With French troops across the Rhine in the Coblenz and Mainz bridgeheads, it had been a club held over Germany's head, necessitating the patient indirect policy of Stresemann. With the removal of this club, 12 years of pent-up nationalist fervour exploded, leading all 24 political parties to demand treaty revision[11] and sending 6.5 million voters to the support of Adolf Hitler in the hope of eliminating the last traces of the 1918 humiliation and restoring the glories of prewar Germany, colonies and all. His party was against much and for little, essentially 'a catch-all party of protest'[12] indicating dislike of the Weimar Republic.

As it is simplistic to argue that the Depression caused Hitler's accession to power, so it is even more simplistic to argue that Hitler's 1930 victory caused the Depression. None the less, the sudden Nazi surge accelerated the Depression's advent in central Europe and heightened its severity there. After the election the Brüning Cabinet tried to counter the Nazi threat by embarking on a more aggressive foreign policy, particularly regarding Austria. This set off within eight months a chain reaction of banking crises from Austria to Germany and eventually to Britain. More immediately, investors reacted swiftly to the German election. The Berlin stock exchange plummeted downward and a massive withdrawal of capital from Germany ensued as the short-term notes were called in. Within three months, at least 1.3 milliard marks were withdrawn, over a third of the foreign exchange then invested in Germany and the equivalent of about three-quarters of the 1930-31 Young annuity. French, Belgian, Swiss and some American financiers withdrew their loans while German liberals and German Jews sent their funds to safety elsewhere. Few new credits replaced the old. While German economic problems were manageable in August 1930, by December the situation had become acute as unemployment soared. And in the winter of discontent, depression and misery, the year turned, ushering in what Arnold Toynbee soon was to term '*annus terribilis*'.[13]

* * *

1931 was aptly named. It proceeded from calamity to calamity, all of them terrible. The year began with a crisis over the prospect of *Anschluss* shaking the foundations of both the Paris peace settlement and the fragile financial structure of central Europe. The spreading stain of the Depression crept onward, with occasional sudden lurches into the abyss of major banking failures and concomitant business bankruptcies, causing more unemployment. The black cloud of the Nazi menace loomed ever larger and more thunderous. Meanwhile in an extraordinary irony of mistiming, plans for the long-heralded 1932 disarmament conference also crept along, the planners themselves trying to overlook mounting German, Italian and Japanese militancy, along with obvious Russian and German rearmament. Neither to the diplomatists nor to the politicians did it occur that rearmament was the swiftest cure for unemployment and depression. On the contrary in most countries, as tax revenues fell, government expenditure was initially cut, thus increasing unemployment and reducing tax revenues further. Finally, *annus terribilis* closed with a bang, a shooting war in East Asia, demonstrating to those who still cherished hopes that the League of Nations could not keep the peace. All in all *annus terribilis* destroyed many illusions. When it ended, while few could envisage the full horrors ahead, there was no longer talk of an extended era of peace and prosperity. Instead many were asking whether Western civilisation could endure.

When *annus terribilis* began, the European world was still optimistically discussing disarmament. As government budgets shrank, it seemed reasonable that armaments should be the first category of expenditure to be slashed. Thus hopes remained high at Geneva although, in the Foreign Ministries, hardheaded diplomatists were doubtful, noting the continuing Franco-Italian naval squabble and the fact that Germany was building an extraordinary new warship with plans for more to follow. The *Deutschland,* launched with full ceremony by Hindenburg on 19 May, was a pocket battleship or heavy cruiser and a triumph of naval engineering. While technically within Versailles Treaty limits, it combined such speed and firepower that it could sink any ship afloat speedy enough to catch it and outrun any ship powerful enough to sink it. Funds for a sister ship (Cruiser B) were voted by the Reichstag on 20 March 1931 and plans for a third (Cruiser C) were well advanced. Throughout the tangled crises of reparations, loans, Austrian alarms, and rearmament which dominated the remainder of the year, Brüning steadfastly refused to delay construction of Cruiser B or jettison plans for Cruiser C, explaining when necessary that the project was particularly dear to the heart of the 'Old Gentleman'.[14]

The voting of funds for Cruiser B stirred Europe's chanceries only moderately because the first major crisis of *annus terribilis* erupted the next day and engulfed lesser matters: 21 March brought confirmation of rumours about a plan for an Austro-German customs union. This had been under consideration since February 1930, but had been given new impetus by Austria's economic plight and Germany's political condition. Throughout, Austrian motives were economic, including overtures to France and Italy, while German aims were political, seen by some as Berlin's first overt act toward a new imperialism.[15] Not only was Brüning eager to steal Nazi thunder and Curtius to set Germany astride the Danube, but there was a wider goal to dominate central Europe, strangle Poland economically, and then force political concessions from it, liberating what Bernhard von Bülow of the Foreign Ministry called 'occupied territories'.[16]

The Treaties of Versailles and Saint-Germain forbade *Anschluss.* While a customs union was not *Anschluss,* it was widely regarded as a giant step in that direction. Moreover the 1922 Geneva Protocol for Austria's financial reconstruction banned any measure affecting Austria's economic independence. Thus the Vienna Protocol of 19 March 1931 embodying the customs union project was drafted to circumvent these restrictions. In addition the Vienna Protocol was a completed treaty slightly rephrased to look like a draft proposal in hopes of soothing the susceptibilities of foreign leaders to whom no warning had been given that such a bombshell would burst. Finally, the announcement was timed to coincide with the meeting of the committee considering Briand's plan for European union so as to give the customs union project an aura of respectability. As von Bülow said: 'We will dress the matter up with a pan-European cloak.'[17]

Nobody was deceived, and the startling absence of diplomatic preparation drew a sharp reaction. France in particular took alarm and was in a position to take action, especially since its currency was now the strongest on the continent. Protests to Germany were unavailing as Brüning threatened his own resignation and the advent of Hitler in an effort to carry the customs union, so pressure was put on the weaker partner. In early April an Austrian request for a French loan gave rise to political conditions, including an Austrian promise to postpone further negotiations on the customs union. As efforts toward a common front with Britain failed, France combined the carrot and the stick, offering loans, concessions and cartels in return for an end to Austro-German revisionism. Germany turned a deaf ear, but Austria was in no position to do so. On 11 May the Creditanstalt, largest of Austrian banks, in whose direction French interests were conspicuous, reached a state of virtual collapse. While French action had not caused its difficulties, which stemmed from earlier failures of smaller banks, Parisian interests may have affected the timing of disclosure of the failure. As the Creditanstalt's balances constituted three-eighths of the total holdings of all Austrian banks combined and 70 per cent of Austrian commerce and industry depended upon it, it could not be permitted to close its doors, but massive government intervention to save it led to an appeal under the 1922 Geneva Protocol for new loans to stave off another national bankruptcy. Thus in short order, the Austrian financial crisis linked the customs union project to its chief obstacle, the 1922 Protocol.

Austria soon lost heart, especially as France, the primary source of new loans, insisted in a three-hour ultimatum upon abandonment of the customs union. Germany remained truculent despite its own mounting financial crisis. In the end, despite German objections, the legal questions surrounding the customs union

were referred to the Permanent Court of International Justice at
The Hague. On 5 September, in a decision based more on legal
than on political considerations, the Court narrowly ruled by a
vote of eight to seven that the Vienna Protocol did not violate the
Treaty of Saint-Germain but, by the same vote, that it did violate
the 1922 Geneva Protocol.[18]

* * *

By then the customs union project was dead, but, in the interim,
its repercussions had deepened the European financial crisis as
the Creditanstalt collapse triggered a new flight of capital from
both Germany and Austria. The Bank of England rushed to
Vienna's rescue with short-term loans which only exacerbated
Britain's own financial crisis late in the summer, causing the credits to be withdrawn in August. Germany's close association with
Austria generated a new rush to withdraw credits, culminating in a
German banking crisis in July. As the flight of both German and
foreign capital intensified, Berlin began a vehement informal
agitation for reparations relief while refusing concessions on the
customs union, Cruiser B, or the army budget, which was nearly
triple that of Britain. Berlin believed that the alarm of private
American investors over the German credit crisis could be
exploited to reduce reparations. Tending to blame all distress on
reparations rather than on Weimar's financial and political prac-
tices or world-wide economic trends, the Cabinet campaigned
through May and June for revision of the Young Plan, to the
further detriment of German credit. An extraordinarily pessimistic
government manifesto on 6 June accelerated the credit débâcle.

American investors were indeed alarmed, not only the huge
New York banks which had committed so much capital in Germany
but Middle Western and New England financial consortia which
also had invested heavily.[19] As the German credit crisis had
reached proportions endangering the American banking structure, and as a psychological victory over the Depression was sorely
needed, on 20 June Hoover unilaterally proposed a one-year moratorium commencing on 1 July for all intergovernmental debts, stat-
ing that: 'The American Government proposes the postponement
during one year of all payments on intergovernmental debts, reparations and relief debts, both principal and interest, of course not
including obligations of governments held by private parties.'[20]

While cancellation of war debts remained politically impossible, postponement was feasible, particularly to ensure the safety of private investment. In a sense, for all creditor nations, namely the United States and those Allies receiving German reparations, private investments were put ahead of public accounts and the immediate interests of the ordinary taxpayer. While self-interest in Wall Street and the City of London contributed much to this decision, it is also true that a massive Anglo-American banking collapse would have brought untold misery throughout the world.

There were several difficulties with Hoover's proposal. Its sudden announcement without diplomatic preparation, while arising from domestic American political considerations, smacked of an ultimatum. Also, though Berlin had already decided upon a postponement, Hoover pre-empted its declaration, offering far more than it had expected to receive. Since the moratorium was a gift, not a concession triumphantly wrested from the foe, Brüning gained no political advantage from it. Finally, Hoover's proposal offered much relief to British and American private investors and to the German government, but it provided no consolation to France, which would lose substantially more than it would gain. Predictably, Paris protested, pointing out that Germany's problem was credit, not reparations, and arguing that, since its budget was virtually balanced (unlike that of most European countries) even with reparations, it surely could pay the unconditional portion of the Young annuities. The British Treasury conceded that this was so – and in fact Berlin had expected to pay that much – but insisted that nothing less than a full moratorium would satisfy panicky private investors.[21]

Frantic Franco-American negotiations ensued. As the Americans were inexperienced in the intricacies of reparations, they relied on British experts for advice. French leaders saw that the Hoover moratorium was inescapable, so they angled for German political concessions, especially abandonment of Cruiser B and the customs union, but to no avail. Paris was also determined to retain at least a paper fiction of partial payment, partly for political reasons and partly out of realisation that once reparations were entirely halted, they would never resume, though the war debts which they were expected to cover would remain to be paid. After much debate, the American negotiators agreed that Germany technically would pay unconditional annuities to the

Bank for International Settlements while actually receiving most or all of them back as a reloan. But Germany refused this arrangement, so, in the end, Germany paid the money to itself, but the fiction of reparations payments was precariously maintained. The Hoover moratorium thus went into effect on 6 July. When news of final agreement reached Washington, the French ambassador called for champagne and offered the prophetic toast: 'To the crisis we have just avoided and to the catastrophe which will follow.'[22]

Catastrophe came swiftly. While much of the Hoover year was consumed by debate over what to do when it ended, at first there was no time to think ahead. The moratorium came too late to salvage German credit, especially since futile British efforts toward all-around cancellation of debts and reparations aggravated the German situation. By mid July failure of a major German firm endangering two large banks set off an unequalled financial panic, generating a new flight from the mark and massive withdrawals of short-term credits, together with forced closure of all German banks for two days, permanent collapse of one very large bank, and closure of the German Stock Exchange for two months. The credit crisis continued to mount while the German standstill led to bank failures and closures all over central Europe along with a sharp withdrawal of foreign funds from London. Britain could not advance additional credits and France would not consider a long-term loan without an equally long-term political moratorium. But Brüning, continually facing Nazi pressure, refused to affirm the political *status quo*. Further American loans were not forthcoming as Berlin refused to restrict the flight of capital and the Federal Reserve thus saw no future in pouring funds into a leaky vessel.

At this juncture, Germany entered upon rule by presidential decree without hope of return. Through the emergency presidential powers, Brüning imposed restriction after unpopular restriction upon the suffering German people, cutting wages, centralising power in a Cabinet without political support, and regimenting the economy to a degree rivalling that of totalitarian Russia, thus unintentionally laying a basis for the Hitlerian transformation to come. Cutting prices and wages deepened the German depression as firms failed and unemployment mounted. However, while most states initially would not risk the untried tactics of deficit spending, public works and inflationary policies,

Germany could not. Domestically, memories of the 1923 inflation only eight years before were too harrowing to render such a course feasible, while internationally the imperatives of German credit and Young Plan requirements rendered it equally impossible.

The German situation soon became so critical that the Bank for International Settlements was asked to appoint a Banker's Committee representing central banks to recommend a solution. In mid-August it produced an ambivalent report, offending nobody but providing no clear-cut guidance, primarily because financial remedies depended on major political decisions which few countries were willing to face.[23] By this time, too, attention had shifted to London, where withdrawal of foreign credits had reached panic proportions as a result of depression-generated budget deficits, unfavourable trade balances, and heavy British loans to other beleaguered nations. Many of these loans were being frozen in a well-intentioned effort to prevent further deterioration in central Europe. As speculation against the pound mounted, emergency credits on 1 August from the Bank of France and the Federal Reserve failed to stem the tide. By 26 August they had largely evaporated as withdrawals continued. Since additional credits were not forthcoming without excruciatingly unpopular financial stringencies, the Labour Cabinet resigned, to be replaced by a three-party emergency National Government with MacDonald continuing as Prime Minister and Lord Reading, a Liberal, as Foreign Minister. In November he was replaced by another Liberal, Sir John Simon, after an election had confirmed the national coalition in office.

* * *

Annus terribilis took a heavy toll of the world's political leadership. Russia's largely closed and regimented command economy moved on, impervious to free-market fluctuations though the world price collapse forced it to sell twice as much wheat to purchase machinery. Its relative stability led many unemployed young Western intellectuals to conclude that while capitalism was dying, communism was the wave of the future and also led to American diplomatic recognition in 1933 for economic reasons. Of the major western countries, France weathered the crisis least agonisingly with its strongly restored currency, evenly balanced economy and lesser dependence on the sharply contracting international market.

Even so, the aged and enfeebled Briand, while lingering on at the Quai d'Orsay, was severely weakened politically and lost the presidential election of 1931 as a consequence of the customs union proposal. Curtius, too, was a victim of the customs union project, and Brüning became his own Foreign Minister when it was abandoned. In the industrial countries, large and small, and in many less developed regions, human misery was extreme, and regimes correspondingly precarious. In far-off Japan the moderate ministry was losing its grip. And in 1932 the Depression was to claim among its victims Brüning, Hoover, and the Herriot ministry in France which fell in December when it attempted payment on the American debt.

When the first of the new depression-generated governments, the British national coalition, took office in late August 1931, it faced acute financial emergency. Additional French and American credits provided a brief respite, but speculative pressure on the pound soon resumed. As Paris and New York could no longer afford massive credits, on 21 September the new Cabinet took the drastic step of abandoning the Gold Standard, the first major power to do so. The pound ceased to be a key reserve currency, and Britain abandoned its historic role as the world's financial leader – with no replacement in sight. Henceforth the pound sterling would no longer be convertible to gold at a fixed rate. In effect the pound was devalued in relation to other currencies to stop the panic and to stimulate exports by lowering the price of British goods abroad. While devaluation did not work an instant cure for Britain's adverse trade balance of imports over exports, it stemmed the London panic, but at the cost of a new collapse in stock prices on the continent, in the United States and in Japan. In Germany the Stock Exchange closed again on the day of British devaluation for nearly seven months.

The Depression was a global phenomenon which dominated the 1930s and made all problems worse, including national emotional and psychological ones. Internationalism was discredited and the democracies were self-absorbed, passive and committed to disarmament, while social unrest led some states to forceful foreign policies to distract from domestic woes and thus to rearmament, which provided jobs and economic stimulus. Britain and France were distracted by empire and focused on it to avoid imports costly in foreign exchange. This left Germany free to dominate east central Europe economically, creating dependence by exchanging German goods for the area's agricultural surpluses and – throughout the interwar era – linking economic and foreign policy, as Britain and France did not. In this respect and others, the Depression damaged what remained of the postwar treaty system and dented faith in international political solutions. It also reduced Britain's and France's world economic and political roles as they and the United States were preoccupied and disarmed, passively favouring peace through much of the decade in the face of potential threats to it.

In 1931 after the British devaluation, everywhere interest rates soared, firms failed, unemployment mounted and *annus terribilis* became more terrible as a chain reaction forced country after country to abandon or suspend the Gold Standard, which had been the world's financial yardstick. Others, including France and Italy, responded to the British devaluation by erecting high tariff barriers against potential British dumping of low-priced goods on their sickly markets. International trade contracted still further, and everywhere the Depression worsened, bringing more bank failures, more corporate failures, more unemployment and more stock-market collapses. In a burst of economic nationalism, desperate governments turned to import quotas, trade wars, high tariffs and export drives, most of which aggravated the situation. The Depression fed upon itself as every disaster in the interlocking industrial, commercial and financial world immediately generated many more, both within a given country and in the furthest reaches of the globe, demonstrating the horrifying interrelatedness of absolutely everything.

The reason why the Depression was so universal and so severe was that, in the twentieth century, the world's financial structure and trade patterns had become entirely interlocking. In the eighteenth century, the French government could reach virtual bankruptcy without Japan even knowing about it, much less being affected, but no longer. Late nineteenth-century imperialism, political and economic, had knit the world together. Now Britain and the United States were the two world-wide financial powers. Of these Britain had colonies and investments all over the globe and was heavily dependent on world trade. But it had spent its treasure in the First World War, remained in precarious economic and financial condition through the 1920s and was sensitive to economic contractions in the United States both directly and through reactions in central Europe, where the Bank of England was deeply committed financially. The United States had also become heavily involved in world trade as it acquired an empire and sought markets abroad for its endless bounty. More importantly the United States, which emerged from the First World War with its abundant wealth intact and no war debts to mention,[24] had now become the world's banker, everyone's source of investment capital and government loans. A precarious world-wide financial structure based on unsecured short-term loans had developed. If investor confidence remained unshaken and loans were not recalled, all was well, but when panic set in on Wall Street, Britain's problems multiplied. As the loss of confidence soon became universal, the chain reaction of disaster became global. The catastrophe was so unprecedented that nobody knew what to do.[25]

* * *

Before anybody could do anything, war broke out in East Asia. The new crisis exacerbated the old as the Tokyo stock exchange reacted violently, adding to the woes of other nations, particularly those several Western countries with substantial investments in Japan or China, the other party to the conflict. Here, by 1930, Chiang Kai-shek had become dominant and had gained control of much of China, including the allegiance of the local Manchurian warlord, but none the less Nationalist control of this northernmost region was nominal. Even so, Japan's treaty rights from 1915, including control of the South Manchurian Railway, seemed threatened. On 18 September 1931 an explosion on the railway north of Mukden (Shenyang) served as a pretext for skirmishes between Japanese troops guarding it and nearby Chinese forces, and for the enlargement of Japanese military activity thereafter toward the conquest of Manchuria.

The hostilities in Manchuria had been set off by local Japanese forces without the consent of the moderate Tokyo Cabinet. As the Japanese troops advanced, meeting little resistance because Chiang was too politically precarious to shift troops northward, they were not to be denied, and the progressively more feeble Tokyo government quickly lost control of the situation. In both China and Japan the pressures of public opinion escalated the affair into a major conflict, even creating a brief semblance of unity in China.

On 21 September the Chinese Nationalist regime appealed to the United States under the Kellogg-Briand Pact and to the League under Article 11 of the Covenant, which did not automatically require League action.[26] From the first, Chiang saw Manchuria as a prelude to a Japanese-American war which would save China. At the behest of Western leaders, who wanted to minimise both the conflict and League responsibility to act, he refrained from citing Articles 10 and 16, which would have required League action against Japan; he also refrained from declaring war and made no military resistance. Thus he was criticised for failure to defend nominally Chinese territories, and much was made of the fact that since neither party had declared war, no legal state of war existed.

The outbreak of hostilities and the consequent Chinese appeal caused much confusion at Geneva. The Depression had so thoroughly dominated all thought and action that the world of diplomacy was taken by surprise. Little reliable information was available about actual conditions in Manchuria and, given the slowness of communication then from that remote spot, little more was available for weeks to come. As there was a universal disinclination to act, much emphasis was placed on China's lack of control in Manchuria, on Japan's treaty right to station troops there, and on the argument that therefore events in Manchuria did not constitute the invasion of one sovereign state by another. On 30 September the League Council passed an empty resolution and adjourned, hoping that the situation would resolve itself. Meanwhile Japanese military advances continued.

Armed with the advantage of hindsight and possibly with a pro-Western bias, history has condemned Japan for the conquest of Manchuria. At the time, however, Western opinion was divided, with much sympathy for Japan as the representative of the civilised West in the barbarous east. As the ancient Chinese culture was non-Western, it was thought at best quaint and at worst primitive. The Chinese economy was chaotic and the political situation turbulent, so much so that some doubted China constituted a sovereign state within the meaning of the Covenant. Through the 1920s, rising Chinese nationalism had caused anti-foreign demonstrations and efforts to end the extra-territorial privileges of foreign settlements there, evoking hostility from Western powers determined to hold what they had. Japan, on the other hand, had Westernised with frenetic haste in the late nineteenth century to escape China's fate. Its law codes, government structure, industrial organisation and armed forces all imitated Western models. Its economy was sophisticated, its country apparently united, and its ministry moderate. In short, it was a 'civilised' nation to which many Western powers had close economic ties.

Even if the fact that Japan was engaged in conquering Manchuria was faced, what could be done? The League could hardly uphold Japan's action. Neither could it condemn or expel it, as Japan would veto motions to such ends. Even the lesser act of sending a commission of inquiry might inflame Japanese national-ism and doom the moderate ministry, whose lack of control was not widely recognised. Idealists talked of the force of world opinion, but it had no force as opinion was divided and Japan, where the war was immensely popular, was indifferent to it. Realists recognised that only military force could stop Japan, but who would supply it? For most countries, the League's concept of collective security rested upon an assumption that somebody else would supply the security. In fact keeping the peace depended, as always, upon the great powers. However, even in Britain, the major power where popular support for the League was strongest, the ordinary citizen assumed that other states would do the shooting, should matters ever come to that. In no nation was there much popular support for military action against Japan and no government seriously consid-ered it. In fact the only League members with any prospect of action were Britain and France and, in reality, neither could act nor considered Manchuria a vital interest. Britain had no fleet east of Malta and France none east of Algeria. After years of budget slash-ing, shrinking armies and naval disarmament, neither had the mili-tary power to embark on a course which, in any event, would probably bring down their depression-burdened Cabinets and invite Japanese retaliation against their trade and their Asian colonies. In 1932 in response to the crisis, Britain tacitly dropped its rule dating from 1919 that no war was to be expected in the next decade, allowing the military services to plan but not to spend, and resumed construction of a naval base at Singapore though govern-ment leaders – if not ardent imperialists – knew that Britain could not defend its Asian interests if war in Europe also threatened.[27]

The other two powers with the theoretical possibility of action were not members of the League. Russia remained warily neutral, as it was preoccupied with European and domestic problems and unprepared for an Asian war. While starting a rapid military build-up in lightly defended Siberia and denouncing Japanese imperialism, the Soviet Union even-handedly remarked that it differed little from Western imperialism in China.[28] Britain quietly echoed this sentiment in other terms, noting that in view of its own actions at Shanghai in 1927, it could hardly condemn Japan.

As those few who sought action looked for somebody else to take it, the last remaining somebody was the United States where the prevailing mood was overwhelmingly isolationist, racist, hostile to the League, and preoccupied with the Depression. Neither Chinese nor Japanese were popular after decades of talk about the 'yellow peril'. Recent landings in several circum-Caribbean states tied up troops and created an embarrassing comparison, while a tiny army and a navy noticeably smaller than Japan's also inhibited action. In Washington there was comprehension of military inadequacy but only moderate awareness of the possibility of future Japanese-American conflict. While counsels were divided, Manchuria was not a vital American interest and there was a general inclination to let the League take the lead. Like everybody else, Washington said, 'After you'.

In the circumstances it is not surprising that nothing was done. Disarmament, disunity, depression and public indifference had rendered impossible any collective action against open aggression by a major power, if indeed it ever had been possible. The League, unable to evade the issue altogether, assiduously avoided action and limited itself to hollow phraseology. As Japan bombed Manchurian towns, China gained a special session of the League Council in mid-October with an American observer actually in attendance. The Council passed a resolution urging Japanese withdrawal within three weeks, which was not binding as Japan voted against it, and adjourned until mid-November. In Manchuria the Japanese troops marched on, undeterred by an increasingly chaotic China or by political and economic upheavals in Japan.

When the Council met in November Japan rejected Chinese offers of arbitration or judicial settlement. In secret sessions accompanied by small-power protests and further Japanese advances in Manchuria, Britain strenuously opposed economic

sanctions, knowing by then that the United States would not participate and that sanctions could thus accomplish little except
Japanese retaliation against Britain's battered trade balance.
Finally, in open sessions on 9 and 10 December, the Council again
called for Japanese withdrawal but without a time limit. Japan
could, however, pursue 'bandits', a loophole affording ample
excuse for further military activity. The League also authorised a
five-man commission representing the four major European
powers and the United States, with Chinese and Japanese assessors
attached, to investigate on the spot. Thereupon it adjourned, able
to delay any further action until the commission's report was
received.

The commission, led by Lord Lytton of Britain, embarked on a
slow journey across the Atlantic, the United States and the Pacific,
reaching Tokyo more than two months later on 29 February 1932.
By then Japan had gained effective control of Manchuria, and on
9 March the puppet state of Manchukuo (Manzhouguo) was established under Japanese auspices. In anticipation of either a puppet
state or outright annexation, Washington had, for lack of an alternative, in January proclaimed Stimson's doctrine of non-recognition of the legality of either the *de facto* situation or any treaty
arising from it.[29] While this declaration aided China not one whit,
it was the first moral condemnation of Japanese aggression. The
other powers remained silent. In January, too, Japanese forces at
Shanghai's International Settlement became involved in conflict
with the Chinese and fighting continued for more than a month,
alarming Western powers which had economic interests there.
Stimson had wanted to warn Japan away from Shanghai and to
reinforce the Anglo-American contingents there, but the British
refused. As fighting continued, Stimson favoured naval demonstrations at a safe distance and appeal to the 1922 Nine Power Pact,
but Britain, torn between offending Japan and offending the
United States, waffled and wavered, so nothing was done. By early
March a ceasefire was in effect in Shanghai and the Japanese soon
began to withdraw.

Throughout the months the League waited to hear from Lord
Lytton, while small powers with a vested interest in maintaining the
League's viability and no risk of direct involvement themselves
protested major power inaction. Their efforts led the Assembly on
11 March to salvage its honour by endorsing non-recognition.

While this would not save Manchuria, the great powers would not go further as each was preoccupied with the Depression and domestic politics. London, further preoccupied with Empire and the forthcoming Ottawa Conference, was increasingly hostile to Japan but unwilling to act without Paris and Washington. In both capitals elections soon ruled out any action, while all three states lacked the military capacity to act. Thus the powers pursued a very limited policy with even more limited results.

* * *

While Japan was mopping up Manchuria, the Disarmament Conference opened at Geneva on 2 February 1932, delayed so the League Council could address the fighting at Shanghai. The mistiming was typical of its history. Among the 59 delegations the conference's saddest figure was its chairman and only true believer, Arthur Henderson, the former British Labour Foreign Secretary.[30] If one man's will could have made the conference a success, it would have been. Henderson had devoted much of his life to disarmament and regarded the conference as the pinnacle of his career. His superhuman efforts were unavailing and he was a broken man when the conference ended, dying soon thereafter. The failure of the conference was foreordained. Most delegates knew that the time was not ripe for disarmament, what with battleships abuilding in Germany, sabres rattling in Italy, bombs bursting in Manchuria, and rearmament in progress in Russia and also in France to a degree. Furthermore: 'The Germans demanded payment in the coin of French and Polish disarmament; the French in the coin of British and American commitments; the British in the coin of French disarmament and American commitments – and so on through the whole catalogue of sovereign self-centred nations.'[31]

Beyond that, the irreducible problem dominating the several intermittent sessions of the conference through 1932 and 1933 was that Germany demanded equality while France insisted upon security, but if Germany gained equality, France had no security since Germany was larger and fundamentally stronger. Repeatedly Germany argued that other powers should disarm to its level (i.e., Versailles Treaty limits as adapted to the relative strength of the countries concerned) or variously that it should be allowed to rearm without restriction. A fear-driven France with an inherently weaker power-base and broader commitments could accept neither argument. There was much 'public pronouncing and private conversing'[32] and frequent adjournments when deadlock was reached. When meetings resumed after more private diplomacy, one delegation or another, often that of Britain, would present an elaborately worded scheme to paper over the divide. Proposal after proposal foundered on the sharp rock of irreconcilable conflict between German equality and French security.[33]

* * *

Throughout the interminable disarmament debates, Brüning and his successors argued that concessions must be made to Berlin to prevent Hitler's accession to power, as Brüning had insisted ever since September 1930. No evidence suggests that additional concessions would have had any effect beyond generating demands for even more, but in 1932 events in Germany seemed to give some force to the argument, for the Hitlerian tide was at the flood. Germany had four national elections in 1932: two presidential and two for the Reichstag, along with state and municipal elections. In all the Nazis did well. Hindenburg was re-elected President, but Hitler finished a solid second in both the initial round and the run-off, collecting 11 million votes. He was now established as the second man in Germany, and since the first was 85 years old and semi-senile, Hitler was marked as the coming man. Brüning was responsible for Hindenburg's victory and so the Old Gentleman, with his customary gratitude, dismissed him on 30 May 1932, ending the last German ministry with a vestige of legitimacy. Brüning's successors, Franz von Papen and General Kurt von Schleicher, were unknown figures lacking popular support. Foreign policy remained unchanged, particularly in demanding concessions to forestall Hitler, but they governed by presidential decree, especially since the Nazis hit their peak in the Reichstag elections of July 1932, taking 37 per cent of the vote, 230 seats and the presidency of the Reichstag as the largest party. The miseries of the Depression sent many to the support of the man who vowed to break the Versailles *Diktat* and rearm Germany. It was cold comfort to nervous neighbouring states that in another Reichstag election in November, the Nazis lost seats. Their interior disarray and financial distress were not public knowledge, and the Nazis remained Germany's largest party.

Germany was not the only country to undergo political turbulence during 1932. Elsewhere the leadership was also aged, ailing and failing. In Poland the elderly Pilsudski was enfeebled. In France Briand, frail and semi-senile, was forced from office by a Cabinet crisis in January to that end.[34] He died in March, leaving only Chamberlain of the Locarno triumvirate alive but inactive. In the course of parliamentary elections early in May, which showed a swing to the left, the President of France was assassinated, causing an intense crisis and new presidential elections. Herriot formed a ministry and survived in power until December. In Britain the elderly MacDonald continued in office, but failing eyesight necessitated repeated surgery and a less detailed direction of policy. His Foreign Secretary, Simon, was competent in the daily conduct of affairs but without commitment to any course of action. Across the Atlantic, the November election repudiated Hoover as the Depression worsened. In the four month hiatus before Franklin Roosevelt could be inaugurated, the United States ground to an economic standstill.

Throughout 1932 economic turbulence also continued unabated, even more widespread than political instability. Prices tumbled and tariff walls rose. During the year, a universal tariff war developed as each country tried to protect sinking domestic markets from foreign competition. Britain, which in 1931 had legislated its proudest interwar achievement, transforming part of the British Empire into the British Commonwealth of Nations, complicated the tariff tangle by gaining at the Ottawa Conference of August 1932 an increase in imperial or commonwealth preference, the tariff reduction given among members of the British imperial family. This helped British exports but not those of countries outside the family, particularly since protectionist new duties were imposed against non-members. As the world economic situation deteriorated still further with normal trade channels entirely clogged and currencies unstable, some nations, Russia among them, reverted to primitive barter arrangements for exchange of goods without reference to money. In paralysed central Europe, barter became commonplace.

As central Europe demonstrated, one effect of the Depression was to exacerbate existing problems, be they social, political, financial, or ethnic. In hitherto stable Czechoslovakia where the German minority had largely come to accept and participate in the existing regime, the Depression hurt the industrialised Germanic borderlands far more than the agricultural Bohemian plains. While Prague took energetic relief measures, Germanic discontent swelled for Hitler to capitalise on later. Yugoslavia nearly shattered into its component parts as an Italian-supported Croatian revolt broke out in 1932. Even Western Europe showed ethnic strains as tension in otherwise peaceful Belgium mounted between Flemings and Walloons. Austria was spared ethnic problems but had all others. A weak financial structure weakened further as Austria was the first country to collapse. Tension between the ruling conservative Catholic party and the socialists of Vienna intensified steadily. As in Czechoslovakia, local Nazis were preparing the future. In addition a right-wing nationalist *putsch* in September 1931 was suppressed at socialist insistence, but the Catholic party remained in control of the government. Incidents between it and the Vienna socialists, along with Nazi-generated unrest, led to the abandonment of parliamentary democracy early in 1933 and the advent of rule by decree.[35]

From one end of Europe to the other, politics veered to the extremes of left and right. The trend was perhaps most marked in Spain where, having nudged its king into exile in 1931, the country suffered an alternating series of right-wing and left-wing regimes, completely divided on matters social, religious and political, until the Spanish Civil War of 1936–9 settled the matter bloodily. In Germany not only Nazism but also communism gained adherents, and the two movements battled in the streets. As there were so many unemployed, there were plenty to fight. In Bulgaria there was a sharp swing to the left, not only nationally but in the Sofia municipal elections, which the Communists won in 1932. Greek politics entered a state of total flux with acute tension between the rising royalists and ebbing republicans. The failure of republican *coups* in 1933 and 1935 led finally to restoration of the monarchy and soon to dictatorship.

Dictatorship seemed the only solution to the social and political pressures generated by the Depression, especially in countries lacking a long tradition of political stability. Stalin had no unrest to contend with. Nor did Pilsudski and Mussolini. While both states suffered economically and Italy was nearly forced off the Gold Standard, dictatorship ensured political and social stability. Romania and Yugoslavia went into royal dictatorship in 1931. In

Hungary a financial collapse caused by the Austrian banking crisis led to League intervention, unpopular financial stringencies, and Fascist dictatorship in 1932. Other countries took a little longer to reap the whirlwind. For some, the harvest did not come home until the Second World War. But misery was universal in 1932, and everywhere most people hoped to alleviate their distress at the expense of some other social, political, or ethnic entity. This fact had been evident during meetings in London in August 1931 to work out some technicalities of the Hoover moratorium and became increasingly apparent as the end of the Hoover year neared.

* * *

Through the mounting distress of 1932, while harried Cabinets coped with immediate political, economic and social problems, they had another worry: what to do when the Hoover moratorium expired on 1 July? As Congressional hostility to debt cancellation precluded further action by Hoover in a presidential election year, reparations and war-debt payments would resume unless some solution were found. Of necessity Hoover left it to the European powers. It was fairly widely recognised that neither Germany nor its creditors were in fit condition to pay what they owed. Berlin insisted that sweeping concessions, preferably cancellation, were as essential in reparations as in disarmament, both for financial reasons and to halt Hitler. Germany's hard-pressed creditors, several of them fearful for their security, were reluctant to see the end of reparations or to abandon any prospect of their own financial relief, particularly since war debts would remain to be paid, whatever happened to reparations. They tended to argue that if Germany could afford to rearm, it could afford to pay reparations. France sought a German political moratorium regarding the Polish Corridor in particular and modification of the Versailles Treaty in general in return for a cancellation which it was reluctant to make but soon recognised to be inescapable.[36] Germany, knowing also that cancellation was obtainable, held firm against endorsement of the political *status quo* and, as negotiations progressed, pointed to its electoral returns.

The probability of some variety of cancellation heightened as an intense Congressional reaction prevented extension of the Hoover moratorium and British financial circles threw their weight behind outright cancellation. Then another special committee of the

Bank for International Settlements, convened under clauses of the Young Plan concerning postponement of German annuities, reported in late December 1931 that postponement of the conditional annuities would be appropriate but entirely inadequate. The committee hinted in the broadest terms at the necessity for all-around cancellation of reparations and war debts to hasten economic recovery.[37]

Britain summoned a conference of the Young Plan countries at Lausanne in January 1932. It was postponed first by a long French political crisis, then by French and German elections, and finally by lack of agreement on what to do. Britain, Germany and Italy wanted full cancellation of reparations; France did not. It was willing to reduce reparations to the extent that its debts were reduced and to be accommodating about modes of payment, but not to forego the net profit it gained in the reparations-debts cycle of the Young Plan. As Britain, Germany and the United States all had serious credit problems, they wished to give priority to private debts over public. France had nothing to gain and much to lose from such a move, but much to gain from a united Anglo-French front against Washington on the debt question. Britain refused that. As each country sought maximum advantage, London and Paris discussed an all-European moratorium on reparations and debts, leaving the American question for post-election resolution. Britain and France could not agree on its duration, while Berlin abruptly declared that no moratorium of any length was acceptable.[38] Only outright cancellation in full would, in its eyes, restore the German economy and financial structure. While the absolute conjunction between reparations and the German financial crisis was absurd over-simplification, it was widely believed by the German citizenry and, not surprisingly, Berlin adhered without deviation to this line.

The end of the Hoover year was approaching. Accordingly, while little was agreed, Britain and France drafted a masterly invitation, which avoided all mention of reparations or war debts, for a conference at Lausanne in mid-June to effect a 'lasting settlement'.[39] By the time that it met, the disarmament conference was nearing the end of its first long dreary session, which adjourned on 23 July. Two simultaneous huge conferences strained diplomatic resources to the limit as skeleton staffs tended Foreign Ministries at home while harried statesmen shuttled from Geneva to

Lausanne. When Germany recognised that full cancellation was not obtainable, it tried to link the two conferences, demanding full rearmament as the price for one final token reparations payment.

When the Lausanne Conference convened on 16 June with MacDonald presiding, it first suspended German reparations and inter-Allied non-American debt payments for the duration of the conference, thus obviating the need to finish before 1 July. It also agreed to hold the American problem in abeyance until the European one was solved. Then agreement ceased. It took all of MacDonald's genial skill as chairman to avoid collapse. In the end agreement was reached only because the sole alternative of reversion to the Young Plan was out of the question. Accordingly several misleading documents were initialled on 9 July.[40]

Under the Lausanne Convention, Germany was to make a final lump-sum payment of three milliard gold marks in government bonds to the Bank for International Settlements immediately after the Convention was ratified and entered force. After a three-year moratorium, the Bank could market the bonds if German financial conditions permitted. As the Lausanne Convention was never ratified, the bonds were never transferred. That this prospect had been considered is evident in the fact that allocation of the three milliard was left for later decision and in the signature by the four principal recipients of a 'Gentleman's Agreement' that they would not ratify the Convention until war-debt relief was obtained from Washington. The moratorium on inter-Allied debts and German payments would continue until the Lausanne Convention went into effect, cancelling the reparations clauses of the Young Plan and Hague Agreements. Subsidiary documents extended the moratorium on non-German reparations until December and established a committee to work out a solution in the interim, created another committee to tackle the financial and economic reconstruction of central and eastern Europe, and issued a call for a world economic and monetary conference to seek solutions to the world crisis.[*]

Thus ended reparations. The Lausanne Agreements sparked

---

[*] When the World Economic Conference finally met in June 1933, its efforts at currency stabilisation were torpedoed by Roosevelt's refusal to cooperate. Thereafter it died a lingering death. On this topic see Patricia Clavin, *The Failure of Economic Diplomacy: Britain, Germany, France and the United States, 1931–36* (New York, 1996).

much resentment in Germany, where full cancellation had been anticipated as an absolute right. Since the Gentleman's Agreement and Washington's refusal of debt cancellation were published at once, it was obvious that the final payment was merely a paper fiction, a sop to French opinion, but Germany was insulted and the results showed in the July election returns. The Gentleman's Agreement called in effect for another conference if the Lausanne Convention failed of ratification, but it was never held as reparations were overtaken by events and the futility of inviting Hitler to discuss payment was evident to all. Reparations quietly fell into limbo, a victim of German revisionism and world depression. Over the years from the Armistice to the Hoover moratorium, Germany had paid about 21.5 milliard marks, slightly over the amount it was committed by the Versailles Treaty to pay by 1 May 1921.[41] This not very grand total, less than a third of it in cash – mostly borrowed, included credits for transferred properties and deliveries in kind under the Versailles Treaty and all subsequent reparations plans. Hungary and Bulgaria had paid some reparations, mostly in properties ceded, but not much. Turkey and Austria had effectively paid nothing at all. The tangled history of reparations demonstrated the futility of imposing large indemnities on destitute or powerful nations. The smaller states could not pay and Germany would not. While it is arguable whether Germany could have entirely fulfilled the 50 milliard marks of the original London Schedule of Payments, it could have paid more than it did, had it seen any reason to do so. But as it chose not to pay, it won in the end at tremendous cost to itself and others. Reparations generated a huge bureaucracy, endless conferences and intense ill-will, all for very little. Their failure only increased the power imbalance, as debt and reconstruction costs were transferred from Germany to the victors. In the end they contributed to and complicated the Great Depression, but their concealed demise did nothing to alleviate the economic crisis.

Reparations were laid to rest, but war debts were not. In December some governments managed to scrape up their payments while others defaulted. In France the Herriot government fell over the issue. In 1933 everybody defaulted except three non-European countries and Finland, each with small debts and correspondingly minuscule payments, which continued regularly. However, First World War debts to the United States were not cancelled, and the United States Treasury continued to compute the amounts owed, which multiplied as interest compounded.[42]

* * *

While the European powers struggled toward a reparations settlement in the spring and summer of 1932, they put far-away Manchuria out of mind, but the Lytton Commission was at work investigating the situation in Japan, Manchuria and China. Its unanimous report was signed in Peking (Beijing) on 4 September and shipped to Geneva via the trans-Siberian railway, arriving too late for the Assembly meeting in mid-September. When the contents of the report became known in early October, there was dismay in Geneva. By then most countries had accepted the *fait accompli* in Manchuria and hoped that time would bury the matter. The Lytton Report[43] did not accelerate that process.

The all-Western Lytton Commission praised Japanese Westernisation, criticised Chinese lack of it, and lauded Japanese contributions to Manchuria's economic development, but it sustained China on the key points, judging that Japan was responsible for the puppet regime, which lacked any local Chinese support. The report recommended its removal, restoration of Chinese sovereignty, and autonomy for Manchuria, along with numerous foreign advisers, many of them Japanese. The League Council met in late November to consider these unwelcome proposals, which ignored reality on the ground, and passed the problem to the Assembly, which met in early December. There some small states urged condemnation of Japan while the major powers stressed 'complexities' and 'conciliation'.[44] As agreement seemed impossible, a committee was charged with seeking one. It devoted the next two months to a hopeless task.

Yet still the East Asian crisis, like the continuing disarmament deadlock, would not subside quietly. On 1 January 1933, after another suspicious railway incident, Japanese forces crossed the Chinese frontier into the province of Jehol (Rehe),[45] which Japan claimed was part of Manchuria. They progressed easily, generating Western scorn at Chinese weakness and taking the provincial capital on 4 March. The primacy of the military in Japanese policy formulation was now clear. By then the League Assembly had on 24 February 1933, in the face of renewed Japanese aggression, finally adopted the Lytton Report, with 42 states voting for it, Japan voting against it, and Siam abstaining. After 17 months of dither, this completed League action. The Japanese delegation left the hall. In March it left Geneva altogether as Japan formally withdrew from the League, the first great power to do so, but retained its island mandates.

Meanwhile the Depression deepened again and the disarmament disputes dragged on, with German representatives rarely in attendance. But events elsewhere overshadowed the squabbles of Geneva and European eyes turned to Berlin, where on 30 January 1933 Adolf Hitler became the last Chancellor of the Weimar Republic. That long-dreaded event had finally occurred and, in the months to come, the Hitlerian transformation of the Weimar Republic into the totalitarian Third Reich dominated diplomatic concern, especially in neighbouring states but throughout Europe as well, as each nation sought to assess what the new situation meant for it. Few of Europe's leaders thought the change boded better times ahead. The three years past had destroyed optimism and drained hope almost to the dregs.

6   The End of Old Illusions

Some have assumed that most Western leaders were slow to recognise what Hitler's accession to power meant. One hears about relief that Germany's political turbulence had ended and that finally Germany had a government which could command a majority in the Reichstag, along with hope that power would tame Hitler and that he really did not mean what he said. Such notions were common and perhaps understandable, but they were rarely found in the ministries of European governments. Nobody fully envisaged the horrors ahead and most Western diplomatists misjudged Hitler's intentions towards Poland, thinking that like his predecessors he sought frontier revision, when in fact he cast Poland as an obedient satellite and then, after Poland rejected this role, saw it as an entity to be destroyed *en route* to Russia.[1] But on the main issue there was, especially at first, little illusion. Most of Europe's leaders realised that Nazism was a threat to Europe's peace and that in the long run Hitler intended war. In April 1933 Herriot informed an American visitor, 'we shall have to fight them again',[2] whereas MacDonald told his son, 'I shall not see peace again in my lifetime; I hope you will see it in yours.'[3]

Such illusions as existed arose from desperation and were nourished by Hitler's early diplomatic caution. As he had insisted upon coming to power legally rather than by a putsch, so also was he Adolf *légalité* in foreign affairs until he had established control in Germany, ended unemployment by rearmament and public works with military application such as highways, and multiplied the military instruments at his command. In October 1933, Hitler withdrew Germany from the Disarmament Conference and from the League, dismaying but not astounding most diplomatists. None the less, he continued to speak the language of Geneva. It suited Hitler to talk of peace while he prepared for war.

* * *

Under the circumstances, the German people were as unclear as electorates elsewhere about Hitler's intentions. He was immensely popular, especially as 'Nazi propaganda portrayed Hitler as a man of peace pursuing justifiable revisions of the humiliating Versailles Treaty',[4] one topic on which a divided nation was entirely unified and on which Hitler skilfully enlarged the national sense of grievance. At first his foreign policy seemed traditional in methods and goals, but breaking the last Versailles Treaty fetters and fully restoring Germany's great power status were only prerequisites to wider aims.

These aims rested on an ideology of race and space (meaning arable land), but far more literally than most realized. Psychologically bruised Germans needed somebody to sneer at. Hitler gave them the Jew – and they did not know that his anti-Semitism would go to its ultimate logical conclusion: mass extermination of millions. To Germans, space meant regaining territories lost under the Versailles Treaty and absorbing other Germanic areas. Hitler obliged, completing Weimar's goals, with mass support through 1938. However, his aims were initially pan-European, later nearly global, and his intended instrument was war. By late 1937, Germany was Europe's strongest power, rearming briskly, and Hitler was set upon war. But in September 1938, Berliners demonstrated their opposition to war, forcing – with other factors – Hitler to delay military conquest for almost a year.

His territorial goals expanded over time, but the European ones were fixed from the outset. Though France must be humiliated to avenge 1918, space meant the Russian plains in a state he deemed both Jewish and communistic; here a pure Germanic master race, untainted by inferior blood or by physical, psychological or mental defects, would create an agricultural peasant society – with the 'subhuman' Slavs expelled, enslaved, or slaughtered. Hitler planned in stages toward this end and later larger ones, but was flexible and opportunistic about the means to them, especially when some states, such as Poland and Britain, did not play their assigned roles. He personally dictated foreign policy and was hard-headed about international politics as he sought a free hand to conquer Europe and continuous expansion. In large part, he dictated events in the 1930s and others reacted. Hitler capitalised on the West's fear of war and love of peace, knowing that democracies rarely engage in preventive wars, which cost lives. In those years, especially at first, he concentrated on rearmament, economic self-sufficiency, economic domination of the distressed Balkans, and gaining the last advantage from the Versailles Treaty, return of the Saar Basin in 1935, meanwhile speaking in pacific tones.

* * *

Among those who were not deceived by Hitler's protestations of peaceful intentions was Stalin. Anti-imperialist propaganda ceased abruptly and Litvinov remained Foreign Minister until 1939 while Hitler put his anti-Semitic creed increasingly into practice in Germany. In September 1934, Russia joined the League of Nations, which it had for so long denounced, and Litvinov was soon Geneva's leading apostle of collective security. Stalin foresaw war and wished to remain neutral until other powers were exhausted and Russia could be decisive. He also feared isolation and a possible capitalist war against him; this fear dictated alliance with or against Germany. So he played a double game, approaching both the West and Hitler, who had cancelled the Rapallo tie and who denounced communism regularly. In 1935, he signed a defensive alliance with Paris to which neither power was truly committed, and a contingent one with Prague, whereby Russia would defend the Czechs if France did. But after Stalin's purges of potential opponents from 1936 on decimated his military leadership, Britain and France, who were almost as hostile as Hitler to communism, dismissed the Red Army's potential. Like other nations, Russia hoped to divert Hitler elsewhere; it feared that the West sought a German-Soviet war just as the Western powers feared Stalin was trying to lure them into war against Germany; as with other states, in threatening times national interest took precedence over ideology. In 1939 Stalin accepted that the West wanted him to fight Hitler without territorial reward and that Britain and France, especially Britain, were not serious about an alliance. Hitler suddenly offered much Polish and Baltic territory in return for Soviet non-belligerence; Stalin accepted, enabling Hitler's invasion of Poland a week later on 1 September 1939, launching the Second World War in Europe.[5]

Meanwhile, Czechoslovakia had felt the force of Nazi propaganda in its large German minority early on.[6] It reinforced its security by the pact with Russia and moved to strengthen the Little

Entente into a formal organisation with a permanent structure. Moves to this end had begun in 1929 in response to Mussolini's attempt to dominate Danubia, but the organisation envisaged then and in 1932 planning sessions had become far more extensive by 1933, including regular general-staff consultations, partly in response to Hitler's advent.[7] The new organisation did immediate and successful battle in 1933 against Mussolini's proposal for a Four Power Pact.

This proposal was Mussolini's reaction to Hitler's accession. While relieved that Hitler displayed no concern for the Germanic South Tyrol, Mussolini was alarmed by his obvious interest in Austria. So Mussolini not only sought to strengthen his diplomatic position by a plan to revive a great power Concert of Europe but also, by proposing territorial revisions, to distract Hitler from the Danube and appease him at the expense of Poland. As the equally threatened Little Entente reacted sharply, France could hardly jettison all its eastern allies at once and so declined to sign Mussolini's document until it was diluted to the point of meaning-lessness. Hitler himself had no interest in the Polish corridor and much disliked multilateral pacts, preferring bilateral treaties as easier to break when the time came. He too signed the Four Power Pact, one of the few multilateral arrangement he ever accepted, only when it had been thoroughly emasculated.[8]

Italy was not strong enough to disrupt world peace greatly, but its local power could threaten both Britain and France in the Mediterranean and, having rearmed early, it had a serious military force in being. For these reasons, because it could block *Anschluss*, and to keep it from joining Germany, Britain and France courted Mussolini, Britain persistently but without much real effect, France until his appetite for French territory in Africa and Europe became evident. Despite this attention, Mussolini soon felt overshadowed by Hitler, despite much flattery from him. Mussolini also sought war, but only small ones, preferably outside Europe. These impulses led his erratic personality and policy into conquest of Ethiopia in 1935–6 and substantial involvement in the Spanish Civil War of 1936–9 – along with Germany's lesser role there. These in turn led to isolation except for Hitler's support and thus lured him into the Nazi camp, removing the barrier to *Anschluss* which occurred in March 1938. Anglo-French reactions to Mussolini's actions were weak and ambivalent owing to disarmament (particularly in relation to large commitments), dread of war and of losing Italy to Germany, depression, domestic division in France and electoral politics in Britain, and especially reluctance to take their eyes off the main threat which they knew to be Hitler.[9]

Poland was nearly paralysed with fear. Under the leadership of the failing Pilsudski, it came to terms with Hitler and signed a Polish-German Non-aggression Declaration in January 1934 to match the similar treaty with Russia signed in July 1932.[10] What else to do? To seek any real refuge in Russia's arms was unthinkable. Thereafter Poland, whose concerns were peace and the *status quo*, tried to maintain a precarious balance between its two dangerous neighbours. The tension eased for a time as Hitler chose to placate Poland temporarily, but the Franco-Russian alliance raised new fears of domination from the other direction. Poland's dilemma of equal perils from east and west engendered continuing paralysis until the German and Russian armies almost simultaneously invaded in 1939. To the south, Austria was similarly paralysed, especially after an abortive Nazi *coup* in Vienna in 1934. On that occasion Mussolini massed troops on the Brenner Pass. Thereafter a frightened Austria, torn by domestic dissension, placed its hopes in Italian protection, which ebbed as Hitler courted Mussolini.[11]

In the West paralysis set in to a degree in Belgium as well but took a little longer. It pressed on with new vigour to complete its frontier fortifications and, unlike France, proceeded to rearm regardless of budget deficits, assuming another war to be inevitable. Belgium also wasted no time in seeking a British guarantee. As early as February 1933, the Belgian Foreign Ministry began a series of efforts to this end. With their failure, Belgium displayed a certain fatalism along with growing fear that French commitments in eastern Europe, especially the Russian tie, would drag Belgium into an unwanted war with Germany. As a consequence, Belgian policy became increasingly ostrich-like.[12]

In France, too, the initial reaction was swift. In March 1933 the French Premier and Foreign Minister were startlingly forthright in spelling out the danger to their British counterparts.[13] Completing the Maginot Line, rebuilding the navy, and reorganising the air force were urgent, but military appropriations were slashed at first to balance budgets shrunk by the depression, and then rearmament was slowed until late 1936 by the knowledge of a succession of weak cabinets that deficit financing could not carry the

Chamber. As additional security was imperative, especially as France was now in the 'lean years' of a smaller army because of a lower birth rate during the First World War, Louis Barthou, a man of no illusions, moved in 1934 toward an eastern Locarno and, with its failure, on toward alliance with Russia, despite Polish dismay. But with his assassination in October 1934 during a state visit by King Alexander of Yugoslavia, the momentum slackened. As early as 1933, French leaders believed that Germany had already achieved numerical military superiority.[14] With continuing evidence of German rearmament and Nazi belligerence, especially the 1934 attempt in Austria and Hitler's announcement in March 1935 of open rearmament, France became more frightened. But the country was riven by divisive political scandals in 1934, and thereafter there was no agreement on how to face the external threat. Instead a bitter ideological battle was fought over whether to join Russia against Germany, to join Germany against Russia, or to stand fast against Germany without contaminating oneself by association with communism. The disunity and passivity damaged the eastern alliances[15] and caused a paralysis of the will evident in 1936 when Hitler openly remilitarised the Rhineland, repudiating the Locarno pacts and putting his army on France's frontier. In that year as well, advent of a leftist Popular Front coalition brought overdue but mistimed labour reforms which reduced production by 17%.[16] But late in 1936 a major military appropriation made the start of serious rearmament possible at last.

In Britain as in France, many people were reluctant to draw close either to communism or to Nazism. They tended to hope that Russia and Germany would fight and destroy each other, conveniently resolving the problem. The Foreign Office was less sanguine. The Hitlerian menace was recognised at once, but the instinct was to temporise, especially with Simon at the helm, while exhorting France to rearm. In January 1933, the British were delighted that the new French Air Minister was committed to disarmament. Their tune soon changed as they urged France to shoulder the burden but refused joint staff talks.[17] The traditional British disinclination to become committed on the continent was combined with growing awareness of the extreme inadequacy of Britain's military forces. Britain officially abolished its rule that no war need be expected for ten years in late 1933 after Hitler's advent,[18] but rearmament was slowed by economic and political factors. Shifting scarce skilled workers to defence contracts would snuff out a budding recovery in depressed industries, and in 1935 all three parties, sensing the prevailing mood, fought the general election on the incongruous platform of disarmament and collective security. Winston Churchill was in the political wilderness partly because he called for rearmament. The British people put their faith in collective security to be provided by somebody else and managed to believe, because they wanted to believe, that an enfeebled and discredited League, once its members were thoroughly disarmed, could stop aggression by Europe's most powerful and belligerent nation. When the election was safely past, the new Conservative government began quiet rearmament, but such a process, especially when quiet, requires much time.

British policy in the late 1930s was dominated by Neville Chamberlain (younger half-brother of Austen Chamberlain), the most forceful Cabinet member well before he became Prime Minister in 1937. He had a visceral hatred of both communism and war, a clear appreciation that Britain was badly over-extended and that war would end its great power status, and a stubborn faith, never abandoned, that Hitler was moderate and reasonable and so could be appeased by offering chunks of territory from his eastern neighbours. Chamberlain shared the national guilt complex about the Versailles Treaty[19] and felt that if Germany's grievances were addressed, it would settle down and war could be avoided, a view reinforced by some Dominions. As Hitler progressively proved him wrong, he did not reconsider.[20]

An additional complicating factor in the 1930s was deterioration of the crucial Anglo-French relationship, for Britain's mostly Francophobe leaders blamed France for Hitler's advent and for much thereafter,[21] including failure to meet German demands about rearmament and African colonies. The two countries appeased separately and together; Britain more often actively, France sometimes by doing nothing. Each was painfully aware of military weakness.[22] They found each other impossible but indispensable, and each assumed the other would be at its side should war come. But in 1935 Britain signed a naval accord with Germany in violation of the Versailles Treaty without consulting France, which fumed impotently, too dependent in view of its economic, demographic and military deficits to protest much. But it retaliated in kind in its dealings with Italy, contributing to the advent of the Italo-Ethiopian war. France focused entirely on Europe, not defending its interests vigorously. Britain of necessity had a broader view but defined its European interests very narrowly, not asking whether maintenance of France's evaporating power was a British interest and not granting staff talks until the spring of 1939. Both powers were half-hearted at best about the *status quo* and international order, seeking deals with Hitler, not facing his preference for war. The policies of both were born of weakness but often led to greater weakness. By late 1937 both were seriously rearming, but Germany had a sizeable head start.

In the United States, the situation was similar though rearmament came later. The nation was engulfed in Depression and overwhelmingly preoccupied with domestic concerns. Isolationist sentiment was all-powerful, particularly since the Atlantic Ocean seemed a more adequate barrier than the English Channel. Roosevelt, whose inclinations were internationalist but whose political instincts were acute, effectively withdrew from Europe altogether in 1933 when he put domestic politics ahead of international economic cooperation, indicating that the United States was no more selfless than other nations. While Roosevelt harboured no illusions about Hitler or about where Washington's interests lay, he gave primary attention to the domestic emergency and held foreign policy within the narrow limits prescribed by public opinion. As late as October 1937, Roosevelt tested the atmosphere with a speech proposing that international troublemakers be quarantined, but the reaction indicated that isolationism remained dominant. So also was pacifism. As the distance from Europe was greater, the American people insisted longer than their British brethren upon beating their swords into ploughshares. Chamberlain's tendency to dismiss the United States as all talk and no action did not encourage greater awareness. However, by the spring of 1939, Hitler forced reassessments in the Western democracies. Quiet Anglo-American cooperation began, as did Anglo-French staff talks, British and French opinion shifted, and the Anglo-French relationship improved as illusions about a reasonable Hitler faded.

* * *

It is because the Western democracies were slow to rearm that some have thought their leaders were slow to recognise the Hitlerian menace. On the contrary, the slowness of rearmament arose from the fact that these countries were democracies. Dictators do not have to concern themselves with public opinion, and Germany, Russia and Italy all rearmed rapidly. Japan, where the military men were now dominant, did the same, and in 1937 invaded China, setting off the Second World War in East Asia. But in the Western democracies such speedy rearmament was generally not possible. The Depression, with its almost universal initial credo of budget-balancing and fiscal stringency, played a role in deferring heavy military expenditures, as did acute internal dissension in some countries. In the first years after Hitler's accession, Belgium could abandon financial orthodoxy in favour of deficit spending for rearmament because it was united in its recognition of the threat and the appropriate response. An utterly divided France could not. But beyond these problems lay a deeper difficulty: the overwhelming commitment of Western Europeans and Americans to peace and disarmament.

Public opinion rarely participates to any large degree in the formulation of foreign policy, but it does set the outer limits of policy, especially when there is a strong tendency in any one direction. In the first years after Hitler's accession, the limits were narrow as popular enthusiasm for disarmament necessarily rendered impossible any policy with the slightest risk of force. Once public opinion is firmly set, it is usually slow to change unless an immediate, direct threat is perceived. Hitler was careful not to provide that threat for several years. In the interim the education of public opinion to a new view progressed, as always, very slowly except in some of Germany's immediate neighbours. And until public opinion shifted, there was no prospect that massive budgets for rearmament would be approved by parliaments, national assemblies, and congresses.

In part the Western democracies were reaping the harvest of the disarmament conference. In 1931 in anticipation of its commencement and in hopes of ensuring its success, there had been an intense world-wide propaganda campaign in favour of disarmament. While this effort had no effect in Italy or Russia, its message took root most deeply in the English-speaking world where, in those days, it was needed least. In 1931 the Oxford Union, cradle of future British political leaders, debated and carried a resolution that 'this House will not fight for King and Country'. Across the Atlantic, there was a widespread and growing belief that 'the munition makers were the merchants of death', a view soon reinforced by sensational public Congressional hearings on the armaments industry. In both countries peace movements were strong and becoming stronger.

Just as the Disarmament Conference opened in early 1932, Britain's leaders recognised the country's extreme military weakness and the need to educate the nation to the dangerous condition of the country's defences. However, they could hardly do so with disarmament hugely popular, the government officially committed to it, and a distinguished British statesman working desperately at Geneva to lead the nations to the light of disarmament and peace. Long before Hitler withdrew from the Disarmament Conference, French and British leaders realised that the deadlock could not be resolved and that nothing could be expected from the conference. Yet they did not know how to extricate themselves from it. Having just convinced the citizenry that disarmament was a sure and swift route to peace, and economical besides, they could hardly sound the tocsin, repudiate the conference, and demand expensive armaments. As no government wanted to incur the onus of killing the conference, it lingered on in diminished form into 1935, thus further postponing the reeducation of Europe's idealists. Then came the 1935 British election, which no party wished to lose by telling the unpalatable truth.

In time, Hitler provided enough direct threats to reverse public opinion, sooner in states close to Germany than in those more distant, but rarely soon enough. As long as he took Germanic areas – through 1938 – electorates and some governments saw at least partial justification for his actions. The failure of Britain and France to defend Czechoslovakia, which they deemed indefensible in view of their own weakness, and the great power conference at Munich (at Hitler's insistence without the Soviet Union, despite its treaty ties[23]) in September 1938 to give him the Germanic Czech borderlands he claimed caused some protest but no great outcry in the West, though it infuriated Hitler who had wanted war. But in March 1939, he seized the non-German remnant of Czechoslovakia, causing a revolution in public opinion in several states and a shift of policy by some governments, notably those of Britain and France. But this was less than six months before Hitler set off the Second World War by invading Poland.[24] Most political leaders in the democracies were prisoners of their electorates by choice or necessity, following more than leading. By the time those electorates faced the danger, the hour was late, particularly since modern weaponry cannot be created overnight. Through a number of crucial years, the politicians had told the people what they wanted to hear and had led them to accept the illusion of peace rather than taking the painful and costly decisions necessary to ensure its reality.

* * *

In 1918–19 at least a theoretical possibility existed of bringing Germany to recognise its defeat and of achieving a *modus vivendi* for coexistence with Soviet Russia, building a peace on what these great powers would accept. Fear of Bolshevism and lack of awareness of German opinion were only two of many reasons that this was not done, along with Allied division, preoccupation with the peace conference, and the miscalculations of mere mortals. In any event, devising a more stable basis for the states between Germany and Russia would have been very difficult at best as the peace settlement reduced but did not eliminate ethnic grievances, especially those of Germans, who often assumed that German rule over Poles was just but that the reverse was unjust. While the Versailles Treaty was far from a perfection which could not exist, it was also far from the degree of harshness ascribed to it in Germany and the English-speaking world. However, the belief that it was unjust was an important part of the interwar reality, as was the Anglo-American guilt complex, contributing substantially to the subsequent lack of enforcement[25] and the crumbling process, thus rendering the peace more unstable.

Throughout the interwar year, there was no firm foundation for permanent peace since three of the four strongest continental powers were intensely dissatisfied with the *status quo*. Italy lacked the power to disturb Europe's peace greatly, but Germany and Russia were strong states, steadily becoming stronger. As their strength grew so did their appetites, and they viewed the small nations on their borders as tempting morsels to be devoured at the first opportunity. Under the circumstances, the existing international structure lacked any aura of permanence. Yet, as crises mounted in the late 1930s, there was no agreement on whether, where, or when to make a stand. New World blacks fought for Ethiopia, European and American leftists in Spain for the

Republic, and British liberals demanded defence of Czechoslovakia, but the British and French Cabinets, weak, fearful and unwilling to risk loss of their great power status, chose none of these, miscalculating often and hoping that appeasement could avoid war and solidify peace.

It is a striking fact that, throughout the 1920s and to a degree in the 1930s, both the statesmen and the ordinary peoples of Europe kept searching for a basis for permanent peace but never found it. Subconsciously they seemed aware that the existing structure lacked solid foundations and provided little security to anybody. As the interwar era brought the democratic experiment to areas where it had hitherto been unknown and the war had heightened the political consciousness of voters in Western countries with longer democratic traditions, the statesmen could not ignore the deep-seated yearnings for peace of ordinary citizens. But as the statesmen could not build a stable peace on the foundation erected at Paris after the war, they fed their electorates on false hopes and pacified them with the illusion of peace. The camaraderie at Locarno and Thoiry, the solemn signing of the Kellogg-Briand Pact, the Hague's Conference on the Final Liquidation of the War, the soaring oratory of Geneva vowing eternal dedication to the impossible dream of collective security, and even the Munich Conference in part with Chamberlain's announcement of 'peace for our time', were all designed to reassure the nervous citizenry that the foundations of peace were firm. Over and over again, from 1920 on, the peoples of Europe were told that true peace had come at last, but somehow, despite a natural inclination to swallow the hopeful illusion, they sensed that it had not, recognising that the situation was inherently volatile. Unfortunately, as the threat to peace grew through the 1930s, so also did the tendency to take refuge in illusion.

That era both destroyed old illusions and created new ones as the late 1930s reaped what the 1920s had sown. Allied division and distrust, dislike of the ubiquitous Beneš (which affected events in 1938), economic frailty and ethnic hatred, disarmament and fear of Germany were all features of the 1920s, as was the collapse of democracy in so many states, starting with Italy, although that trend, like others, accelerated in the 1930s. The disintegration of the League was progressive as challenges became more acute, but after its failure in the Ethiopian crisis of 1935–6, it was dismissed as irrelevant, and few seriously believed any longer in collective security or the efficacy of disarmament to prevent war. The illusion that a fading France was 'too strong' was gone as well. Some still believed that Germany would settle down if given what it sought, responsibility might still tame Hitler, and that he did not mean what he said, but these were new illusions, born mostly of desperation. Equally illusory were widespread hopes that Japan would confine itself to China and that Germany and Russia would conveniently destroy each other, Belgium's effort to escape the storm by retreat into neutrality, and Chamberlain's beliefs that Britain could salvage its great power status if it avoided war, that France could protect Britain, and that he could bluff Berlin into quiescence by empty overtures to Moscow. Throughout the two decades and until the moment Hitler invaded Poland, both the miscalculations and the perpetual search for peace continued.

* * *

Clearly one of the leading characteristics of interwar Europe was instability of all varieties, political, economic, social and diplomatic. With rare exceptions, such domestic political and social stability as European countries enjoyed arrived in the wake of dictatorship, as one central or east European country after another abandoned any effort to impose democracy on unprepared populations, with the Balkans subsiding in the 1930s into royal or royal-backed dictatorships increasingly committed economically – and thus soon politically – to Germany.[26] Economically even the patchy prosperity of the late twenties rested on an impermanent and precarious base which shattered with startling suddenness. The fragile collective security afforded by the League of Nations proved to be similarly ephemeral. While small nations clung desperately, despite growing evidence to the contrary, to the hope that the League could save them from mighty and rapacious neighbours, the great powers devoted their oratory to concealing the fact that it could not and their energies to propping up a very fragile structure in hopes that its total collapse could be averted. The period 1935–6 showed that it could not.

One of the several causes of instability in interwar Europe was the fact that the political fragmentation inherent in the postwar peace settlement was either too great or not great enough. No serious consideration was given after the First World War to the forcible break-up of Germany and Russia, as both would have required the sustained use of arms and prolonged occupation, prospects unattractive to the war-weary victors, and even then, enforcement of German disunification – which the peacemakers did not desire – would be improbable without the unlikely cooperation of Soviet Russia. On the other hand, it was impossible to revert to prewar boundaries as the Habsburg Empire could not be reconstituted except by extended use of force, Poland could not be re-created without the transfer of some districts from Germany, and Communist Russia could not, given the prevailing climate of opinion, be allotted any more territory than the unavoidable minimum. And so the peacemakers chose a middle course, with all the dangers inherent in solutions which satisfied almost nobody and particularly dissatisfied those nations with the latent strength to alter the *status quo* in time. Clearly, the creation of a host of small, relatively weak states partly out of defunct empires, but also at the expense of great nations whose power had not been significantly reduced, generated a potentially explosive situation. While the fuse proved to be 20 years long, it was evident from the outset that the *cordon sanitaire* was ineffectual in every sense and an invitation to German and Russian aggression once the time was ripe and the fuse had burnt down.

Another cause of instability was the fact that political fragmentation necessitated a compensatory economic integration which did not occur. Indeed, ancient hostilities and rivalries, heightened by the creation of east European national states and the advent of intense political and economic nationalism, rendered economic cooperation an impossibility despite the obvious need and the heartfelt hopes of both the peacemakers and Europe's business leaders. Above all, interwar Europe was dominated by political and ethnic nationalism, invariably strident and jealous, almost always selfish and short-sighted. Perhaps the eruption of this pent-up nationalism was inescapable in the aftermath of a war which dissolved the restraints which had contained it for a century. Yet its tactless exercise contributed to the development, once the new and inadequate restraints of the Versailles Treaty had also dissolved, of the most virulent and dangerous nationalism of all, that of Nazi Germany under Adolf Hitler.

In retrospect much of the instability of the interwar international structure arose from Germany's consistent refusal to accept its circumstances. Without German revisionism to disturb the tranquillity of Europe, many problems would probably have dissipated over time as new nations became more mature and their minorities partially assimilated. But the advent of Hitler indicated that Germany's discontent was being translated into the will and capacity to act forcibly. Most West European leaders knew how fragile the foundation of peace was and recognised at once that Hitler intended to smash it.[27] They knew too, that only the Western democracies, possibly in reluctant combination with the distrusted Soviet regime, had sufficient power potential to counter this obvious threat to peace. Yet they were unable to meet the threat because public opinion had swallowed the comforting illusion that peace could be ensured by collective security entrusted to a limping League of disarmed nations. Given Adolf Hitler in full control of Europe's most powerful and most dissatisfied state, it certainly could not, if ever it could have been. It is not only ironic but also tragic that, aside from Hitler's aggressive aims and his single-minded pursuit of them, the major factor forcing Europe toward the Second World War was the intense yearning of the Western democracies for peace, however illusory.

Chronological Table

1915	18 January	Japan's 21 Demands on China
	26 April	Allied-Italian Treaty of London
	25 May	Sino-Japanese agreements
	24 October	McMahon Pledge to Sharif Hussein
1916	16 May	Sykes-Picot agreement on Middle East
1917	2 November	Balfour Declaration on Palestine
	7 November	Lenin's *coup* in Russia
1918	8 January	Wilson's Fourteen Points
	17 February	British forces land in Transcaucasus
	3 March	Russo-German Treaty of Brest-Litovsk
	5 April	Japanese occupy Vladivostok
	23 June	British forces land at Murmansk
	4 October	Germany requests an armistice
	30 October	Turkish unconditional surrender
	3 November	Austro-Hungarian Armistice
	6 November	Pre-Armistice agreement with Germany
	11 November	German Armistice
1919	18 January	Paris Peace Conference opens
	14 February	League of Nations Covenant approved
	4 March	Comintern founded at Moscow
	24 March	Council of Four begins
	28 March	Hungary invades Slovakia
	29 March	China leaves Peace Conference
	7 May	Versailles Treaty presented to Germany
	28 June	Versailles Treaty signed; First Minorities Treaty

	10 September	Treaty of Saint-Germain-en-Laye with Austria
	12 September	D'Annunzio seizes Fiume
	12 October	British evacuate Murmansk
	27 November	Treaty of Neuilly with Bulgaria
1920	10 January	Versailles Treaty enters into force
	2 February	Russo-Estonian peace treaty of Tartu (Dorpat)
	16 March	Allies occupy Constantinople
	19 March	Final US Senate defeat of Versailles Treaty
	4 April	France occupies Frankfurt
	18–26 April	San Remo Conference
	25 April	Polish offensive against Russia
	4 June	Treaty of Trianon with Hungary
	6 July	Russian offensive against Poland
	12 July	Russo-Lithuanian peace treaty of Moscow
	16 July	Spa Protocol on reparations
	10 August	Treaty of Sèvres with Turkey
	11 August	Russo-Latvian peace treaty of Riga
	14 August	Czech-Yugoslav alliance
	14–16 August	Poles defeat Russians at Warsaw
	7 September	Franco-Belgian military convention
	9 October	Poland seizes Vilna
	14 October	Russo-Finnish peace treaty of Tartu
	28 October	Bessarabian Accord
	12 November	Italo-Yugoslav treaty of Rapallo
1921	19 February	Franco-Polish alliance
	3 March	Polish-Romanian pact against Russia
	8 March	Entente occupation of Düsseldorf
	16 March	Anglo-Soviet trade agreement
	18 March	Russo-Polish peace treaty of Riga
	20 March	Upper Silesian plebiscite
	27 March	Habsburg *coup* in Hungary fails
	5 May	London Schedule of Payments
	5 June	Czech-Romanian alliance
	7 June	Yugoslav-Romanian alliance
	25 August	US-German peace treaty of Berlin
	21–25 October	Habsburg *coup* in Hungary fails
	12 November	Washington Conference opens
	6 December	Anglo-Irish peace agreement

1922	6–13 January	Cannes Conference
	6 February	Five Power Treaty on Naval Limitations; Nine Power Treaty on China; Four Power Treaty on Pacific Islands
	15 March	Russo-German military agreement
	10 April–19 May	Genoa Conference
	16 April	Russo-German treaty of Rapallo
	1 August	Balfour note on war debts
	4 October	Geneva Protocol for Austrian financial reconstruction
	11 October	Mudanya armistice ends Chanak crisis
	25 October	Japanese evacuate Vladivostok
	28 October	Mussolini becomes Italian Prime Minister
	26 December	Reparation Commission declares German timber default
1923	9 January	Reparations Commission declares German coal default
	10 January	Lithuania occupies Memel
	11 January	Ruhr occupation begins
	19 January	German passive resistance begins
	30 January	Greco-Turkish convention on minorities exchange
	24 July	Treaty of Lausanne with Turkey
	31 August	Italy occupies Corfu
	12 September	Draft Treaty of Mutual Assistance
	17 September	Italy seizes Fiume
	26 September	German passive resistance ends
	29 October	Turkish republic declared
	20 November	German currency stabilised
1924	25 January	Franco-Czech alliance
	27 January	Italo-Yugoslav treaty of Rome
	1 February	Britain recognises Soviet government
	9 April	Dawes Plan issued
	18 April	League reorganises Hungarian finances
	5 July	Britain rejects Draft Treaty of Mutual Assistance
	16 July–16 Aug.	London Reparations Conference

	2 October	Geneva Protocol for Pacific Settlement of International Disputes
	25 October	Zinoviev letter published
1925	15 February	IMCC Final Report
	10 March	Britain rejects Geneva Protocol
	27 August	Last French troops leave the Ruhr
	16 October	Locarno treaties initialled
	22 October	Greece invades Bulgaria
	1 December	Locarno treaties signed
1926	31 January	First Rhineland zone evacuated
	17 March	Brazil blocks German League entry
	26 March	Polish-Romanian guarantee treaty
	24 April	Russo-German treaty of Berlin
	10 June	Franco-Romanian friendship treaty
	12 June	Brazil leaves the League
	17 August	Greco-Yugoslav friendship treaty
	10 September	Germany enters the League
	11 September	Spain leaves the League
	16 September	Italo-Romanian friendship treaty
	17 September	Thoiry talks
	26 September	International Steel Agreement
	3–6 October	First Pan-European Congress, Vienna
	27 November	Italo-Albanian treaty of Tirana
1927	31 January	IMCC abolished
	25 February	British forces mass at Shanghai
	5 April	Italo-Hungarian friendship treaty
	2–23 May	World Economic Conference, Geneva
	27 May	Britain breaks relations with Russia
	20 June–4 Aug.	Geneva Naval Conference
	11 November	Franco-Yugoslav treaty of understanding
	10 December	Polish-Lithuanian state of war ends
1928	27 August	Kellogg-Briand Pact
	16 September	Geneva communiqué on Rhineland and reparations
1929	9 February	Litvinov Protocol
	11 February	Lateran Accords

	7 June	Young Report issued
	31 August	Hague Conference Protocol on Young Plan
	6 September	Briand speech on European union
	3 October	Anglo-Russian relations restored
	29 October	New York Stock Exchange collapse
	13 November	Bank for International Settlements established
	30 November	Second Rhineland zone evacuated
1930	3–20 January	Second Hague Conference
	18 Feb.–24 March	Geneva tariff conference
	22 April	London Naval Treaty
	17 May	Young Plan into force; Briand memo on United States of Europe
	30 June	Last Rhineland zone evacuated
	14 September	German Reichstag elections (107 Nazis)
1931	20 March	Reichstag appropriation for Cruiser B
	21 March	Austro-German customs union announced
	11 May	Austrian Creditanstalt fails
	19 May	*Deutschland* launched
	20 June	Hoover Moratorium proposed
	11 August	London Protocol on Hoover Moratorium
	5 September	PCIJ ruling on Austro-German customs union
	18 September	Mukden incident
	21 September	Britain abandons Gold Standard
	11 December	Statute of Westminster
1932	7 January	Stimson note on non-recognition
	21 January	Russo-Finnish non-aggression pact
	22 January	Second Russian five-year plan
	28 January	Sino-Japanese clash at Shanghai
	2 February	Geneva Disarmament Conference opens
	5 February	Russo-Latvian non-aggression pact
	9 March	Manchukuo proclaimed
	11 March	League adopts non-recognition
	4 May	Russo-Estonian non-aggression pact

	16 June–9 July	Lausanne reparations conference
	21 July–20 Aug.	Imperial Economic Conference, Ottawa
	25 July	Russo-Polish non-aggression pact
	29 November	Russo-French non-aggression pact
1933	30 January	Hitler becomes German Chancellor
	16 February	Little Entente Pact of Organisation
	24 February	League adopts Lytton Report
	14 March	Mussolini's Four Power Pact proposal
	23 March	German Enabling Law
	27 March	Japan leaves the League
	31 May	Sino-Japanese truce of Tang-Ku
	7 June	Four Power Pact initialled
	12 June–27 July	World Economic Conference, London
	15 July	Four Power Pact signed at Rome
	14 October	Germany leaves League and Disarmament Conference
1934	26 January	German-Polish non-aggression pact
	12–16 February	Civil war in Vienna
	29 May	Disarmament Conference ends (except for Bureau)
	30 June	Hitler's Night of Long Knives
	25 July	Failure of Nazi putsch in Vienna
	2 August	Death of Hindenburg; Hitler chancellor and Führer
	18 September	Russia enters League
	9 October	Assassination at Marseilles of Louis Barthou and King Alexander of Yugoslavia
	5–6 December	Wal Wal incident, Ethiopia
1935	7 January	French-Italian agreements, Rome
	13 January	Saar plebiscite
	16 March	German conscription introduced
	11–14 April	Stresa Conference
	2 May	Russo-French mutual assistance treaty
	16 May	Russo-Czech mutual assistance treaty

	18 June	Anglo-German Naval Accord
	27 June	British Peace Ballot results published
	31 August	Neutrality Act signed, Washington
	15 September	Nuremberg Laws
	3 October	Italy invades Ethiopia
	14 November	British general election
	6–7 December	Hoare-Laval plan
1936	6 March	Franco-Belgian military accord abrograted
	7 March	Hitler remilitarises Rhineland and denounces Locarno pacts
	5 May	Ethiopian war ends
	18 July	Spanish Civil War begins
	1 November	Rome-Berlin Axis proclaimed
	24 November	Anti-Comintern Pact (Germany and Japan)
1937	7 July	Sino-Japanese war begins
	5 October	Roosevelt's quarantine speech
	5 November	Hossbach conference
	11 December	Italy leaves the League
1938	12 March	*Anschluss*
	29 September	Munich Conference
	9–10 November	*Kristallnacht*
1939	12 March	Pope Pius XII crowned
	14–15 March	Germany occupies Czechoslovakia
	23 March	Germany occupies Memel
	28 March	Spanish Civil War ends
	31 March	Britain (and then France) guarantees Poland
	7 April	Italy seizes Albania
	22 May	German-Italian Pact of Steel
	23 August	Russo-German Non-Aggression Pact
	1 September	Germany invades Poland
	3 September	Britain and France declare war

Notes and References

Note: Wherever possible, citations are made to English language published works.

Abbreviations

AA, T-120	Selected Foreign Ministry Records, T-120. Auswärtiges Amt, Germany, serial/reel/frame
AR, Kab	Germany [Weimar Republic]. *Akten der Reichskanzlei*, 25 vols (Boppard am Rhein, 1968–89), cabinet minutes
BMAE	Belgian Foreign Ministry files, Brussels
CAB 2/-, CAB 23/-	Cabinet Papers, Public Record Office (PRO), London
Cmd.	Parliamentary Command Papers, London
DBFP	Foreign Office, *Documents on British Foreign Policy, 1919–1939*, 65 vols (London, 1946–85).
DD	Ministère des Affaires Étrangères, *Documents diplomatiques*, various, Paris
DDB	Académie Royale de Belgique, *Documents diplomatiques belges, 1920–1940*, 5 vols (Brussels, 1964–8)
DIA	Royal Institute of International Affairs, *Documents on International Affairs*, London, annual
FMAE	French Foreign Ministry files, Quai d'Orsay, Paris
FO 371/-	Foreign Office files, Public Record Office (PRO), London
FRUS	Department of State, *Papers Relating to the Foreign Relations of the United States*, Washington, DC, annual
FRUS PPC	Department of State, *The Paris Peace Conference, 1919*, 13 vols (Washington, DC, 1942–7)
Hymans/-	Papers of Paul Hymans, Archives générales du Royaume, Brussels

SD-   Department of State, decimal files, National
                Archives, Washington
SIA   Royal Institute of International Affairs, *Survey of
                International Affairs,* London, annual

1. The Pursuit of Peace

1. The classic work on the Inquiry is Laurence E. Gelfand, *The Inquiry: American Preparations for Peace, 1917–1919* (New Haven, CT, 1963). Most of the experts of the large American delegation came from the Inquiry, not the State Department. A few of them were more influential than some of the plenipotentiaries. House is often referred to as Colonel House, but he was a Texas colonel, not a veteran of the US Army.

2. On Wilson's vacuity, see Charles Seymour, *Letters from the Paris Peace Conference* (New Haven, CT, 1965) pp. xxx–xxxii, 10, 20–6; and Robert Lansing, *The Big Four and Others of the Peace Conference* (Boston, MA, 1921) pp. 40–2.

3. For details, see J. W. Wheeler-Bennett, *The Nemesis of Power: The German Army in Politics, 1918–1945* (New York, 1964).

4. The full annotated text of the Fourteen Points and the subsequent Wilsonian pronouncements may be found in Ferdinand Czernin, *Versailles, 1919* (New York, 1965 edn.) pp. 10–22.

5. The standard study of the Armistice remains Harry Rudin, *Armistice, 1918* (New Haven, CT, 1944).

6. Klaus Schwabe, 'Germany's Peace Aims and the Domestic and International Constraints', and Fritz Klein, 'Between Compiègne and Versailles: The Germans on the Way from a Misunderstood Defeat to an Unwanted Peace', both in Manfred F. Boemeke, Gerald D. Feldman and Elisabeth Glaser (eds), *The Treaty of Versailles: A Reassessment after 75 Years* (Cambridge, 1998), both quoting Ernst Troeltsch.

7. Schwabe, 'Germany's Peace Aims', in Boemeke et al., addresses German governmental policies. Expectations of a population much distracted by domestic political and social crises were less realistic. Helmut Heiber, *The Weimar Republic,* tr. W. E. Yuill (Oxford, 1993) p. 36. See also Hans Mommsen, *The Rise and Fall of Weimar Democracy,* tr. Elborg Forster and Larry Eugene Jones (Chapel Hill, NC, 1996) p. 72. The United States officially but very discreetly reminded German representatives during negotiations on Armistice details at Trier on 8 March 1919 that Germany had lost the war and warned that its interpretation of the Fourteen Points was unacceptable, but no public statement was made. *AR, Kab Scheidemann* (1971) p. 28. See also Peter

Krüger's penetrating analysis, 'German Disappointment and Anti-Western Resentment, 1918–19', in Hans-Jürgen Schröder (ed.), *Confrontation and Cooperation: Germany and the United States in the Era of World War I, 1900–1924* (Providence, RI, 1993) pp. 323–35.

8. For wartime Czech efforts, see Vera Olivová, *The Doomed Democracy: Czechoslovakia in a Disrupted Europe, 1914–1938* (London, 1972).

9. A convenient summary of the secret treaties may be found in H. W. V. Temperley, *History of the Peace Conference of Paris*, 6 vols (London, 1920) I.

10. On the confusing Russian situation, the clearest work is Evan Mawdsley, *The Russian Civil War* (Boston, MA, 1987). For Soviet policy, see Richard K. Debo, *Revolution and Survival* (Toronto, 1979) and *Survival and Consolidation* (Buffalo, NY, 1992).

11. See Laurence W. Martin, *Peace without Victory* (New Haven, CT, 1958); N. Gordon Levin, Jr, *Woodrow Wilson and World Politics* (London, 1968); and Harold Nicolson, *Peacemaking, 1919* (London, 1933).

12. On the Shantung question, see Russell Fifield, *Woodrow Wilson and the Far East* (New York, 1952), which has not been superseded. A broader study is Roy W. Curry, *Woodrow Wilson and Far Eastern Policy, 1913–1921* (New York, 1957).

13. See Ann Williams, *Britain and France in the Middle East and North Africa, 1914–1967* (London, 1968), and Peter Mansfield, *The Ottoman Empire and its Successors* (London 1973). See also n. 42.

14. Warren F. Kuehl, *Seeking World Order: The United States and International Organization to 1920* (Nashville, TN, 1969) p. 199. See also Thomas J. Knock, *To End All Wars: Woodrow Wilson and the Quest for a New World Order* (New York, 1992), and George W. Egerton, *Great Britain and the Creation of the League of Nations* (Chapel Hill, NC, 1978).

15. The standard work on this subject is Z. A. B. Zeman, *The Break-up of the Habsburg Empire, 1914–1918* (London, 1961).

16. See F. L. Carsten, *Revolution in Central Europe, 1918–1919* (Berkeley, CA, 1972), and also John Bradley, *Allied Intervention in Russia, 1917–1920* (New York, 1968). Despite factual errors, Edmond Taylor, *The Fall of the Dynasties: The Collapse of the Old Order, 1905–1972* (New York, 1963) is also useful.

17. Stephen A. Schuker, 'The Rhineland Question', in Boemeke et al., p. 301.

18. Literature on the League of Nations from start to finish tends to be skimpy, but David Hunter Miller's *The Drafting of the Covenant*, 2 vols (New York, 1928) provides a detailed participant's account of the deliberations at Paris. On the history of the League, see F. S. Northedge, *The League of Nations* (New York, 1986).

19. On Hankey's important role, see S. W. Roskill's excellent *Hankey: Man of Secrets* (London 1972) II.

20. Christopher Seton-Watson, *Italy from Liberalism to Fascism, 1870–1925* (London 1967) p. 537. See also H. James Burgwyn, *The Legend of the Mutilated Victory* (Westport, CT, 1993).

21. A detailed and sympathetic study of the German delegation may be found in Alma Luckau, *The German Delegation at the Paris Peace Conference* (New York, 1941).

22. For the full annotated text of the Treaty of Versailles, see *FRUS PPC*, XIII.

23. The essential introduction to the peace conference in general is Alan Sharp, *The Versailles Settlement* (London, 1991). Key works on the German treaty, in addition to Boemeke *et al.*, include Inga Floto, *Colonel House in Paris* (Princeton, NJ, 1980), and Lorna S. Jaffe, *The Decision to Disarm Germany* (Boston, MA, 1985).

24 This attitude is explored by Martin and Levin.

25. In 1921, Lord Curzon, then Foreign Secretary, complained that 'we cannot trust them'. G. H. Bennett, *British Foreign Policy during the Curzon Period, 1919–24* (New York, 1995), p. 22.

26. Harold Nelson, *Land and Power: British and Allied Policy on Germany's Frontiers, 1916–19* (Toronto, 1963) studies German territorial issues. On Poland, Kay Lundgreen-Nielsen, *The Polish Problem at the Paris Peace Conference*, tr. Alison Borch-Johansen (Odense, 1979) is definitive.

27. Czernin, p. 31.

28. On this and other aspects of the reparations question at the peace conference, see Sally Marks, 'Smoke and Mirrors', in Boemeke et al.

29. On the impracticality of collective security, see Inis L. Claude, Jr, *Swords into Plowshares, the Problems and Progress of International Organization* (New York, 1971 edn.) ch. 12.

30. See, among others, Thomas A. Bailey, *Woodrow Wilson and the Lost Peace* (New York, 1944) pp. 312–14, and Erich Eyck, *A History of the Weimar Republic*, 2 vols, tr. Harlan P. Hanson and Robert G. L. Waite (Cambridge, MA, 1967) I, pp. 80–5. Note also Jacques Bainville's 'too mild for its severity' in *Action Française*, 8 May 1919, as cited by A. Lentin, *Lloyd George, Woodrow Wilson, and the Guilt of Germany* (Baton Rouge, LA, 1985) p. 30.

31. The classic exposition of this view is John Maynard Keynes, *The Economic Consequences of the Peace* (London, 1919). It should be read in conjunction with Étienne Mantoux, *The Carthaginian Peace, or the Economic Consequences of Mr. Keynes* (Oxford, 1946), and in awareness of Keynes's guilt as a pacifist at having aided Britain's war effort and his passion for a German reparations expert.

32. Heiber, p. 38.

33. *AR, Kab Scheidemann*, pp. 28, 78–90, 146–8; *FRUS PPC*, II, p. 139, XII, pp. 12–13, 16–26, 33, 82–6. See also Eyck, I, p. 103; Robert Waite,

172   NOTES AND REFERENCES

Vanguard of Nazism (Cambridge, MA, 1952) pp. 6–8; J. W. Wheeler-Bennett, *Hindenburg: The Wooden Titan* (London, 1936) pp. 215–21, 229, 235–8; A. J. Nicholls, *Weimar and the Rise of Hitler,* 2nd edn (London, 1979) pp. 53–61. See also Klein, 'Between Compiègne and Versailles', and Schwabe, 'Germany's Peace Aims', in Boemeke *et al*; Richard Bessell, *Germany after the First World War* (Oxford, 1993) pp. 254–5; Eberhard Kolb, *The Weimar Republic,* tr. P. S. Falk (London, 1988) pp. 30–1; Krüger in Schröder (ed.) p. 332; and Mommsen, pp. 75–6.

34. For texts of all four treaties, see Fred L. Israel (ed.), *Major Peace Treaties of Modern History, 1648–1967,* 4 vols (New York, 1967) III.

35. On this fear, see Levin and especially Arno Mayer, *Politics and Diplomacy of Peacemaking: Containment and Counterrevolution at Versailles, 1918–1919* (New York, 1967).

36. On the Austrian financial collapse and its aftermath, see Karl R. Stadler, *The Birth of the Austrian Republic, 1918–1921* (Leyden, 1966); and Barbara Jelavich, *Modern Austria* (Cambridge, 1987); as well as C. A. Gulick, *Austria from Habsburg to Hitler,* 2 vols (Berkeley, CA, 1948); and Stanley Suval, *The Anschluss Question in the Weimar Era* (Baltimore, MD, 1974).

37. On the negotiation of the Treaty of Trianon, see Mária Ormos, *From Padua to the Trianon,* tr. Miklós Uszkay (New York, 1990).

38. Zsuzsa L. Nagy, 'Revolution, Counterrevolution, Consolidation', in Peter F. Sugar, Péter Hanák, and Tibor Frank (eds), *A History of Hungary* (Bloomington, IN, 1990) p. 316.

39. Barbara Jelavich, *History of the Balkans: Twentieth Century* (Cambridge, 1983) p. 166.

40. See Paul C. Helmreich, *From Paris to Sèvres* (Columbus, OH, 1973).

41. *DBFP*, First Series, VIII, p. 9.

42. For all the texts concerned and an Arab analysis of them, see George Antonius, *The Arab Awakening* (New York, 1939), as well as an anti-Arab treatment in Elie Kedourie, *In the Anglo-Arab Labyrinth* (Cambridge, 1976). A popular work on the Middle Eastern settlement in general, focusing on Britain, is David Fromkin, *A Peace to End All Peace* (New York, 1989). Two studies using the same archival material to reach opposite conclusions are Isaiah Friedman, *The Question of Palestine,* 2nd edn (New Brunswick, NJ, 1992), and A. L. Tibawi, *Anglo-Arab Relations and the Question of Palestine, 1914–1921* (London, 1978).

43. On all three questions, see René Albrecht-Carrié, *Italy at the Paris Peace Conference* (New York, 1938). See also Burgwyn, *Mutilated Victory*; Ivo Lederer, *Yugoslavia at the Paris Peace Conference* (New Haven, CT, 1963); and, on the Greek end, N. Petsalis-Diomedes, *Greece at the Paris Peace Conference, 1919* (Thessaloniki, 1978), as well as the broader

study by Michael Llewellyn Smith, *Ionian Vision: Greece in Asia Minor, 1919–1922*, 2nd edn (London, 1998).

44. On the Turkish national movement, see Mansfield and also Bernard Lewis, *The Emergence of Modern Turkey* (London, 1968 edn), and Erik J. Zürcher, *Turkey, A Modern History* (London, 1997). For the Treaty of Lausanne, standard works are S. R. Sonyel, *Turkish Diplomacy, 1918–1923* (London, 1975), and Bülent Gökay, *A Clash of Empires* (London, 1997). For a classic brief account of its negotiation, see Roderic H. Davison, 'Turkish Diplomacy from Mudros to Lausanne', in Gordon A. Craig and Felix Gilbert (eds), *The Diplomats, 1919–1939* (Princeton, NJ, 1953). The negotiations may also be traced in *DBFP*, First Series, XVIII.

45. William M. Hale, *Turkish Foreign Policy, 1774–2000* (London, 2000) p. 45.

46. Raymond Pearson, *National Minorities in Eastern Europe, 1848–1945* (New York, 1883); Mark Mazower, *Dark Continent, Europe's Twentieth Century* (New York, 1999); and Séamus Dunn and T. G. Fraser (eds), *European Ethnicity* (London, 1996) provide recent estimates.

47. Sharp, p. 132.

48. For example, Eyck, I, p. 106.

49. For details, see Joseph Rothschild, *East Central Europe between the Two World Wars* (Seattle, WA, 1974).

50. The late correspondent and Professor Elizabeth Wiskemann so remarked to the author, London, March 1971.

51. Emile Cammaerts, *Albert of Belgium, Defender of Right* (London, 1935) p. 347.

52. For text, see Israel, III.

2. The Effort to Enforce the Peace

1. Senator Kenneth Wherry of Nebraska in 1940, as quoted by T.R.B. (Richard L. Strout), 'The Tarnished Age', *New Republic* (26 Oct 1974) p. 4.

2. Leonard Mosley, *Curzon: The End of an Epoch* (London, 1960) p. 210.

3. José Ortega y Gasset, *The Revolt of the Masses* (New York, 1930, 1957 edn) p. 55. See also his ch. 14, urging both European union and the necessity for European domination of the world.

4. Maj.-Gen. Sir C. E. Callwell, *Field Marshal Sir Henry Wilson, His Life and Diaries*, 2 vols (London, 1927) II, p. 193.

5. Olivová provides a convenient summary of the central-European ramifications of the Russo-Polish conflict.

6. The standard source is Piotr Wandycz, *Soviet-Polish Relations, 1917–1921* (Cambridge, MA, 1969). For a summary treatment, see

Norman Davies, *God's Playground: A History of Poland*, 2 vols (New York, 1982) II.

7. *FRUS PPC*, XIII, p. 8.
8. Comment by Salvador de Madariaga cited in Ruth Henig, 'Britain, France, and the League of Nations in the 1920s', in Alan Sharp and Glyn Stone (eds), *Anglo-French Relations in the Twentieth Century* (New York, 2000) p. 129.
9. *DBFP*, First Series, XVI, p. 864.
10. This nervousness is clearly revealed in Committee of Imperial Defence papers and meetings. See, for example, CAB 2/3, *passim*. See also *I Documenti Diplomatici Italiani, Settima Serie*, II, p. 320.
11. *DBFP*, First Series, XVI, p. 862.
12. Rothschild, p. 5. The opening chapter of this book is particularly valuable.
13. Sally Marks, *The Ebbing of European Ascendancy* (London, 2002) p. 276.
14. Michael E. Howard, *The Continental Commitment* (London, 1972) p. 78.
15. D. W. Brogan, *The Development of Modern France* (New York, 1966 edn) p. 543.
16. Alan Sharp, 'Anglo-French Relations from Versailles to Locarno', in Sharp and Stone (eds), pp. 122, 126.
17. Imanuel Geiss, 'The Weimar Republic between the Second and Third Reich', in Michael Laffan (ed.), *The Burden of German History, 1919–45* (London, 1988) pp. 66–9; Krüger in Schröder (ed.), pp. 328–32.
18. Mommsen, pp. 75–6
19. Bessel, pp. 254–5; Krüger in Schröder (ed.), p. 332.
20. Pierre Rain, *L'Europe de Versailles* (Paris, 1945) p. 141.
21. Sir Robert Vansittart, 'An Aspect of International Relations in 1931' (n.d.), p. 29, FO 371/15205.
22. The standard work is Magda Ádám, *The Little Entente and Europe (1920–1929)*, tr. Mátyás Esterházy (Budapest, 1993).
23. *AR, Kab Scheidemann*, pp. 78–88.
24. The Spa negotiations may be traced in *DBFP*, First Series, VIII. The Spa Protocol dividing reparations was published as Cmd. 1615 (London, 1922). The Yugoslav share, originally 6 per cent, was reduced to 5 per cent in 1921.
25. Gaston A. Furst, *De Versailles aux experts* (Nancy, 1927) pp. 124–6, 133–4, 346. Also indispensable on any question concerning German reparations is Étienne Weill-Raynall, *Les Réparations allemandes et la France*, 3 vols (Paris, 1947).
26. The text of the London Schedule appears in Reparation Commission, *Official Documents* (London, 1922) I. The London Conference may be traced in *DBFP*, First Series, XV.
27. For the Franco-Belgian negotiations, see *DDB*, I. For the eastern

alliances, see Piotr Wandycz, *France and her Eastern Allies, 1919–1925* (Minneapolis, MN, 1962).

28. On the Washington Conference, see Roger Dingman, *Power in the Pacific* (Chicago, 1976), and Erik Goldstein and John Maurer (eds), *The Washington Conference, 1921–22* (London, 1995). There is a summary account in *SIA*, 1920–1923. For documents, see Cmd. 1627 (London, 1922); *DD, Conférence de Washington* (Paris, 1923); and especially *FRUS*, 1921, I, and 1922, I. Minutes of meetings may be found in United States, 67th Congress, Second Session, Senate Document No. 126, Conference on the Limitation of Armament (Washington, DC, 1922).

29. Joel Blatt, 'France and the Washington Conference', in Goldstein and Maurer (eds), pp. 192–219, also Joel Blatt, 'The Parity that Meant Superiority', *French Historical Studies* XII (1981) 223–48.

30. See Georges Suarez, *Briand: sa vie, son oeuvre*, 6 vols (Paris, 1938–52) V.

31. Frank Owen, *Tempestuous Journey: Lloyd George, his Life and Times* (New York, 1955), pp. 598–9. On the Anglo-French negotiations, see also Cmd. 2169 (London, 1924) and *DD, Documents rélatifs aux négociations concernant les garanties de sécurité* . . . (Paris, 1924).

32. Jacques Bardoux, *Lloyd George et la France* (Paris, 1923) pp. 18, 19, 30.

33. On the Genoa Conference in general and the Rapallo treaty in particular, see Carole Fink, *The Genoa Conference* (Chapel Hill, NC, 1984).

34. For details, see Aleksandr Nekrich, *Pariahs, Partners, Predators: German-Soviet Relations, 1922, 1941*, ed. and tr. Gregory L. Freeze (New York, 1997). For the memoir of a participant, see Gustav Hilger and Alfred G. Meyer, *The Incompatible Allies, German-Soviet Relations, 1918–1941* (New York, 1953), especially chs VI and VII.

35. *Le Temps* (4 May 1922 *et seq.*).

36. *AR, Kab Cuno* (1968) p. 192.

37. See Cmd. 1812 (London, 1923); Cmd. 2258 (London, 1924); and *DD, Demande de moratorium du gouvernement allemand* . . . (Paris, 1924).

38. Stephen A. Schuker, *The End of French Predominance in Europe* (Chapel Hill, NC, 1976) pp. 6, 12, 16; Schuker, *American 'Reparations' to Germany, 1919–33* (Princeton, 1988) p. 22; Heiber, pp. 42–5, 73–4, 86; Kolb, pp. 40–41; Mommsen, p. 117; Nicholls, pp. 75, 125; Niall Ferguson, *The Pity of War* (London, 1999) pp. 391, 411–2, 414. Carl-Ludwig Holtfrerich, *The German Inflation, 1919–1923*, tr. Theo Balderston (Berlin, 1986) dissents, pp. 137–55, especially 153–4, but has proved in 'Internationale Verteilungsfolgen der deutschen Inflation, 1918–1923', *Kyklos* XXX (1977) 271–92, that foreign investment in Germany lost in the inflation constituted a real transfer of wealth amply covering reparations paid to 1923. Bruce Kent, *The Spoils of War* (Oxford, 1989) announces at the outset a 'cornerstone assumption'

that reparations were unpayable. Holtfrerich, Gerald D. Feldman in *The Great Disorder: Politics, Economics, and Society in the German Inflation, 1914–1924* (New York, 1993), and Manfred Berg in 'Trade, Debts, and Reparations', in Schröder (ed.), make a key distinction between economic feasibility and political possibility.

39. FO memo (23 Nov. 1922) FO 371/7487.

40. Nicholls, p. 74; Heiber, p. 73.

41. A very long payment period with low annual payments in the early years implied cancellation or reduction when politics permitted; a modest interest rate effectively cancelled about a third of the British debt. Later settlements with continental victors forgave roughly twice that or more. Stephen A. Schuker, 'Origins of American Financial Policy in Europe', in Schröder (ed.), p. 399.

42. Crowe memo (27 Dec. 1922) FO 371/7491; Ryan to Lampson (5 Jan. 1923), no number, FO 371/8626. See also J. F. V. Keiger, *Raymond Poincaré* (Cambridge, 1997) pp. 290–9, and Sally Marks, 'Poincaré-la-peur: France and the Ruhr Crisis', in Kenneth Mouré and Martin S. Alexander (eds), *Crisis and Renewal in France, 1918–1962* (New York, 2002) pp. 28–45.

43. Commission des Réparations, *Rapport sur les travaux de la commission des réparations de 1920 à 1922*, 2 vols (Paris, 1923) I, pp. 241–7, II, pp. 465–88, 430–1.

44. For text, see Cmd. 1812.

45. Godley to War Office (7 Jan. 1923), tel. CO 371/7/1; FO 371/8703; Crewe to Curzon (11 Feb. 1923), tel. 173, FO 371/8712; Cabinet 10 (23) (15 Feb. 1923) CAB 23/45.

46. *DD, Demande de moratorium . . .*, pp. 93–7; Grahame to Curzon (1 Mar. 1923) tel. 39, FO 371/8718; Crewe to Curzon (14 July 1923) no. 680, FO 371/8643; Phipps to Tyrrell (8 Sept. 1923), Phipps to Crowe (6 Nov. 1923), Phipps papers (Cambridge). To this should be added the substantial evidence from French sources in Schuker, *French Predominance*, pp. 20–4, 117, 123, 179. See also n. 42.

47. AR, *Kab Cuno*, pp. 158–9.

48. Degoutte to Maginot, (7 Jan. 1923), 99 3/4, Maginot to Degoutte (17, 24 Jan. 1923), E 7642, 182 PC/4, Papers of Gen. J.-J.-M. Degoutte/7N3489, Service Historique de l'Armée, Vincennes; Payot instruction (8 Jan. 1923), 8727/CRW, FMAE Série B/141; Tirard to Poincaré (30 Jan. 1923), tel. 58, FMAE B/197; de Gaiffier to Jaspar (7 Feb. 1923), no. 1877/970, BMAE Correspondance politique, France/1923; Delacroix to Theunis (6 Feb. 1923), no. 60105, BMAE Classement B-10.071.

49. Cole to Wigram (30 Jan. 1923) FO 371/8709; Ramsbottom to Bennett (24 Aug. 1923) FO 371/8651; Board of Trade memo (25 Aug. 1923) FO 371/8651.

50. Heiber, p. 43.
51. Stephen D. Carls, *Louis Loucheur and the Shaping of Modern France, 1916–1931* (Baton Rouge, LA, 1993) p. 9; Mommsen, p. 144.
52. For details, see V. R. Berghahn, *Modern Germany* (Cambridge, 1987) or Nicholls.
53. Ultimately, nearly 900 million gold marks or almost £45 million. *FRUS PPC*, XIII, p. 785.
54. Most published accounts of Rhenish separatism are unreliable. Materials on the subject may be found in FO 371/8682–8691, FO 371/9770–9776; Henri Jaspar Papers (Archives générales du Royaume, Brussels), files 235, 240, 240B; FMAE, Série Z, Rive Gauche du Rhin, files 30–47, Série B/352–3; BMAE France/1923, B-10.440–4. Poincaré was surprised and dismayed by the separatist outbreak in the Palatinate engineered by the French Army commander there but did not repudiate it.
55. For text, see Reparations Commission, *Official Documents*, XIV (London 1927).
56. Schuker, *French Predominance*, p. 184.
57. SD 462.00R 296/376. Most experts at the time agreed.
58. For heavily edited minutes of the technical work of the London Conference, see Cmd. 2258 (London, 1924), and Cmd. 2270 (London, 1924). There were no minutes kept of political discussions except those with Germany (CAB 29/104). The least inadequate notes were those of Paul Hymans, Belgian Foreign Minister (Hymans/157). Stresemann's exchanges with Berlin are also helpful (AA, T-120, 3398/1736). For texts of agreements, see Cmd. 2259 (London, 1924).
59. Schuker, *French Predominance*, pp. 302–18, 349–53.

3. The Revision of the Peace

1. For Soviet diplomacy in the 1920s, see Jon Jacobson, *When the Soviet Union Entered World Politics* (Berkeley, CA, 1994).
2. The early negotiations may be traced in *DBFP*, First Series, VIII, XII, and Degras, Soviet *Documents*, I.
3. *The Times* (London, 25 October 1924).
4. On the Comintern, see Tim Rees and Andrew Thorpe (eds), *International Communism and the Communist International, 1919–1943* (Manchester, 1998); Julius Braunthal, *History of the International*, 2 vols (New York, 1967) II; and Günther Nollau, *International Communism and World Revolution* (New York, 1961).
5. Nollau, p. 62.
6. The definitive study is James Barros, *The Corfu Incident of 1923:*

Mussolini and the League of Nations (Princeton, NJ, 1965). See also Joel Blatt, 'France and the Corfu-Fiume Crisis of L 923', *The Historian* L (1988) 234–59.

7. Alan Cassels, *Mussolini's Early Diplomacy* (Princeton, NJ, 1970) pp. 116–19. Most probably, the culprits were Albanians.

8. League of Nations Covenant, Article 15.

9. Very little has been written about the Draft Treaty. However, some material may be found in: Bruce Williams, *State Security and the League of Nations* (Baltimore, MD, 1927); Francis P. Walters, *A History of the League of Nations* (London, 1952); and J. T. Shotwell and Marina Salvin, *Lessons on Security and Disarmament* (New York, 1949).

10. Leading contemporary accounts are David Hunter Miller, *The Geneva Protocol* (New York, 1925), and Philip J. Noel-Baker, *The Geneva Protocol for the Pacific Settlement of International Disputes* (London, 1925). See also David Marquand, *Ramsay MacDonald* (London, 1977), and David Dutton, *Austen Chamberlain* (New Brunswick, NJ, 1985).

11. Final Report, IMCC, 15 Feb. 1925, FO 371/10708.

12. For D'Abernon's role, see F. G. Stambrook, ' "*Das Kind*" – Lord D'Abernon and the origins of the Locarno Pact', *Central European History* I (September 1968).

13. Hindenburg was 78 years old and living in a retirement home. Mommsen, p. 236.

14. Textual comparison of Cabinet instructions to Stresemann before Locarno (Deutschen Demokratischen Republik, Ministerium für Auswärtige Angelegenheiten, *Locarno-Konferenz, 1925: Eine Dokumentensammlung*, Berlin, 1962, p. 143), British minutes of meetings (FO 371/10742), and Vandervelde's reports to Brussels (*DDB*, II) with Stresemann's diary accounts (Eric Sutton (ed.), *Gustav Stresemann: His Diaries, Letters, and Papers*, 3 vols, London, 1937 II, pp. 180–201) and AA, T-120, 4509H/2270 and 3123H/1512 supports this conclusion and indicates some fudging. However, his accounts are usually more reliable than Briand's.

15. For similar assessments based on different evidence, see Kolb, p. 58; Mommsen, pp. 200–7; Annelise Thimme, 'Stresemann and Locarno', in Hans Gatzke (ed.), *European Diplomacy between Two Wars* (Chicago, 1972). The best book-length studies of Stresemann in English remain Henry A. Turner, Jr, *Stresemann and the Politics of the Weimar Republic* (Princeton, NJ, 1956), and Hans Gatzke, *Stresemann and the Rearmament of Germany* (Baltimore, MD, 1954).

16. Suarez, *Briand*, VI, lacks the detail and documentation of the earlier volumes.

17. See Dutton and also Sir Charles Petrie, *The Life and Letters of the Right Honourable Sir Austen Chamberlain*, 2 vols (London, 1940) II.

18. For Vandervelde's attitude, which expressed the reaction of socialists

everywhere to the Matteotti murder, see Pierre van Zuylen, *Les Mains libres: politique extérieure de la Belgique, 1914–1940* (Brussels, 1950) pp. 215–16. For the Matteotti murder itself, see Alan Cassels, *Fascist Italy*, 2nd edn (Arlington Heights, IL, 1985) or Philip Morgan, *Italian Fascism, 1919–1945* (New York, 1995).

19. Sir Ivone Kirkpatrick, *Mussolini: A Study in Power* (New York, 1964) p. 249.

20. Ibid. See also Emery Kelen, *Peace in their Time* (London, 1964) pp. 155–6.

21. Stresemann, *Diaries*, II, p. 228.

22. The negotiations may be traced in FO 371/10726–10744, FMAE, Série Z, Grande-Bretagne, files 72–88, and AA, T-120, 4509H/2269–71 and 3123H/1509–12.

23. For example, Loc/122/Con, FO 371/10744.

24. The only detailed reports of the work of the jurists are *DDB*, II, pp. 316–25, and AA, T- 120, 4509H/2271/E12877–83, and 3123H/1512/ D644530–51, D644592,

25. For the public aspect of Locarno, see Kelen, pp. 152–61.

26. For text, see *DDB*, II, pp. 345–6.

27. From the outset, the British guarantee was the decisive factor in France's reluctant acceptance of a pact restoring Germany to diplomatic equality. Massigli note, 6 March 1925, FMAE note, 6 March 1925, draft instructions, 12 March 1925, FMAE Z/Grande-Bretagne/73; 2 Herriot notes, 16 March 1925, FMAE Z/Grande-Bretagne/74.

28. Kelen, pp. 159, 161; van Zuylen, p. 217; Petrie, II, pp. 287–90; Suarez, VI, pp. 129–30.

29. For texts of the Locarno treaties, see Cmd. 2525 (London, 1925).

30. Stresemann, *Diaries*, II, pp. 216–17; van Zuylen note, 8 June 1932, Hymans/151. For a detailed examination, see Manfred J. Enssle, *Stresemann's Territorial Revisionism* (Weisbaden, 1980).

31. See Wandycz, *France and her Eastern Allies*, pp. 361–8; For Poland, Anna Cienciala and Titus Komarnicki, *From Versailles to Locarno: Keys to Polish Foreign Policy, 1919–1925* (Lawrence, KA, 1984), which is less reliable on the Czechs; F. Gregory Campbell, *Confrontation in Central Europe; Weimar Germany and Czechoslovakia* (Chicago, 1975).

32. *DDB*, II, p. 2l3.

33. *DBFP*, Series IA, I, pp. 249–51.

34. See George A. Grün, 'Locarno, Idea and Reality', *International Affairs* xxxi (1955) 477–85.

35. In a closed meeting, Stresemann told his political party that Germany had only renounced regaining Alsace-Lorraine by force and hinted that even this renunciation would be temporary since any treaty (he said) is governed by the principle of *rebus sic stantibus*, wherein a

change of circumstances [such as regaining the necessary military force] voids the treaty. Henry Ashby Turner, Jr, 'Eine Rede Stresemanns über seine Locarnopolitik', in *Vierteljahrshefte für Zeitgeschichte* xv (1967) 425.

36. Gordon A. Craig, *Germany, 1866–1945* (New York, 1980) p. 519.
37. Minutes of the 1 December 1925 talks are to be found in *DBFP*, Series IA, I.
38. Michael Laffan, 'Weimar and Versailles: German Foreign Policy, 1919–33', in Laffan (ed.), p. 92.

4. The Years of Illusion

1. On this episode, see James Barros, *The League of Nations and the Great Powers: The Greek-Bulgarian Incident, 1925* (Oxford, 1970).
2. *SIA*, 1926, p. 3.
3. Walters, p. 319.
4. See Erik Lönnroth, 'Sweden: the diplomacy of Östen Undén', in Craig and Gilbert (eds), *The Diplomats*.
5. For text, see *SIA*, 1927.
6. D'Abernon to Foreign Office (11 Aug. 1926) tel. 202, FO 371/11270; Cab 33 (26) (19 May 1926) CAB 23/53; Chamberlain to D'Abernon (13 Aug. 1926) tel. 93, FO 371/11270.
7. Suarez, vi, p. 197.
8. Walters, p. 343.
9. Ibid., pp. 342–3.
10. Stephen Bonsal, *Unfinished Business* (Garden City, NY, 1944) p. 26.
11. Walters, p. 346.
12. Cf. Stresemann, *Diaries*, iii, pp. 17–26, Suarez, vi, pp. 219–27, and the fuller, less tactful version of Stresemann's account in AA, T-120, 7332H/3146/H162515–29. The French version is inaccurate, Briand having much exceeded his instructions, for Poincaré opposed any territorial *quid pro quo*. Stresemann's fuller version is probably essentially accurate in most particulars – with a bit of spin. Jacques Bariéty, 'Finances et relations internationales: à propos du "plan de Thoiry"; septembre 1926', *Relations Internationales* 21 (1980) 51–70, especially 65–9.
13. On the Belgian and Polish crises, see Richard H. Meyer, *Bankers' Diplomacy* (New York, 1970). On Stresemann's eastern manoeuvres, see Robert Mark Spaulding, 'The Political Economy of German Frontiers, 1918, 1945, 1990', in Christian Baechler and Carole Fink (eds), *The Establishment of European Frontiers after the Two World Wars* (Bern, 1996), pp. 229–48. On the French situation, see Jon Jacobson, *Locarno Diplomacy* (Princeton, NJ, 1972), pp. 84–90. While inclining habitually

to Stresemann's view, Jacobson provides a valuable study of the period 1926–9.

14. See Ervin Hexner, *The International Steel Cartel* (Chapel Hill, NC, 1943).

15. On Coudenhove-Kalergi and the pan-European movement, see Carl H. Pegg, *Evolution of the European Idea, 1914–1933* (Chapel Hill, NC, 1983).

16. Cassels, p. 390. This is the best study of Mussolini's diplomacy in the 1920s.

17. Mussolini's enthusiasm for Adolf Hitler derived in part from the fact that, alone among German nationalists, he was from the first prepared to abandon all claims on behalf of the south Tyrolese.

18. For text, see *SIA*, 1927.

19. Ibid., 1927.

20. Ibid., 1926.

21. On Franco-Italian relations from the French side, see William I. Shorrock, *From Ally to Enemy: The Enigma of Fascist Italy in French Diplomacy, 1920–1940* (Kent, OH, 1988).

22. For text, see *SIA*, 1926.

23. For France's relations with the Little Entente and Poland, see Piotr Wandycz, *The Twilight of French Eastern Alliances, 1926–36* (Princeton, NJ, 1988).

24. For text, see *SIA*, 1927.

25. On Mussolini's east European revisionism, see H. James Burgwyn, *Italian Foreign Policy in the Interwar Period, 1918–1940* (Westport, CT, 1997) especially pp. 35–41, 51–5.

26. Cassels, p. 313.

27. The negotiations may be traced in *DBFP*, Series IA, III. On Anglo-American naval policy in general and the Geneva conference in particular, see S. W. Roskill, *Naval Policy between the Wars*, 2 vols (London, 1968; Annapolis MD, 1976) I.

28. R. H. Ferrell, *The American Secretaries of State and their Diplomacy*, XI: *Frank B. Kellogg, Henry L. Stimson* (New York, 1963) pp. 171–2.

29. See *DIA*, 1930, for texts. The negotiations may be traced in *DBFP*, Second Series, I. A good account of the London conference may be found in David Carlton, *MacDonald versus Henderson* (New York, 1970) ch. 6.

30. A summary may be found in *SIA*, 1929, pp. 101–8. *The New York Times* also provided excellent coverage (May 1927).

31. On Stresemann's machinations, see Spaulding, 'German Frontiers', in Baechler and Fink (eds), pp. 233–8.

32. For text, see *SIA*, 1926.

33. On French-Polish relations in the late twenties, see Wandycz, *Twilight*.

34. J. Korbel, *Poland between East and West* (Princeton, NJ, 1963), p. 223.

35. Petrie, II, p. 304.
36. For example, D'Abernon to Foreign Office (25 Sept. 1926) no. 664, FO 371/11279; Belgian Army G/S, Study of German Army Budget (25 Feb. 1926) Vicomte Prosper Poullet papers (Brussels), file 232; *DBFP*, Second Series, II, pp. 585–7.
37. *DBFP*, Series IA, I, p. 381.
38. For text of speech, see *DIA*, 1928.
39. The negotiations may be traced in Cmd. 3109 (1928) and Cmd. 3153 (1928). For final text, see Cmd. 3410 (1929) or *DIA*, 1928. The leading study is R. H. Ferrell, *Peace in their Time* (New Haven, CT, 1952).
40. *DDB*, II, p. 528.
41. Stresemann, *Diaries*, III, pp. 383–92; Hymans notes (28 Aug. 1928) Hymans/159; *DDB*, II, pp. 528–30.
42. For text, see *DIA*, 1928, or *DBFP*, Series IA, V, p. 335.
43. For French policy, see Philipp Heyde, 'Frankreich und das Ende der Reparationen', *Vierteljahrshefte für Zeitgeschichte* XLVIII (2000) 37–73.
44. The handiest compendium, containing background, text, analysis, account of subsequent events through the Hague Conferences, and conference documents, is Denys P. Myers, *The Reparations Settlement* (Boston, 1929 [1930]). David Carlton, *MacDonald versus Henderson: The Foreign Policy of the Second Labour Government* (New York, 1970) provides a clear narrative of both the Labour government's response to the Young Plan (ch. 2) and the restoration of relations with Russia (ch. 7).
45. Texts may be found in Myers or *DIA*, 1929.
46. Though erratic, Cornelia Navari, 'The Origins of the Briand Plan', *Diplomacy and Statecraft* III (1992) 74–104 provides information on this topic and its links to the pan- European movement, business interests and fears of American economic dominance.
47. For details, see Nicholls, pp. 100–01, or K. D. Bracher, *The German Dictatorship* (New York, 1970) pp. 160–2.
48. John Hiden, *Republican and Fascist Germany* (London, 1996) p. 27.
49. For texts, see Myers or Cmd. 3484 (1930), Cmd. 3763 (1931), and Cmd. 3766 (1931).
50. For text, see *DBFP*, Second Series, I, pp. 487–8.
51. Eyck, II, pp. 263–4.
52. *DBFP*, Second Series, I, p. 486.
53. For text, see *DBFP*, Second Series, I, pp. 314–24 or *DIA*, 1930.
54. Navari, p. 99.

5. The Crumbling of Illusion

1. Tyrrell to Henderson (14 Jan. 1931) no. 37 (France, Annual Report, 1930) FO 371/15646.

2. Granville to Henderson (16 Feb. 1930 no. 150 (Belgium, Annual Report, 1930) FO 371/15632.

3. For texts, see *DIA*, 1929.

4. On the international effects of the Lateran accords, see Peter C. Kent, *The Pope and the Duce* (New York, 1981)

5. Vansittart memo, 'An Aspect of International Relations in 1931' (n.d.) FO 371/15205.

6. For example, Belgian General Staff note (30 July 1930), Comte Charles de Broqueville papers (Brussels), file 650; Belgian Study of German Reichswehr Budget (n.d.) 1931, de Broqueville/648; D'Abernon to Foreign Office (31 March 1926) no. 178, FO 371/11279; Tyrrell to Henderson, no. 661, FO 371/15187; *DBFP*, Second Series, II, pp. 515–25.

7. Campbell to Vansittart (25 Aug. 1931) pers., FO 371/15195.

8. See William S. Allen, *The Nazi Seizure of Power* (Chicago, 1965) pp. 12, 24, 34; Kolb, p. 102; Berghahn, pp. 133–4; Eyck, II, pp. 278–9.

9. In this connection, it should be noted that in November 1932, when the Depression had become truly acute in Germany, unemployment had doubled, and the onset of winter was making a severe situation worse, the Nazi vote dropped significantly.

10. *DBFP*, Second Series, I, p. 502.

11. Zara Steiner, 'The League of Nations and the Quest for Security', in R. Ahmann et al. (eds), *The Quest for Stability: Problems of West European Security, 1918–1957* (New York, 1993) p. 54.

12. Hans Mommsen, 'The Breakthrough of the National Socialists as a Mass Movement in the Late Weimar Republic', in Laffan (ed.), pp. 106–8.

13. See his essay under this title, *SIA*, 1931.

14. Newton to Foreign Office (1 July 1931), tel. 91, FO 371/15184.

15. Mommsen, 'Breakthrough', in Laffan (ed.), p. 127.

16. F. G. Stambrook, 'The German-Austrian Customs Union Project of 1931', in Gatzke (ed.), p. 98. The best studies of the customs union proposal are Stambrook, Stanley Suval and Edward W. Bennett, *Germany and the Diplomacy of the Financial Crisis, 1931* (Cambridge, MA, 1962), to which this analysis of the events of 1931 owes much. A simplified account of the Austrian crisis may be found in Carlton, ch. 10. The negotiations over the customs union may also be traced in *DBFP*, Second Series, II.

17. Bennett, p. 48.

18. For text, see *DIA*, 1931.

19. In July 1931, German debts to American citizens and banks amounted to almost $2.5 milliard (nearly 9.5 milliard gold marks). Robert H. Ferrell, *American Diplomacy in the Great Depression* (New Haven, CT, 1957) p. 117.

20. For text, see *FRUS*, 1931, I, pp. 33–5.
21. Tyrrell to Foreign Office (22 June 1931) tel., no number, FO 371/15182.
22. Bennett, p. 177.
23. For text, see *DIA*, 1931.
24. The United States quickly paid off its domestic war debt and had no foreign one. Throughout the 1920s, government budgets were small and balanced and the dollar was unassailable.
25. On the Wall Street crash and the depression, see Derek H. Aldcroft, *From Versailles to Wall Street* (Berkeley, CA, 1977); John Kenneth Galbraith, *The Great Crash, 1929* (Boston, MA, 1988 edn); Patricia Clavin, *The Great Depression in Europe, 1929–1939* (New York, 2000); and Charles P. Kindleberger, *The World in Depression, 1929–1939* (London, 1973).
26. On the Manchurian crisis, see Christopher Thorne, *The Limits of Foreign Policy* (London, 1972); Parks Coble, *Facing Japan: Chinese Politics and Japanese Imperialism, 1931–1937* (Cambridge, MA, 1991); James William Morley (ed.), *Japan Erupts* (New York, 1984); Sadako N. Ogata, *Defiance in Manchuria* (Berkeley, CA, 1964); Ian Nish, *Japan's Struggle with Internationalism: Japan, China and the League of Nations, 1931–3* (London, 1993); and You-li Sun, *China and the Origins of the Pacific War, 1931–1941* (New York, 1993). The diplomatic manoeuvres may be traced in *DBFP*, Second Series, VIII–XI.
27. Howard, pp. 97–101.
28. See, for instance, *Izvestiia* article (22 Nov. 1931) in Xenia Joukoff Eudin and Robert M. Slusser (eds), *Soviet Foreign Policy, 1928–1934, Documents and Materials* (University Park, PA, 1966) I, pp. 345–7
29. For text, see *FRUS, Japan, 1931–1941*, I, p. 76. The doctrine of non-recognition had also been used in 1915 to oppose Japan's 21 Demands on China.
30. See the portrait by Henry R. Winkler in Craig and Gilbert (eds), *The Diplomats*, and also Carlton.
31. Toynbee, *SIA*, 1932, p. 175.
32. Thorne, p. 306.
33. The standard work on the Disarmament Conference is still J. W. Wheeler-Bennett, *The Pipe Dream of Peace* (London, 1935). The negotiations may be traced in *DBFP*, Second Series, III–VI.
34. Tyrrell to Foreign Office (13 Jan. 1932) tel. 19S, FO 371/16369.
35. On the Austrian situation, see Gulick, II, or Jelavich, *Modern Austria*.
36. On French policy, see Heyde.
37. For text of report, see *DIA*, 1931.
38. Memo on German reparations (31 May 1932) FO 371/15910.
39. Tyrrell to Simon (16 Jan. 1933) no. 70 (France, Annual Report, 1932) FO 371/17299.

40. Key documents may be found in *DIA*, 1932. The negotiations may be traced in *DBFP*, Second Series, III. The standard work is J. W. Wheeler-Bennett, *The Wreck of Reparations* (London, 1933).

41. Estimates vary from about 20.5 milliard gold marks to 22.9 milliard. For a detailed breakdown, see Schuker, American 'Reparations', pp. 107–8.

42. The curious may consult the *World Almanac, 1974*, p. 510. During the winter war of 1939–40, Finland gained enormous American sympathy as 'the only country to pay its war debts'.

43. Extracts may be found in *DIA*, 1932.

44. Thorne, pp. 332–3.

45. No longer a province. Now divided between Hebei and Liaoning.

6. The End of Old Illusions

1. Gerhard Weinberg, *The Foreign Policy of Hitler's Germany: Diplomatic Revolution in Europe, 1933–36* (Chicago, 1970) p. 14. This work and its sequel, *The Foreign Policy of Hitler's Germany: Starting World War II, 1937–1939* (Chicago, 1980), are definitive on this subject. For a brief introduction to Nazi foreign policy, see either William Carr, *Arms, Autarky, and Aggression* (New York, 1972), or Klaus Hildebrand, *The Foreign Policy of the Third Reich*, tr. Anthony Fothergill (Berkeley, CA, 1973).

2. Edgar B. Nixon (ed.), *Franklin D. Roosevelt and Foreign Affairs*, 3 vols (Cambridge, MA, 1969) I, p. 122.

3. David Marquand, *Ramsay MacDonald* (London, 1977) p. 749.

4. David Welch, *Hitler, Profile of a Dictator* (London, 1994) p. 59. This short work serves as a useful introduction before one tackles the many massive biographies.

5. On Soviet policy, see Geoffrey Roberts, *The Soviet Union and the Origins of the Second World War* (New York, 1995).

6. On Nazi penetration in Czechoslovakia, see Elizabeth Wiskemann, *Czechs and Germans* (London, 1967 edn).

7. Rothstein, pp. 149, 152–5. See also Robert Machray, *The Struggle for the Danube and the Little Entente, 1929–38* (London, 1938). Text of the Statute of the Little Entente may be found in *DIA*, 1933.

8. For final text, see *DIA*, 1933. The negotiations may be traced in *DBFP*, Second Series V.

9. On Italian policy, see Burgwyn, *Italian Foreign Policy*; R. J. B. Bosworth, *Italy and the Wider World, 1860–1960* (London, 1996); or Philip Morgan, *Italian Fascism, 1919–1945* (New York, 1995). The best survey of the crises of the 1930s is P. M. H. Bell, *The Origins of the Second World War in Europe* (London, 1986). See also Gordon Martel (ed.), *'The*

Origins of the Second World War' Reconsidered, 2nd edn (London, 1999). Brief clear studies of the confusing Spanish war are George Esenwein and Adrian Shubert, *Spain at War* (New York, 1995), and Gabriel Jackson, *A Concise History of the Spanish Civil War* (London, 1974).

10. For texts, see Poland, Ministry of Foreign Affairs, *Official Documents concerning Polish-German and Polish-Soviet Relations, 1933–1939. The Polish White Book* (London, n.d.) pp. 20–1, and Leonard Shapiro (ed.), *Soviet Treaty Series,* 2 vols (Washington, DC, 1950) II, pp. 55–6. For analysis of the German treaty, see Weinberg, I, ch. 3. On the Russian pact, see Bohdan B. Budorowycz, *Polish-Soviet Relations, 1932–1939* (New York, 1963) ch. 1.

11. On Polish and other east European reactions to Hitler, see Anita J. Prażmowska, *Eastern Europe and the Origins of the Second World War* (London, 2000).

12. Clerk to Simon, 27 Jan. 1934, no. 57 (Belgium, Annual Report, 1933); FO 371/17616; Simon to Bland (10 July 1933), FO 371/17282; Sargent to Ovey (31 July 1934) FO 371/17630; FO Memo (30 May 1934) FO 371/17630. On Belgian policy, see D. O. Kieft, *Belgium's Return to Neutrality* (Oxford, 1972), and Martin S. Alexander, *The Republic in Danger: General Maurice Gamelin and the Politics of French Defence, 1922–1940* (Cambridge, 1992).

13. Minutes of meeting at French Ministry of War (10 March 1933) FO 371/16668. On France's dilemmas, see Robert J. Young, *France and the Origins of the Second World War* (New York, 1996).

14. Minutes of meeting at French Ministry of War (10 March 1933) FO 371/16668.

15. The standard work is Wandycz, *Twilight.*

16. Michael Dockrill, 'France's Economic and Financial Crisis', in Sharp and Stone (eds), p. 209.

17. Tyrrell to Foreign Office (31 Jan. 1933) tel. 20S, FO 371/17290; Campbell to Simon (30 Nov. 1934) tel. 130, FO 371/17670; Clerk to Eden (13 Nov. 1936) no. 1469, FO 371/19860.

18. Thorne, p. 267.

19. For example, see Ferguson, p. 397.

20. The best study is R. A. C. Parker, *Chamberlain and Appeasement* (New York, 1993).

21. See, for example, Maarten L. Pereboom, *Democracies at the Turning Point* (New York, 1995), p. 176, and Richard Davis, *Anglo-French Relations Before the Second World War* (London, 2001) p. 14. Davis provides a new examination of the Anglo-French relationship in the Ethiopian and Rhineland crises. On this relationship thereafter, see Martin Thomas, *Britain, France, and Appeasement* (Oxford, 1996).

22. See Stephen A. Schuker, 'France and the Remilitarization of the Rhineland, 1936', *French Historical Studies* (spring 1986), and Donald

Cameron Watt, *Too Serious a Business: European Armed Forces and the Approach to the Second World War* (Berkeley, CA, 1975) pp. 21, 74, 100–2.

23. For the Soviet reaction, including dismissal of collective security, see Michael Jabara Carley, *1939: The Alliance that Never Was and the Coming of World War II* (Chicago, 1999). This work effectively represents the Soviet viewpoint.

24. On events after Munich, see Donald Cameron Watt, *How War Came* (New York, 1989). For French opinion, see William D. Irvine, 'Domestic Politics and the Fall of France in 1940', in Joel Blatt (ed.), *The French Defeat of 1940: Reassessments* (Providence, RI, 1998) pp. 85–99.

25. Antony Lentin, ' "Appeasement" at the Paris Peace Conference', in Michael Dockrill and John Fisher (eds), *The Paris Peace Conference, 1919* (New York, 2001) p. 51.

26. By 1939, 70 per cent of Bulgaria's exports went to Germany, with predictable political effects. Prażmowska, p. 211.

27. Hitler's intent was eventually demonstrated not only by the disputed Hossbach memorandum (*Documents on German Foreign Policy, 1918–1945*, Series D, I no. 19) but also by the Blomberg Directive (ibid., VII, App. III k).

Bibliography

Books

For reasons of space, only English language secondary works are listed.

MAGDA ADÁM, *The Little Entente and Europe (1920–1929)*, tr. Mátyás Esterházy (Budapest, 1993).

ANTHONY P. ADAMTHWAITE, *Grandeur and Misery: France's Bid for Power in Europe, 1914–1940* (London, 1995).

FEROZ AHMAD, *The Making of Modern Turkey* (London, 1993).

R. AHMANN et al. (eds), *The Quest for Stability: Problems of West European Security, 1919–1937* (New York, 1993).

RENÉ ALBRECHT-CARRIÉ, *Italy at the Paris Peace Conference* (New York, 1938).

DEREK H. ALDCROFT, *From Versailles to Wall Street, 1919–1929* (Berkeley, CA, 1977).

MARTIN S. ALEXANDER, *The Republic in Danger: General Maurice Gamelin and the Politics of French Defence, 1933–1940* (Cambridge, 1992).

WILLIAM S. ALLEN, *The Nazi Seizure of Power* (Chicago, 1965).

GEORGE ANTONIUS, *The Arab Awakening* (New York, 1939).

CHRISTIAN BAECHLER AND CAROLE FINK (eds), *The Establishment of European Frontiers after the Two World Wars* (Bern, 1996).

THOMAS BAILEY, *Woodrow Wilson and the Lost Peace* (New York, 1944).

IVO BANAČ, *The National Question in Yugoslavia* (Ithaca, NY, 1984).

CORELLI BARNETT, *The Collapse of British Power* (New York, 1972).

JAMES BARROS, *The Corfu Incident of 1923* (Princeton, NJ, 1965).

—— *The League of Nations and the Great Powers* (Oxford, 1970).

RONALD P. BARSTON, *The Other Powers* (New York, 1973).

GÁBOR BÁTONYI, *Britain and Central Europe, 1918–1933* (Oxford, 1999).

P. M. H. BELL, *France and Britain, 1900–1940* (London, 1996).

—— *The Origins of the Second World War in Europe* (London, 1986).

EDWARD W. BENNETT, *German Rearmament and the West* (Princeton, NJ, 1979).

—— *Germany and the Diplomacy of the Financial Crisis, 1931* (Cambridge, MA, 1962).

G. H. BENNETT, *British Foreign Policy during the Curzon Period, 1919–24* (New York, 1995).

V. R. BERGHAHN, *Modern Germany*, 2nd edn (Cambridge, 1987).

RICHARD BESSEL, *Germany after the First World War* (Oxford, 1993).

JOEL BLATT (ed.), *The French Defeat of 1940: Reassessments* (Providence, RI, 1997).

MANFRED F. BOEMEKE, GERALD D. FELDMAN AND ELISABETH GLASER (eds), *The Treaty of Versailles* (Cambridge, 1998).

EUGENE BOIA, *Romania's Diplomatic Relations with Yugoslavia in the Interwar Period* (New York, 1993).

R. J. B. BOSWORTH, *Italy and the Wider World, 1860–1960* (London, 1996).

K. D. BRACHER, *The German Dictatorship* (New York, 1970).

JULIUS BRAUNTHAL, *History of the International*, 2 vols (New York, 1967).

D. W. BROGAN, *The Development of Modern France* (New York, 1966 edn).

BOHDAN B. BUDOROWYCZ, *Polish-Soviet Relations, 1932–1939* (New York, 1963).

H. JAMES BURGWYN, *Italian Foreign Policy in the Interwar Period* (Westport, CT, 1997).

—— *The Legend of the Mutilated Victory: Italy, the Great War, and the Paris Peace Conference* (Westport, CT, 1993).

EMILE CAMMAERTS, *Albert of Belgium, Defender of Right* (London, 1935).

F. GREGORY CAMPBELL, *Confrontation in Central Europe: Weimar Germany and Czechoslovakia* (Chicago, 1975).

MICHAEL JABARA CARLEY, *1939: The Alliance that Never Was and the Coming of World War II* (Chicago, 1999).

STEPHEN D. CARLS, *Louis Loucheur and the Shaping of Modern France, 1916–1931* (Baton Rouge, LA, 1993).

DAVID CARLTON, *MacDonald versus Henderson: The Foreign Policy of the Second Labour Government* (New York, 1970).

WILLIAM CARR, *Arms, Autarky and Aggression: A Study in German Foreign Policy, 1933–1939* (New York, 1972).

F. L. CARSTEN, *Revolution in Central Europe, 1918–1919* (Berkeley, CA, 1972).

GWENDOLEN M. CARTER, *The British Commonwealth and International Security: The Role of the Dominions, 1919–1939* (Toronto, 1947).

LEWIS CARTER, et al., *The Zinoviev Letter* (London, 1967).

ALAN CASSELS, *Fascist Italy*, 2nd edn (Arlington Heights, IL, 1985).

—— *Mussolini's Early Diplomacy* (Princeton, NJ, 1970).

ANNA CIENCIALA AND TITUS KOMARNICKI, *From Versailles to Locarno: Keys to Polish Foreign Policy, 1919–1925* (Lawrence, KA, 1984).

INIS L. CLAUDE Jr, *Swords into Plowshares: The Problems and Progress of International Organization* (New York, 1971 edn.).

PATRICIA CLAVIN, *The Failure of Economic Diplomacy: Britain, Germany, France, and the United States, 1931–36* (New York, 1996).

—— *The Great Depression in Europe, 1929–1939* (New York, 2000).

PARKS COBLE, *Facing Japan: Chinese Politics and Japanese Imperialism, 1931–1937* (Cambridge, MA, 1991).

FRANK COSTIGLIOLA, *Awkward Dominion: American Political, Economic, and Cultural Relations with Europe, 1919–1933* (Ithaca, NY, 1984).

GORDON A. CRAIG, *Germany, 1866–1945* (New York, 1980).

—— AND FELIX GILBERT (eds), *The Diplomats, 1919–1939* (Princeton, NJ, 1953).

ROY W. CURRY, *Woodrow Wilson and Far Eastern Policy, 1913–1921* (New York, 1957).

FERDINAND CZERNIN, *Versailles, 1919* (New York, 1965 edn).

NORMAN DAVIES, *God's Playground: A History of Poland*, 2 vols (New York, 1982).

—— *White Eagle, Red Star: The Polish-Soviet War, 1919–20* (New York, 1972).

RICHARD DAVIS, *Anglo-French Relations Before the Second World War* (London, 2001).

RICHARD K. DEBO, *Revolution and Survival: The Foreign Policy of Soviet Russia, 1917–18* (Toronto, 1979).

—— *Survival and Consolidation: The Foreign Policy of Soviet Russia, 1918–1921* (Buffalo, NY, 1992).

PETER DENNIS, *Decision by Default: Peacetime Conscription and British Defence, 1919–39* (Durham, NC, 1972).

DAVID DILKS (ed.), *Retreat from Power: Studies in Britain's Foreign Policy in the Twentieth Century*, 2 vols (London, 1981).

ROGER DINGMAN, *Power in the Pacific: The Origins of Naval Arms Limitation, 1914– 1922* (Chicago, 1976).

ALEKSA DJILAS, *The Contested Country: Yugoslav Unity and Communist Revolution, 1919–1953* (Cambridge, MA, 1991).

MICHAEL DOCKRILL AND JOHN FISHER (eds), *The Paris Peace Conference, 1919* (New York, 2001).

MICHAEL DOCKRILL AND J. DOUGLAS GOOLD, *Peace without Promise: Britain and the Peace Conferences, 1919–1923* (Hamden, CT, 1981).

PAUL W. DOERR, *British Foreign Policy, 1919–1939* (Manchester, 1998).

IAN M. DRUMMOND, *British Economic Policy and the Empire, 1919–39* (London, 1972).

SÉAMUS DUNN AND T. G. FRASER (eds), *Europe and Ethnicity: World War I and Contemporary Ethnic Conflict* (London, 1996).

DAVID DUTTON, *Austen Chamberlain* (New Brunswick, NJ, 1985).

G. W. EGERTON, *Great Britain and the Creation of the League of Nations* (Chapel Hill, NC, 1978).

L. ETHAN ELLIS, *Frank B. Kellogg and American Foreign Relations, 1925–1929* (New Brunswick, NJ, 1961).

MANFRED J. ENSSLE, *Stresemann's Territorial Revisionism* (Wiesbaden, 1980).

GEORGE ESENWEIN AND ADRIAN SHUBERT, *Spain at War* (New York, 1995).

ERICH EYCK, *A History of the Weimar Republic*, 2 vols (Cambridge, MA, 1962).

GERALD D. FELDMAN, *The Great Disorder: Politics, Economics, and Society in the German Inflation, 1914–1924* (New York, 1993).

NIALL FERGUSON, *The Pity of War* (London, 1999).

R. H. FERRELL, *The American Secretaries of State and their Diplomacy*, XI, *Frank B. Kellogg, Henry L. Stimson* (New York, 1963).

—— *Peace in their Time* (New Haven, CT, 1952).

J. R. FERRIS, *Men, Money, and Diplomacy: The Evolution of British Strategic Policy, 1919–1926* (Ithaca, NY, 1989).

RUSSELL FIFIELD, *Woodrow Wilson and the Far East* (New York, 1952).

CAROLE FINK, *The Genoa Conference* (Chapel Hill, NC, 1984).

—— AXEL FROHN AND JÜRGEN HEIDEKING (eds), *Genoa, Rapallo, and European Reconstruction in 1922* (Cambridge, 1991).

INCA FLOTO, *Colonel House in Paris: A Study of American Policy at the Paris Peace Conference, 1919* (Åarhus, Denmark, 1973).

DAVID S. FOGELSONG, *America's Secret War against Bolshevism* (Chapel Hill, NC, 1995).

ISAIAH FRIEDMAN, *The Question of Palestine* (New Brunswick, NJ, 1992 edn).

DAVID FROMKIN, *A Peace to End all Peace* (New York, 1989).

MICHAEL G. FRY, *Illusions of Security: North Atlantic Diplomacy, 1918–1922* (Toronto, 1972).

JOHN KENNETH GALBRAITH, *The Great Crash, 1929* (Boston, MA, 1988 edn).

LLOYD C. GARDNER, *Safe for Democracy: The Anglo-American Response to Revolution, 1913–1923* (New York, 1984).

HANS GATZKE (ed.), *European Diplomacy between Two Wars* (Chicago, 1972).

—— *Stresemann and the Rearmament of Germany* (Baltimore, MD, 1954).

LAURENCE E. GELFAND, *The Inquiry: American Preparations for Peace, 1917–1919* (New Haven, CT, 1963).

BETTY GLAD, *Charles Evans Hughes and the Illusions of Innocence* (Urbana, IL, 1966).

BÜLENT GÖKAY, *A Clash of Empires: Turkey between Russian Bolshevism and British Imperialism* (London, 1997).

ERIK GOLDSTEIN, *Winning the Peace: British Diplomatic Strategy, Peace Planning, and the Paris Peace Conference, 1916–1920* (Oxford, 1991).

—— AND JOHN MAURER (eds), *The Washington Conference, 1921–22* (London, 1995).

GABRIEL GORODETSKY (ed.), *Soviet Foreign Policy, 1917–1991* (London, 1994).

RICHARD S. GRAYSON, *Austen Chamberlain and the Commitment to Europe* (London, 1997).

CHARLES A. GULICK, *Austria from Habsburg to Hitler*, 2 vols (Berkeley, CA, 1948).

WILLIAM M. HALE, *Turkish Foreign Policy, 1774–2000* (London, 2000).
HELMUT HEIBER, *The Weimar Republic*, tr. W. E. Yuill (Oxford, 1993).
PAUL C. HELMREICH, *From Paris to Sèvres* (Columbus, OH, 1973).
ERVIN HEXNER, *The International Steel Cartel* (Chapel Hill, NC, 1943).
JOHN HIDEN, *The Baltic States and Weimar Ostpolitik* (Cambridge, 1987).
—— *Republican and Fascist Germany* (London, 1996).
—— AND PATRICK SALMON, *The Baltic Nations and Europe*, revised edn
    (London, 1994).
KLAUS HILDEBRAND, *The Foreign Policy of the Third Reich*, tr. Anthony
    Fothergill (Berkeley, CA, 1973).
GUSTAV HILGER AND ALFRED G. MEYER, *The Incompatible Allies:
    German-Russian Relations, 1918–1941* (New York, 1953).
KEITH HITCHINS, *Rumania, 1866–1947* (Oxford, 1994).
MICHAEL HOGAN, *Informal Entente: The Private Structure of Cooperation in
    Anglo-American Economic Diplomacy, 1918–1928* (Columbia, MO, 1977).
JONATHAN HOLLOWELL (ed.), *Twentieth Century Anglo-American
    Relations* (London, 2001).
CARL-LUDWIG HOLTFRERICH, *The German Inflation, 1914–1923*, tr.
    Theo Balderston (Berlin, 1986).
DAGMAR HORNA-PERMAN, *The Shaping of the Czechoslovak State* (Leiden,
    1963).
MICHAEL E. HOWARD, *The Continental Commitment: The Dilemma of British
    Defence Policy in the Era of the Two World Wars* (London, 1972).
GABRIEL JACKSON, *A Concise History of the Spanish Civil War* (London,
    1974).
JON JACOBSON, *Locarno Diplomacy* (Princeton, NJ, 1972).
—— *When the Soviet Union Entered World Politics* (Berkeley, CA, 1994).
LORNA S. JAFFE, *The Decision to Disarm Germany* (Boston, MA, 1985).
BARBARA JELAVICH, *History of the Balkans*, 2 vols (Cambridge, 1983).
—— *Modern Austria* (Cambridge, 1987).
NICOLE JORDAN, *The Popular Front and Central Europe* (New York, 1992).
JAN KARSKI, *The Great Powers and Poland, 1919–1945* (Lanham, MD,
    1985).
ELIE KEDOURIE, *In the Anglo-Arab Labyrinth: The McMahon-Husayn
    Correspondence* (Cambridge, 1976).
EDWARD KEETON, *Briand's Locarno Policy* (New York, 1987).
J. F. V. KEIGER, *Raymond Poincaré* (Cambridge, 1997).
BRUCE KENT, *The Spoils of War: The Politics, Economics, and Diplomacy of
    Reparations, 1918–1932* (Oxford, 1989).
PETER C. KENT, *The Pope and the Duce* (New York, 1981).
WILLIAM R. KEYLOR, *The Legacy of the Great War: Peacemaking, 1919*
    (Boston, MA, 1998).
JOHN MAYNARD KEYNES, *The Economic Consequences of the Peace*
    (London, 1919).

DAVID OWEN KIEFT, *Belgium's Return to Neutrality* (Oxford, 1972).

CHARLES P. KINDLEBERGER, *The World in Depression, 1919–1939* (London, 1973).

SIR IVONE KIRKPATRICK, *Mussolini: A Study in Power* (New York, 1964).

CAROLYN J. KITCHING, *Britain and the Problem of International Disarmament, 1919–1934* (London, 1999).

THOMAS J. KNOCK, *To End all Wars: Woodrow Wilson and the Quest for a New World Order* (New York, 1992).

EBERHARD KOLB, *The Weimar Republic*, tr. P. S. Falk (London, 1998 edn).

J. KORBEL, *Poland between East and West* (Princeton, NJ, 1963).

WARREN F. KUEHL, *Seeking World Order: The United States and International Organization to 1920* (Nashville, TN, 1969).

MICHAEL LAFFAN (ed.), *The Burden of German History, 1919–45* (London, 1988).

IVO LEDERER, *Yugoslavia at the Paris Peace Conference* (New Haven, CT, 1963).

MARSHALL LEE AND W. MICHALKA, *German Foreign Policy, 1917–1933* (Leamington Spa, 1987).

STEPHEN J. LEE, *European Dictatorships, 1918–1945* (London, 1987).

MELVIN P. LEFFLER, *The Elusive Quest: America's Pursuit of European Stability and French Security, 1919–1933* (Chapel Hill, NC, 1979).

GEORGE A. LENSEN, *The Damned Inheritance: The Soviet Union and the Manchurian Crisis, 1924–1935* (Tallahassee, FL, 1974).

ANTONY LENTIN, *Lloyd George, Woodrow Wilson, and the Guilt of Germany* (Baton Rouge, LA, 1985).

N. GORDON LEVIN Jr, *Woodrow Wilson and World Politics* (London, 1968).

BERNARD LEWIS, *The Emergence of Modern Turkey* (London, 1968 edn).

ARTHUR S. LINK, *Wilson the Diplomatist* (Baltimore, MD, 1957).

—— (ed.), *Woodrow Wilson and a Revolutionary World* (Chapel Hill, NC, 1982).

WM. ROGER LOUIS, *Great Britain and Germany's Lost Colonies, 1914–1919* (Oxford, 1967).

ALMA LUCKAU, *The German Delegation at the Paris Peace Conference* (New York, 1941).

KAY LUNDGREEN-NIELSEN, *The Polish Problem at the Paris Peace Conference*, tr. Alison Borch-Johansen (Odense, Denmark, 1979).

MARGARET MACMILLAN, *Peacemakers: The Paris Peace Conference of 1919 and its Attempt to End War* (London, 2001).

PETER MANSFIELD, *The Ottoman Empire and its Successors* (London, 1973).

ÉTIENNE MANTOUX, *The Carthaginian Peace, or the Economic Consequences of Mr. Keynes* (Oxford, 1946).

ANDREW MARGO, *Atatürk* (Woodstock, NY, 2000).

SALLY MARKS, *The Ebbing of European Ascendancy: An International History of the World, 1914–1945* (London, 2002)

—— *Innocent Abroad: Belgium at the Paris Peace Conference of 1919* (Chapel Hill, NC, 1981).

DAVID MARQUAND, *Ramsay MacDonald* (London, 1977).

F. S. MARSTON, *The Peace Conference of 1919: Organization and Procedure* (London, 1944).

GORDON MARTEL (ed.), *'The Origins of the Second World War' Reconsidered* (London, 1999 edn).

LAURENCE W. MARTIN, *Peace without Victory* (New Haven, CT, 1958).

EVAN MAWDSLEY, *The Russian Civil War* (Boston, 1987).

ARNO MAYER, *Politics and Diplomacy of Peacemaking* (New York, 1967).

MARK MAZOWER, *Dark Continent: Europe's Twentieth Century* (New York, 1999).

WALTER A. MCDOUGALL, *France's Rhineland Diplomacy, 1914–1924* (Princeton, NJ, 1978).

WILLIAM C. MCNEIL, *American Money and the Weimar Republic* (New York, 1986).

RICHARD H. MEYER, *Bankers' Diplomacy* (New York, 1970).

ALFRED C. MIERZEJEWSKI, *The Most Valuable Asset of the Reich: A History of the German National Railway*, 2 vols (Chapel Hill, NC, 1999, 2000).

DAVID HUNTER MILLER, *The Geneva Protocol* (New York, 1925).

HANS MOMMSEN, *The Rise and Fall of Weimar Democracy*, tr. Elborg Forster and Larry Eugene Jones (Chapel Hill, NC, 1996).

PHILIP MORGAN, *Italian Fascism, 1919–1945* (New York, 1995).

JAMES W. MORLEY (ed.), *Japan Erupts* (New York, 1984).

LEONARD MOSLEY, *Curzon: The End of an Epoch* (London, 1960).

KENNETH MOURÉ AND MARTIN S. ALEXANDER (eds), *Crisis and Renewal in France, 1918–1962* (New York, 2002).

DENYS P. MYERS, *The Reparations Settlement* (Boston, MA, 1929).

HARRY E. NADLER, *The Rhenish Separatist Movements During the Early Weimar Republic, 1918–1924* (London, 1987).

ALEKSANDR M. NEKRICH, *Pariahs, Partners, Predators: German-Soviet Relations, 1922, 1941*, ed. and tr. Gregory L. Freeze (New York, 1997).

HAROLD NELSON, *Land and Power: British and Allied Policy on Germany's Frontiers, 1916–19* (Toronto, 1963).

KEITH L. NELSON, *Victors Divided: America and the Allies in Germany, 1918–1923* (Berkeley, CA, 1975).

JUKKA NEVAKIVI, *Britain, France, and the Arab Middle East, 1914–1920* (London, 1969).

DOUGLAS NEWTON, *British Policy and the Weimar Republic, 1918–1919* (Oxford, 1997).

A. J. NICHOLLS, *Weimar and the Rise of Hitler* (London, 1979 edn).

IAN H. NISH, *Alliance in Decline: A Study in Anglo-Japanese Relations, 1908–1923* (London, 1972).

—— *Japan's Struggle with Internationalism: Japan, China, and the League of Nations* (London, 1993).

PHILIP J. NOEL-BAKER, *The Geneva Protocol for the Pacific Settlement of International Disputes* (London, 1925).

GÜNTHER NOLLAU, *International Communism and World Revolution* (New York, 1961).

F. S. NORTHEDGE, *The League of Nations* (New York, 1986).

SADAKO N. OGATA, *Defiance in Manchuria: The Making of Japanese Foreign Policy, 1931–1932* (Berkeley, CA, 1964).

VERA OLIVOVÁ, *The Doomed Democracy: Czechoslovakia in a Disrupted Europe, 1914–1938* (London, 1972).

ANNE ORDE, *British Policy and International Reconstruction after the First World War* (Cambridge, 1990).

—— *Great Britain and International Security, 1920–1926* (London, 1978).

ELSPETH Y. O'RIORDAN, *Britain and the Ruhr Crisis* (London, 2001).

MARIA ORMOS, *From Padua to the Trianon, 1918–1920*, tr. Miklós Uszkay (New York, 1990).

JOSÉ ORTEGA Y GASSET, *The Revolt of the Masses* (New York, 1930).

FRANK OWEN, *Tempestuous Journey: Lloyd George, his Life and Times* (New York, 1955).

STANLEY W. PAGE, *The Formation of the Baltic States* (Cambridge, MA, 1959).

R. A. C. PARKER, *Chamberlain and Appeasement* (New York, 1993).

RAYMOND PEARSON, *National Minorities in Eastern Europe, 1848–1945* (New York, 1983).

CARL H. PEGG, *Evolution of the European Idea, 1914–1932* (Chapel Hill, NC, 1983).

MAARTEN L. PEREBOOM, *Democracies at the Turning Point* (New York, 1995).

MARTA PETRICIOLI (ed.), *A Missed Opportunity? 1922: The Reconstruction of Europe* (Bern, 1995).

N. PETSALIS-DIOMIDIS, *Greece at the Paris Peace Conference, 1919* (Thessaloniki, 1978).

VINCENT J. PITTS, *France and the German Problem: Politics and Economics in the Locarno Period, 1924–1929* (New York, 1987)

ANITA J. PRAŻMOWSKA, *Eastern Europe and the Origins of the Second World War* (London, 2000).

GEORGE VON RAUCH, *The Baltic States* (Berkeley, CA, 1974).

TIM REES AND ANDREW THORPE (eds), *International Communism and the Communist International, 1919–1943* (Manchester, 1998).

GEOFFREY ROBERTS, *The Soviet Union and the Origins of the Second World War* (New York, 1995).

ESMONDE ROBERTSON, *Mussolini as Empire Builder, 1932–36* (London, 1977).

STEPHEN W. ROSKILL, *Hankey: Man of Secrets*, 3 vols (London, 1970–4).

—— *Naval Policy between the Wars*, 2 vols (London, 1968, Annapolis, MD, 1976).

JOSEPH ROTHSCHILD, *East Central Europe between the Two World Wars* (Seattle, WA, 1974).

ROBERT L. ROTHSTEIN, *Alliances and Small Powers* (New York, 1968).

HARRY RUDIN, *Armistice, 1918* (New Haven, CT, 1944).

THOMAS SAKMYSTER, *Hungary's Admiral on Horseback: Miklos Horthy, 1918–1944* (Boulder, CO, 1994).

GEORG SCHILD, *Between Ideology and Realpolitik: Woodrow Wilson and the Russian Revolution, 1917–1921* (Westport, CT, 1995).

SCHRÖDER, HANS-JÜRGEN (ed.), *Confrontation and Cooperation: Germany and the United States in the Era of World War I, 1900–1924* (Providence, RI, 1993).

STEPHEN A. SCHUKER, *American 'Reparations' to Germany, 1919–1933* (Princeton, NJ, 1988).

—— *The End of French Predominance in Europe* (Chapel Hill, NC, 1976).

GERHARD SCHULZ, *Revolutions and Peace Treaties, 1917–1920* (New York, 1972).

KLAUS SCHWABE, *Woodrow Wilson, Revolutionary Germany, and Peacemaking, 1918–1919*, tr. Robert and Rita Kimber (Chapel Hill, NC, 1985).

CHRISTOPHER SETON-WATSON, *Italy from Liberalism to Fascism, 1870–1925* (London, 1967).

ALAN SHARP, *The Versailles Settlement* (New York, 1991).

—— AND GLYN STONE (eds), *Anglo-French Relations in the Twentieth Century* (New York, 2000).

WILLIAM I. SHORROCK, *From Ally to Enemy: The Enigma of Fascist Italy in French Diplomacy, 1920–1940* (Kent, OH, 1988).

J. T. SHOTWELL AND MARINA SALVIN, *Lessons on Security and Disarmament* (New York, 1949).

KATHERINE A. S. SIEGEL, *Loans and Legitimacy: The Evolution of Soviet-American Relations, 1919–1933* (Lexington, KY, 1996).

MICHAEL LLEWELLYN SMITH, *Ionian Vision: Greece in Asia Minor, 1919–1922* (Ann Arbor, MI, 1998 edn).

SARA SMITH, *The Manchurian Crisis* (New York, 1948).

SALAHI RAMSDAN SONYEL, *Turkish Diplomacy, 1918–1923* (London, 1975).

SHERMAN D. SPECTOR, *Rumania at the Paris Peace Conference* (New York, 1962).

KARL R. STADLER, *The Birth of the Austrian Republic, 1918–1921* (Leyden, 1966).

STEWART A. STEHLIN, *Weimar and the Vatican, 1919–1933* (Princeton, NJ, 1983).

DAVID R. STONE, *Hammer and Rifle: The Militarization of the Soviet Union, 1926– 1933* (Lawrence, KA, 2000).

PETER F. SUGAR, PÉTER HANÁK AND TIBOR FRANK (eds), *A History of Hungary* (Bloomington, IN, 1990).

SUN, YOU-LI, *China and the Origins of the Pacific War, 1931–1941* (New York, 1993).

STANLEY SUVAL, *The Anschluss Question in the Weimar Era* (Baltimore, MD, 1974).

EDMOND TAYLOR, *The Fall of the Dynasties: The Collapse of the Old Order, 1905–1922* (New York, 1963).

HAROLD W. V. TEMPERLEY, *A History of the Peace Conference of Paris*, 6 vols (London, 1920–4).

MARTIN THOMAS, *Britain, France, and Appeasement* (Oxford, 1996)

JOHN M. THOMPSON, *Russia, Bolshevism, and the Versailles Peace* (Princeton, NJ, 1966).

CHRISTOPHER THORNE, *The Limits of Foreign Policy* (London, 1972).

A. L. TIBAWI, *Anglo-Arab Relations and the Question of Palestine, 1914–1921* (London, 1978).

SETH P. TILLMAN, *Anglo-American Relations at the Paris Peace Conference of 1919* (Princeton, NJ, 1961).

A. J. TOYNBEE (ed.), *Survey of International Affairs, 1920–1923* (*et seq.*), annual (London, 1927–).

MARC TRACTENBERG, *Reparation in World Politics* (New York, 1980).

HENRY A. TURNER Jr, *Stresemann and the Politics of the Weimar Republic* (Princeton, NJ, 1956).

ADAM B. ULAM, *Expansion and Coexistence: The History of Soviet Foreign Policy, 1917–1967* (New York, 1968).

RICHARD ULLMAN, *Anglo-Soviet Relations, 1917–1921*, 3 vols (Princeton, NJ, 1961–7).

ROBERT WAITE, *Vanguard of Nazism* (Cambridge, MA, 1952).

FRANCIS P. WALTERS, *A History of the League of Nations* (London, 1952).

ARTHUR WALWORTH, *Wilson and his Peacemakers* (New York, 1986).

SARAH WAMBAUGH, *Plebiscites since the World War* (Washington DC, 1933).

PIOTR WANDYCZ, *France and her Eastern Allies, 1919–1925* (Minneapolis, MN, 1962).

—— *Soviet-Polish Relations, 1917–1921* (Cambridge, MA, 1969).

—— *The Twilight of French Eastern Alliances, 1926–36* (Princeton, NJ, 1988).

DONALD CAMERON WATT, *How War Came* (New York, 1989).

——*Too Serious a Business: European Armed Forces and the Approach to the Second World War* (Berkeley, CA, 1975).

GERHARD WEINBERG, *The Foreign Policy of Hitler's Germany*, 2 vols (Chicago, 1970, 1980).

DAVID WELCH, *Hitler, Profile of a Dictator* (London, 2001 edn).

K. C. WHEARE, *The Statute of Westminster and Dominion Status* (New York, 1938).

J. W. WHEELER-BENNETT, *Hindenburg: The Wooden Titan* (London, 1936).

—— *The Nemesis of Power: The German Army in Politics, 1918–1945* (New York, 1964).

—— *The Pipe Dream of Peace* (London, 1935).

CHRISTINE A. WHITE, *British and American Commercial Relations with Societ Russia, 1918–1924* (Chapel Hill, NC, 1992).

ANDREW J. WILLIAMS, *Trading with the Bolsheviks* (Manchester, 1992).

ANN WILLIAMS, *Britain and France in the Middle East and North Africa, 1914–1967* (London, 1968).

JOAN HOFF WILSON, *American Business and Foreign Policy, 1920–1933* (Boston, MA, 1973 edn).

HENRY R. WINKLER, *The League of Nations Movement in Great Britain, 1914–1919* (New Brunswick, NJ, 1952).

ELIZABETH WISKEMANN, *Czechs and Germans* (London, 1967 edn).

—— *Fascism in Italy* (London, 1969).

ROBERT J. YOUNG, *France and the Origins of the Second World War* (New York, 1996).

Z. N. ZEINE, *The Struggle for Arab Independence* (Beirut, 1960).

Z. A. B. ZEMAN, *The Break-up of the Habsburg Empire, 1914–1918* (London, 1961).

DRAGAN R. ŽIVOJINOVIĆ, *America, Italy, and the Birth of Yugoslavia* (New York, 1972).

ERIK J. ZÜRCHER, *Turkey, a Modern History* (London, 1997).

Articles Cited

JACQUES BARIÉTY, 'Finances et relations internationales: à propos du "plan de Thoiry"; septembre 1926', *Relations Internationales* (1980).

JOEL BLATT, 'France and the Corfu-Fiume Crisis of 1923', *The Historian* (1988).

—— 'The Parity that Meant Superiority', *French Historical Studies* (1981).

GEORGE A. GRÜN, 'Locarno, Idea and Reality', *International Affairs* (October, 1955).

PHILIPP HEYDE, 'Frankreich und das Ende der Reparationen', *Vierteljahrshefte für Zeitgeschichte* (2000).

CARL-LUDWIG HOLTFRERICH, 'Internationale Verteilungsfolgen der deutschen Inflation, 1918–1923', *Kyklos* (1977).

SALLY MARKS, 'My Name is Ozymandias: The Kaiser in Exile', *Central European History* (1983).

ALFRED C. MIERZEJEWSKI, 'Payments and Profits: The German National Railway Company and Reparations, 1924–1932', *German Studies Review* (1995).

CORNELIA NAVARI, 'The Origins of the Briand Plan', *Diplomacy and Statecraft* (1992).

The New York Times (May 1927).

STEPHEN A. SCHUKER, 'France and the Remilitarization of the Rhineland, 1936', *French Historical Studies* (1986).

F. G. STAMBROOK, ' *"Das Kind"* – Lord D'Abernon and the Origins of the Locarno Pact', *Central European History* (September, 1968).

Le Temps (Paris, 4 May 1922 *et seq.*).

The Times (London, 25 October 1924).

T. R. B. (RICHARD L. STROUT), 'The Tarnished Age', *New Republic* (26 October 1974).

HENRY ASHBY TURNER Jr, 'Eine Rede Stresemanns über seine Locarnopolitik', *Vierteljahrshefte für Zeitgeschichte* (1967).

Index